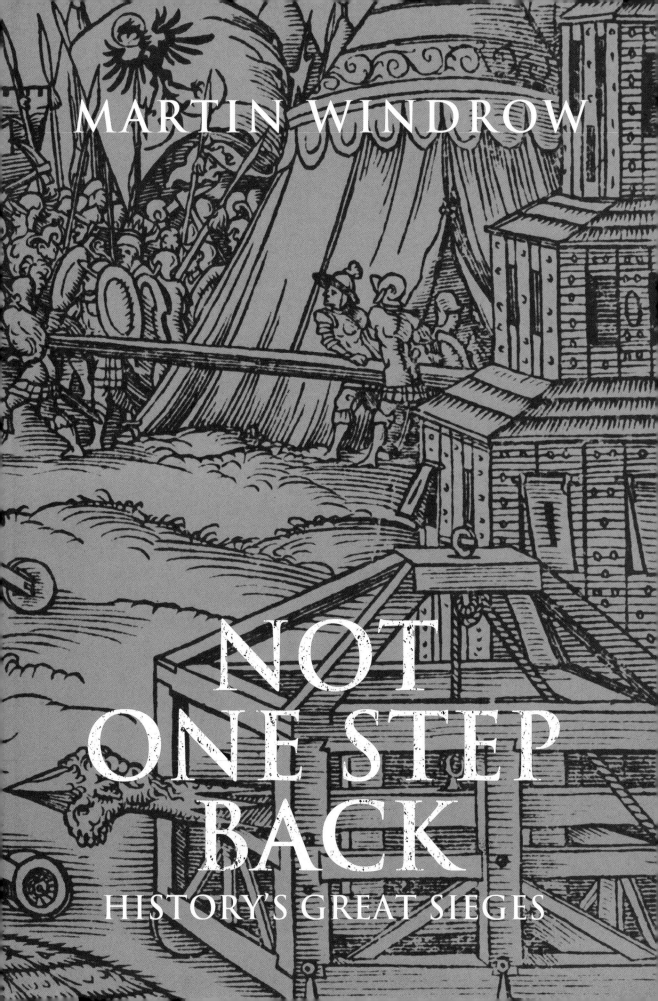

MARTIN WINDROW

NOT ONE STEP BACK

HISTORY'S GREAT SIEGES

CONTENTS

Previous page: **Siege equipment**, from a treatise by Gualtherus Rivius, Nuremberg 1547.

Below: **The relief of Londonderry** in July 1689 from a contemporary painting.

INTRODUCTION

> '*The worst policy of all is to besiege walled cities.*'

SUN TZU, *THE ART OF WAR* (*c.*500 BC)

Over the centuries a stereotypical picture of a siege has formed in the popular mind. This usually involves the hard-pressed defence of ramparts against repeated assaults, while the garrison ekes out its dwindling stores of food and ammunition. As the siege wears on, the defenders watch the horizon for signs of an approaching relief force with increasing desperation, knowing that if the place falls then the winner takes all – including, probably, their lives and those of any civilians they are protecting. The group in jeopardy is one of the most basic of human stories, and because of the tightly focused nature of sieges we cannot help but identify with the garrison at a human level – perhaps especially on that minority of occasions when, against all reason, they successfully hold out against overwhelming odds.

WHY DO SIEGES HAPPEN?

Popular stereotypes are always founded (if sometimes vaguely) on real historical examples that have captured the imagination. However, they often ignore the background factors that actually dictate events on a less immediate level.

A siege is defined as the investment or beleaguering of a town or fortress, and the French root of the word denotes a seat or the act of sitting down. In other words, a siege occurred when armies stopped moving across the countryside and settled down inside and around a defended place. This might be either a purely military stronghold or a walled town; but in each case the key question to ask about a siege is simply, what was the purpose of attacking or defending this place?

The classic military answer is that a fortress provides a local means of frustrating enemy operations, or a local base for friendly operations. It dominates an area of, or corridor through, the local landscape: while men of one army hold it, and are free to make sorties or to shoot from its walls, the other army cannot advance past it in safety. Moreover, if it is well provisioned, and the enemy lack the means to assault it, then it can decide the outcome of a whole campaign. Such defensible places have often been sited deliberately at those points through which moving armies must pass – harbours, river crossings, roads confined by forest or swampland, mountain passes or the mouths of valleys. Around such purpose-built fortresses a science of defence and attack, and a code of customary military behaviour, have evolved steadily over tens of centuries.

However, this answer points us much further back in history, to the ages when the civilian and military worlds were inseparable. It was also on sites dominating the surroundings from high

The Defeat of the Floating Batteries at Gibraltar, painted by John Singleton Copley soon after the long siege of the promontory ended in 1783, shows General George Eliott on horseback

ground, or spaced along the natural routes for travel, that many human communities grew up: in dangerous times people generally settle together in physically defensible places, and for our distant ancestors times were always dangerous. Gradually, some of these natural sites were further protected by the building of earth banks, dry-stone ramparts and timber palisades, and some of them evolved into towns walled with brick or masonry.

A Refuge or a Trap?

These towns provided commercial centres for expanding populations farming the surrounding countryside. In times of anarchy or war, enemies ravaged that countryside; the town offered refuge, so farmers and rural villagers would flee their isolated homes and bring their families, goods and even their beasts inside the notional protection of the walls. This always worsened the balance between the numbers of active defenders and the numbers of mouths that had to be fed, and also increased the risk of disease breaking out. Often military and civilian purposes might become superimposed on the same site: a city might be not merely a militarily desirable but also a rich and politically symbolic prize for an invading army, thus actually exposing the citizens and refugees to additional dangers rather than offering them a haven. In the case of major centres the dilemma for city fathers was that the very importance to which they owed their prosperity now made their community an attractive prey in its own right: '*We have taken Paris*' has always been a much more impressive boast than '*Our army has reached the River Seine*'.

The Defenders' Gamble

The citizens were always confronted by the same calculation that faced the commander of a purely military stronghold: what was the likelihood of an outside force marching to their relief, within the period that they could expect to hold their walls? For civilians the consequences of a wrong choice might be particularly costly.

If a town controlled a bottleneck on the route of a campaigning army, then the attackers' goal might be best achieved by persuading the inhabitants to surrender as rapidly as possible – by visibly cutting them off from easy supply or relief and then offering reasonably humane terms. (Indeed, in medieval Europe there was even a recognized protocol by which garrisons were allowed a certain number of weeks to ascertain if they could expect help.) If the citizens, or any defending soldiers, recognized the inevitable and opened the gates without forcing the attackers to pay the bloody price of assaulting the walls, then their sufferings might be limited; a new garrison sufficient to control the place could then be installed, and the army could move on.

If an attacking army intended to occupy the country in the long term, then the town and its population had a long-term value; self-interest argued for limiting the destruction and bloodshed – although, again, this would depend upon how readily the defenders gave up their keys. (In both these scenarios, the most cost-effective way for attackers to short-circuit the defenders' deliberations was to pay a traitor within to open the gate – the solution that probably concluded the majority of historical sieges.)

The Worst-case Scenario

However, while the purpose of capturing a strategic stronghold was simply to gain freedom of military movement, that of capturing a city might be far more sinister: in the worst cases the prize might not be mobility or even territory, but the population itself. The inhabitants might not have the option of surrendering in order to save their lives: some attacking armies were bent on massacre, pillage and destruction. Ancient invaders often annihilated, expelled or enslaved whole populations, subjecting cities to wholesale massacre, rape, looting and arson simply to vent their blood-lust.

This nightmarish scenario, which occasionally fell not far short of our modern definition of genocide, might spring from violent hatred across racial or religious divides; but it sometimes served the colder political purpose of sending a terrifying message to others – as in ancient Rome's crushing of rebellions within her empire, or the Mongols' lightning advances across great swathes of Asia and Europe. Such atrocities were still being committed by European armies as late as the religious wars of the 17th century; and of course, the sinister euphemism 'ethnic cleansing' is a coinage of our own very recent past.

The Theoretical Equations

While the reasons for laying siege to a defended place might vary, the factors governing the outcome have been fairly constant throughout history, and their balanced interplay at different times and places runs like a thread through any serial account of siege warfare. In every case, the defenders and attackers have been faced by a series of choices.

The defenders have to ask themselves two fundamental and linked questions: what is the purpose of mounting a defence – a wider strategic aim, or mere survival? And how do the chances and rewards of a successful defence compare with the dangers and penalties of a failed attempt? If they do choose to resist, then they face a number of further questions:

* Above all – is there a realistic chance of relief by an outside force, and if so, how long might it take?
* How strong are the defences, and do we have enough men in the garrison to man the length of the perimeter?
* Is sufficient water, food and ammunition available to sustain the garrison's strength, morale and ability to resist for a realistic length of time?

The attackers, in their turn, must also ask themselves questions – though since they enjoy the initiative, they will probably have addressed these at leisure before appearing in front of the walls. Fundamentally, what will be the military, political or other rewards of successfully attacking this place? What is the probable cost in lives and resources, particularly if an actual final assault is required? (Of course, the penalties of failure probably present a less stark calculation than that facing the defenders – a failed attack does not usually leave the attackers helpless at the defenders' mercy.) If the attackers decide to attempt a siege and perhaps an assault, then they face questions that mirror those preoccupying the garrison:

* What is the danger of interference from an outside enemy force, in what strength, and how soon? Do we have enough men available to simultaneously fend off such interference, and to pursue the siege and assault?

* Do we have the necessary equipment and skills to overcome the defences, and how long will it take?

* Is sufficient water, food, fuel and shelter available to sustain the siege army for long enough to achieve success?

HISTORICAL DIFFERENCES AND CONSTANTS

In modern times, with more complex weapons, munitions and other combat equipment, the logistic needs of both defenders and attackers have, of course, multiplied enormously, and by the nature of a siege these needs have usually been the more urgent for the defenders.

Throughout history up to the high medieval period, the irreducible logistic needs of a besieged garrison were simply water, food and perhaps a supply of arrows. From the 15th to the mid-19th century they also needed gunpowder, slowmatch or flints, and shot. Since then, they have increasingly needed cartridge ammunition for a whole range of different small arms and artillery; medical drugs, as the capabilities of medicine (and thus our expectations of it) have increased; and, in the past 90 years, radio batteries for communication (and the power, and thus the fuel, to recharge them).

As in every other more or less sophisticated system, both mechanical and human, the more moving parts there are, the greater the vulnerability to breakdown. There is also a psychological dimension: modern liberal democracies have a reduced public tolerance for the sufferings of the wounded and any besieged civilians, and mass communications reporting in real time have therefore sometimes shortened the endurance of defenders by contrast with those in the theoretically more brutal past.

*　*　*

With the whole of recorded history to consider, the selection of a limited number of individual sieges for a book of this size has naturally been difficult, and any choices I made were bound to dissatisfy some; indeed, a number of obvious contenders were only excluded at the last moment and with real regret. Given the space, the gap in coverage between 1871 and 1941 might have been filled by Port Arthur (1904), Kut el-Amara (1915–16) and the Alcázar of Toledo (1936); but although these were all dramatic episodes, yielding strategic or operational lessons, in the end I had to let them go, since none of them offered important differences in nature – as opposed to differences of degree – from the other examples. The examples that I have chosen were picked to represent a wide range of periods, and also some variations of culture. Some had significant political consequences, others did not; some involved hundreds of thousands of people, others only a few thousands or even hundreds; in most the attackers were successful, but in some the garrison managed to hold out.

Primarily, I have tried to choose subjects that demonstrate the decisive importance, across boundaries of time and place, of many of the factors outlined in the rather dry checklists above – and particularly, the effect of operations by forces elsewhere. Perhaps the decisive factor in most sieges in history was that by the time the stronghold was actually surrounded and cut off, conditions had already been created that made the outcome of any siege highly predictable. That fact adds an extra level of poignancy to the stories of human suffering and courage, since we can understand (as they did) that the defenders were often defying the almost inevitable – yet sometimes they succeeded.

The renowned Victorian soldier General Sir Garnet Wolseley made himself unpopular when he commented that the desperate defence by the tiny garrison of Rorke's Drift in Zululand in January 1879 was hardly surprising, since they had no choice, being *'shut up in buildings ... [where they] fought like rats for their lives which they could not otherwise save'*. Despite his ungracious turn of phrase, this was nothing but the truth. It is the last-ditch aspect of such battles – the tension of watching men who seem to have no way out, defending themselves to the last of their strength – that makes the tales of sieges so grimly compelling, even many centuries after the event.

The fighting for Khe Sanh in 1968 (summarized at the end of this book) has suggested – and more recent events have not refuted – that in modern conventional warfare no stronghold that is supported, with determination, by a world-class air force can truly be said to be besieged. An opinion of Sun Tzu is quoted at the head of this introduction, but the lessons of more than two millennia also suggest that no victory or defeat is inevitable – history does not move in straight lines, but in cycles. The great General von Moltke, the victor in the Franco-Prussian War of 1870–1, was reportedly known to have laughed only twice during his adult life: once when informed of the death of his mother-in-law, and again when he heard a particular fortress described as 'impregnable'.

Martin Windrow
2009

Alexander's masterpiece of
siege warfare TYRE

'*[Alexander was] most brilliant in seizing on the right course of action, even where all was obscure ... most masterly in marshalling an army and in arming and equipping it, and in uplifting his soldiers' spirits...*'

FLAVIUS ARRIANUS, *ANABASIS ALEXANDRI* (SECOND CENTURY AD)

No conqueror in world history has left a more indelible impression on later generations than Alexander of Macedon (r. 336–323 BC), the young king who led his armies from the Balkans to northern India in just five years of the fourth century BC. The story of his siege and capture of the port city of Tyre (in modern Lebanon), written by the Romanized Greek historian Flavius Arrianus in the second century AD (but based largely upon the now-lost memoir of Alexander's general Ptolemy), is the earliest fairly detailed account we have of a systematic amphibious assault on a fortified coastal stronghold. It is also an immediate reminder of the remarkable sophistication of the military technology of 2300 years ago, when every classic problem of pre-gunpowder siege warfare – and the responses developed to overcome them – were already present.

There is no such thing as an impregnable military obstacle, whether it is an ancient walled city or a reinforced concrete 'Maginot line' mounting massive guns. Given the willingness to sacrifice enough lives, and (above all) enough time, an attacker will always find some way in. The essential choice of method is always the same: if you cannot go around an obstacle, then you must either go over it, under it, or through it. By the third century BC techniques and equipment to achieve all these solutions were already being employed.

THE TRIUMPH OF MACEDON

In 358 BC, about 40 years after the end of the ruinous Peloponnesian War (431–404 BC) between Greece's city-states, the energetic Philip II (r. 358–336 BC) came to the throne of Macedon, then a marginal hill kingdom far to the north. This 'barbarian' king quickly proved himself a talented military reformer and general; previously known for its light troops, the new Macedonian army created by Philip was built around massed phalanx formations of heavy infantry pikemen, but he also revived the siege-warfare methods of a previous generation. Philip soon gained control over much of the Balkan peninsula north of Greece – conquests that brought him gold and silver mines, to fund his further ambitions.

In 339 he marched south into central Greece, and the following year, at the Battle of Chaeronea, he defeated an alliance of Thebes and Athens; on that field Philip's 18-year-old son Alexander

Detail of a floor mosaic, depicting Alexander the Great defeating Darius III at the Battle of Issus before continuing down the Mediterranean coast towards the strategic jewel of Tyre.

distinguished himself in command of one wing of the army. Philip employed both force and political guile to bring the chronically competitive Greek city-states into a unity (albeit a restless and fragile one) which they had been unable to achieve for themselves, and all except Sparta – aloof in the far south – subsequently made terms with him. Philip's so-called League of Corinth was intended for an even more ambitious project: the invasion of the Persian empire by a combined army of Greeks and Macedonians. In the latter years of the Peloponnesian War the Persian governors of the Greek-settled provinces in Asia Minor (modern Turkey) had meddled in the conflict; and although Persia was herself too weak to attempt another outright invasion, there were those who argued that the Aegean edge of the Persian empire cast a constant threatening shadow over Greece.

In 336, Philip was assassinated by palace conspirators and succeeded by Alexander. Faced with defections among the Greek cities and uprisings among the northern tribes, he moved with dazzling energy, and simply cowed the cities by the speed with which he brought troops to their gates. When he turned north to crush the Balkan tribes, Thebes alone took the opportunity to rebel against Macedon, and when it refused his terms Alexander stormed and sacked the city. With the mainland garrisoned and secure, he turned to the East once again; and in the spring of 334 BC, the 22-year-old king marched through Thrace and crossed the Dardanelles into Asia Minor, at the head of an army of about 35,000 men.

ALEXANDER IN ASIA

The ostensible aim of Alexander's campaign was to 'liberate' the Greek settlements from Persia, but it is clear that he always intended to invade the Persian heartland in Mesopotamia. The Greek cities of Asia Minor had for many years lived under fairly relaxed Persian suzerainty, juggling their loyalties for immediate advantage. Significant numbers of Greek mercenaries were still fighting for the Persians, and one of the ablest generals serving King Darius III (r. 336–330 BC) was a Greek, Memnon of Rhodes.

At the head of his cavalry, Alexander won a victory of audacious brilliance at the Granicus river (in modern northwest Turkey) in May 334. He spent the year 333 conquering Asia Minor; some cities opened their gates to him, but others remained loyal to Darius. The Persian fleet – in fact largely made up of Phoenicians (from modern Lebanon), Cypriots and Rhodians – was far stronger than Alexander's, and during this campaign it played cat-and-mouse around the coasts, landing troops to attack his rear lines and supplying cities that defied him.

One of the latter was Miletus, in modern southwest Turkey, whose reduction gave Alexander experience in combined land and sea operations. He sent ships to blockade its harbour before bringing up siege towers – a technology learned from his father – to attack its landward walls and capture the city. Alexander went on to take the city of Halicarnassus, but only after both the garrison (under Memnon) and the siege army had employed every known device and method; in the end it only fell to Alexander when the garrison broke out successfully, firing the city before they left.

King Darius led a large Persian force north from Syria, and in November 333 the two armies met on the narrow coastal plain at Issus, just inland from the northeastern 'corner' of the Mediterranean Sea (near the border between present-day Turkey and Syria). Alexander won another brilliant victory, forcing Darius to flee far to the southeast. Meanwhile the Persians' Aegean

GREEK SIEGE WARFARE

Although both were previously known in Mesopotamia, there is no evidence for the use in the Greek world of either siege mining (tunnels, to undermine and collapse a section of a city wall) or of battering rams (beams, swung to knock breaches in walls) before the Peloponnesian War. At the Spartan siege of Athens' allied city of Plataea in 429 BC, Thucydides tells us that the Spartans piled earth around a timber framework to raise a high mound close against the wall, to allow them to shoot down on the rampart; the defenders responded by building their walls higher, and tried to undermine the mound. When the Spartans used battering rams the garrison dangled noosed ropes to catch these, or dropped timber beams to break them. Eventually the Spartans built walls ('of circumvallation') all around the city, and settled down to a blockade to starve the defenders out – which for many centuries remained the most common method of reducing a stronghold (while always seeking a traitor inside to open a gate).

An important cradle of siege warfare was the island of Sicily, where there seems to have been a leap forward in the development of 'siege engines' at the turn of the fifth/fourth centuries. After the destruction of an Athenian army at Syracuse by the Spartans during the Peloponnesian War, the Carthaginians (then a leading naval power, based in modern Tunisia) tried to take over Sicily. When they built movable siege towers to enable troops to shoot down onto the defenders of the walls, the ruler Dionysius of Syracuse resisted with arrow-shooting catapults, from which stone-throwing catapults were later developed. At first these were simply 'giant crossbows', but by the time of Philip of Macedon half a century later improved models powered by torsion springs of twisted hair or sinew cord had been invented.

BATTERING RAMS AND SIEGE TOWERS

These classic mechanical solutions to the problems of getting through or over walls were in regular use by the late fifth century BC by the Carthaginian attackers of Greek towns on Sicily, where in c.398 BC they were copied by Dionysius I (c.432–367 BC), the ingenious Tyrant of Syracuse. They were costly and took a good deal of skilled labour to construct, so their use was probably limited to the armies of larger, wealthier states. They do not seem to have been much employed around the Mediterranean in c.400–350 BC, but they reappeared in the armies of Philip II of Macedon and his son Alexander. The names of some of the chief engineers of the kings of Macedon have survived: Philip was served by Polyidus of Thessaly, and one of his pupils, Diades, was given much credit for his work with Alexander at Tyre.

The purpose of each of these types of machine was to get attacking troops up to the walls under cover from arrows and other missiles; they were both sturdy housings, built on the spot from locally felled timber, and mounted on rollers or rudimentary wheels so that they could be pushed forward against the walls, either by large numbers of men or by teams of oxen. It seems likely that the more complex fittings – such as wheel-trucks, metal ram-heads and pulleys – were prefabricated and carried on campaign.

Battering ram housings were large enough to accommodate a team of men to swing a long, heavy, metal-tipped beam mounted to hang from the roof at its point of balance; repeated impacts on a single spot would eventually smash a hole in the wall. Similar 'tortoises' or rolling sheds could be pushed forward without rams to partly overlap defensive ditches, allowing logs, rocks, bundles of brushwood and earth-baskets to be dropped in to provide a causeway across.

Siege towers provided attackers not only with access but also with 'covering fire'. They were made several storeys tall to overtop the walls, tapering from a broad base to a narrower top for stability, with successive landings reached by ladders. Although they certainly existed, the dimensions claimed for some of them in ancient sources are dismissed by scholars as beggaring belief: Diades is supposed to have recommended one 20-storey monster rising as high as 53 metres (175 ft) – a great deal taller than any known contemporary city wall. Whatever their actual height, the troops climbed up inside them, protected by parapets and hoardings, to shoot down to clear defenders from the ramparts (with their own missile weapons or with catapults), before lowering gangways onto the battlements and storming across.

All these machines naturally drew the defenders' missiles, so had to be protected from fire-arrows and stones by an outer covering of wickerwork, dampened animal hides and/or thick padding; some ancient sources also show metal sheathing.

fleet continued to harry the Macedonians on both the Greek mainland and the islands; before venturing any deeper into Asia, Alexander had to secure his rear. Since his navy was too weak to risk a decisive fleet action, he determined to hamstring the Persian navy by robbing it of its coastal bases in the Eastern Mediterranean.

THE SIEGE OF TYRE

In 332, as Alexander continued his inexorable advance down the coast of Lebanon, most of the Phoenician ports and other cities surrendered to him; but Tyre refused to yield. Its king, Azimilik, was away serving with the Persian Aegean fleet, but since the city had once allegedly withstood an Assyrian siege lasting 13 years, the Tyrians believed it to be impregnable. Its main strength was that part of the city lay on a strongly fortified island perhaps half a mile (0.8 km) off the coast of the mainland Old City, easily supplied and supported from the sea. All numbers in ancient texts are, of course, suspect, but it appears that the garrison of the island was some 8000 strong, protecting perhaps 45,000 civilians, while Alexander had an army of about 30,000 men.

Alexander ordered the building of a causeway or mole out from the waterfront of the Old City. This was a natural extension of the old idea of a siege mound or ramp, and the water was shallow close to shore, with a muddy bottom. Timber piles were driven in first, then stones (from demolition in the Old City) were piled between them, and earth was layered on top; as the causeway progressed the working gangs were protected from the missiles of Tyrian ships by palisades along the sides. This was a massive engineering task – by the time it was finished the mole would reportedly be about 100 metres (330 ft) wide by 900 metres (2950 ft) long; and it became more difficult as it inched forwards, since nearer to the island the seafloor dropped away sharply and became stonier.

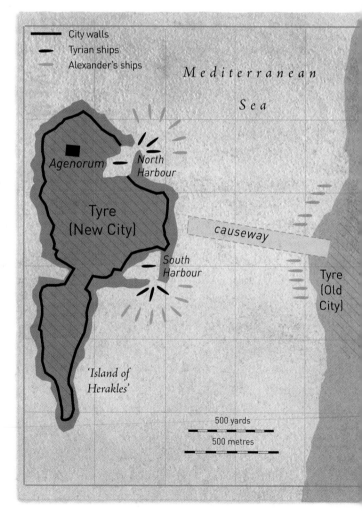

Map showing the island of Tyre, and the causeway (mole) built from the mainland by Alexander.

The builders were frequently raided by Tyrian boat-parties, and as they got closer they came under fire from catapults on the island. When they came within 'artillery' range, Alexander rolled two siege towers up to the head of the causeway and began bombarding the walls. The Tyrians responded by converting a horse-transport into a fireship; weighted at the stern to bring the bows up, this was towed across and beached at the head of the mole, where Alexander's towers were burned down. Tyrian warships showered missiles on the Macedonians attempting to fight the flames, and boats landed raiding-parties to wreck other catapults and palisades on the causeway.

THE TURNING POINT

Patiently, Alexander ordered the causeway to be enlarged (it may have taken the form of two closely parallel moles) and equipped with even more towers and catapults. Meanwhile, since most of the country had surrendered to him, he was able to persuade Phoenicians from Aradus and Byblus to come over to his side – and crucially, with their ships and crews. More ships from Rhodes and Cyprus soon joined him, and with the balance of power at sea tipped in his favour a successful conclusion to the siege was now achievable. He also received some 4000 fresh troops from Greece, and recruited skilled local and Cypriot artisans for construction work.

Against the worsened odds the Tyrian captains could not be lured into leaving their two protected harbours to fight on the open sea. Alexander's strengthened fleet blockaded them in port; he mounted siege engines on lashed-together ships and rafts, and anchored them around the coast of the island. The Tyrians countered by raising the height of their rampart towers, which were

ANCIENT 'ARTILLERY': ARROW-CATAPULTS

The first type of catapult is believed to have been invented in the late fifth or early fourth century BC. Its details – like those of all classical military machinery known only from later and only partly-understood sources – are interpreted in various ways, but there is little doubt that it resembled a giant crossbow. Mounted on a frame, this had a winching system for drawing back the string, and with it a sliding shoe holding a large arrow, along a wooden stock mounted at right-angles to the bowstave; it was released by a trigger mechanism tripping a pivoting claw. Philip II of Macedon is believed to have employed catapults mounted in siege towers in 340 BC.

Soon afterwards a major technical advance took place: the replacement of a single bowstave, storing its energy through compression, by a type with two arms thrust through vertical 'springs' of twisted sinew or hair mounted in frames either side of the forward end of the stock. The spring tension was adjustable by turning cotter-pins in round, notched metal washers at the top and bottom of each spring-frame. It seems to have taken a couple of generations to develop the full potential of this 'torsion' catapult, but by the early third century BC a standard set of tables existed for building them – the relative dimensions were crucial.

ANCIENT 'ARTILLERY': STONE-THROWING CATAPULTS

While the development of the arrow-shooter was still taking place, a similar machine for throwing stones began to be introduced by the armies of Alexander the Great, and was employed alongside arrow-shooters at Tyre. The frames and stock were redesigned and strengthened to take the greater weight and shock of discharge, although the first models probably took only lightweight ammunition. Stone-throwers had an obvious advantage over arrow-shooters: while the latter were anti-personnel weapons, useful for clearing defenders from ramparts or killing close-packed attackers at a distance, the former could – with repetitive hits – actually damage the fabric of fortress walls. By 311 BC, just 21 years after the siege of Tyre, stone balls in various standard weights between 4.4 kilograms (9.7 lbs) and 17.6 kilograms (38.8 lbs) were in use (recovered examples even have carved-in weight markings for the guidance of the catapult crews), and other, undated finds include balls weighing up to 35.7 kilograms (78.6 lbs).

Calculations have suggested that a 30-*mina* (13 kg/28.6 lb) ball shot at an elevation of 43.5° had a range of about 450 metres (1475 ft), but lost much of its impact through air resistance – and, in the air for over 9 seconds, it was easy for defenders to spot and avoid. If the catapult could be brought up to a range of 100–183 metres (330–600 ft) and the ball shot at an elevation of 5.7°–10°, it arrived with maximum impact after a flight of only 1 or 2 seconds.

strongest opposite the advancing causeway, and by dropping boulders into the shallows as ship obstacles. Alexander's sailors and soldiers laboriously dragged these clear, under storms of arrows and rocks. His ships landed men on the island, and fighting began on the narrow fringes of land under the walls. Mutual raiding by and from ships continued, with swimmers and divers cutting enemy anchor-cables; meanwhile, summer storms damaged the mole.

The main Tyrian effort came when 13 of their ships with picked crews managed to slip out of the north harbour and attack blockading Cypriot vessels by surprise while many of the sailors were ashore. Several ships were destroyed or cast adrift to founder; but Alexander immediately went aboard and led a counter-attack around the island, which trapped many of the raiders and drove the rest back into harbour with heavy loss.

THE FINAL ASSAULT

After about six months of relentless labour, the causeway finally reached the island. Siege engines made little impression on the walls, however, and an attempt to bombard and land near the north harbour was also beaten off. Diversionary and probing attacks were made all round the coast, seeking a weak point, from ships brought close in under the walls. Ships fitted with rams and catapult towers at first shook, and then made small breaches in the wall on the southern promontory known as the Island of Herakles, but the first assaults were repulsed. Three days later, at the end of July, Alexander tried again at this vulnerable sector; the breaches were enlarged, and two ships carried up landing bridges for a picked assault force. After their commander fell, Alexander personally led an all-out attack; he got enough men ashore to capture and clear two sections of the walls, while Phoenician and Cypriot ships forced their way into both harbours and landed more troops. The defences began to unravel; one by one towers were captured and the Macedonians advanced, clearing the curtain walls and penetrating deeply northwards into the city.

THE PUNISHMENT FOR DEFIANCE

After seven months, Tyre finally fell to these combined assaults, and the garrison's last stand in the Agenorum citadel turned into a bloody massacre. There was nothing new about the atrocities that followed the capture of the city, and which have been repeated on a greater or lesser scale throughout the history of siege warfare.

According to this grimmest of all the traditional 'customs of war', if a garrison forced its besiegers to go through every stage of the process – enduring months of backbreaking labour while paying a steady toll of deaths from missiles, accidents during engineering work and disease in the crowded siege-camps, and finally facing the inevitably heavy casualties of an assault over breaches in the walls – then that garrison and its citizens could expect no mercy. Generals usually understood that there was no point in trying to control their almost crazed troops during the immediate aftermath of a successful storming; looting, murder and rape simply had to run their horrible course, until the surviving soldiers sickened of it and their madness dissipated in the sleep of drunken exhaustion. When Tyre fell, perhaps as many as 8000 defenders were slaughtered – 2000 of them allegedly being crucified after capture; about 30,000 civilian captives were sold into slavery, although it was said that Alexander's allied troops from Sidon spared perhaps 15,000 of their fellow Phoenicians.

The Destruction of Jerusalem by Ercole de' Roberti (c.1451–96), a sweeping panorama that dramatically depicts the siege and destruction of the city by the Roman army in AD 70.

Europe's first professional army overcomes a desperate but disunited defence JERUSALEM

<small>APRIL–SEPTEMBER AD 70</small>

'What are we doing here? ... We allow three fortified walls to be built to coop us in ... while we sit still within our own walls, simply spectators to what they are doing, with our hands idle and our armour laid by. It seems we are only courageous against one another, while the Romans are likely to gain the city ... by reason of our disunity.'

FLAVIUS JOSEPHUS, *THE JEWISH WAR* (*c.*AD 75)

The siege and storming of Jerusalem, which led to the destruction of the Second Temple – and soon afterwards to the complete extinction of the ancient Jewish state – exemplified several of the key equations of siege warfare, but added another fatal flaw in the defence. The defenders had no hope of relief by an outside force, so the besiegers could work methodically without threat of interference. The defenders were numerous and their fortifications reasonably strong, but they were outclassed by the attackers both in military resources and in engineering skills. Their food stores were inadequate, while the attackers had control of a large area to pillage. Finally, the garrison demonstrated the suicidal folly of indulging in violent factional fighting among themselves, while also brutalizing the civilian population.

THE JUDEAN KINGDOM

In AD 6 the Roman emperor Augustus (r. 27 BC–AD 14) broke the realm of Herod the Great (r. 38–4 BC) , his former client king of Judea, into three parts, to bring an end to civil war between Herod's rival heirs. Judea became an imperial province, with headquarters at the port of Caesarea, and a small garrison installed in the Antonia fortress adjoining the magnificently reconstructed Temple in the northeast quarter of Jerusalem – the showpiece of Herod the Great's reign. Rome's everyday rule was fairly unobtrusive, and many Jews prospered; but Judea was always a troubled province, due largely to dynastic rivalries and religious factionalism. In AD 41 a grandson of Herod then living in Rome, Agrippa I (10 BC–AD 44), was helpful to the newly succeeded Emperor Claudius (r. 41–54), who in gratitude made him the client king of the whole of Herod's former realm. However, when he died three years later his son Agrippa II (27–100) was too young to ascend his throne, and greater Judea reverted to direct Roman rule – including, for the first time, the perennially restless region of Galilee, the heartland of the fundamentalist Zealot sect.

THE JEWISH REVOLT

In the AD 50s a harsh governor provoked widespread Jewish unrest, and Roman reprisals increased the popular following of the Zealots. In 62–4 a weak governor failed to prevent anarchic faction-fighting; in 67 his hard-line successor Gessius Florus provoked such bloody riots in Jerusalem that he had to withdraw from the city. The Zealots took control of much of Jerusalem, massacring both pro-Roman citizens and the surrendered garrison of the Antonia fortress. As inter-ethnic violence and rebellion spread across the country the governor of Syria, Cestius Gallus, marched on Jerusalem and occupied the northern suburbs; but he failed in an assault on the huge Temple complex, and was obliged to withdraw. Harried by guerrillas, Gallus's retreating column was forced to abandon its catapults – which were dragged back in triumph to Jerusalem, where the rebels began improving the fortifications.

The Zealots were always a minority, however, and most Jews looked to the traditional leadership class, who were thoroughly ambiguous about the rebellion. These leaders (including the man who later called himself Flavius Josephus, the commander in Galilee) urged patience, and explored ways to achieve a negotiated outcome, under the hostile scrutiny of the Zealots and their followers.

THE ROMAN MILITARY MACHINE

Waiting out the Romans behind city walls was not a realistic option for the rebels, however. In siege warfare the Romans were the direct heirs to the Greeks, whose techniques and weapons they had consciously adopted since 200 BC; they were masters of practical engineering of all kinds, and their patient, determined, ruthless temperament was well suited to the methodical reduction of fortified strongholds. In 67, the emperor Nero gave command in Judea to a middle-aged soldier of humble background but much experience: some 20 years earlier, Flavius Vespasianus (Vespasian; Roman emperor 69–79) had commanded a legion – a brigade of roughly 5000 professional, long-service heavy infantry – in the storming of hill-forts during the invasion of southern Britain. Now Vespasian sent his son and aide Titus (39–81; Roman emperor 79–81) to Alexandria to mobilize Legio XXII Deiotariana, while he took command of Legiones V Macedonica and X Fretensis in Syria, and marched down the Mediterranean coast to the port of Acre (improved by the Romans, and still to be a strategic harbour a thousand years later). Titus joined him there from Egypt, and this third legion brought his army up to some 50,000 men: 15,000 Roman citizen legionaries; about

FLAVIUS JOSEPHUS (37 – c.100)

We owe the detailed account of the siege to this Jewish turncoat. Joseph ben Matityahu was an educated man of aristocratic priestly background, who made important contacts while on a mission to Rome in 64. As the unenthusiastic commander in Galilee three years later, he contrived to avoid the massacre of his garrison at Jotapata and changed sides, becoming a favoured aide to both Vespasian and Titus. Thereafter he enjoyed a life of privileged wealth among the Romanized élite; his account of the events of the Jewish Revolt is historically important, though it casts Josephus himself in a most unattractive light.

TIMELINE

66 First Jewish-Roman War (or Great Jewish Revolt) begins, sparked by religious tension in Caesarea

67 Nero makes Flavius Vespasianus (Vespasian) commander of Roman forces in Judea

68 Nero commits suicide; chaos reigns during the Year of the Four Emperors

69 Vespasian becomes emperor and restores order

70 Roman legions under Vespasian's son Titus besiege Jerusalem, which falls after five months

72–3 Jewish–Roman War ends with mass suicide of defenders at the Siege of Masada

*c.*75 Titus Flavius Josephus writes his account of the conflict, *The Jewish War*

17,000 long-service auxiliary light infantry and 5500 cavalry raised in the provinces; and perhaps 4000 cavalry and 10,000 archers provided for the short term by Rome's regional client kings. As the Romans rolled through Galilee and Samaria, killing any group and burning any place that resisted them, many towns simply surrendered without a fight.

The fortress at Jotapata, in the hills west of the Sea of Galilee, was commanded unwillingly by the later chronicler Josephus; intending to surrender, he was prevented by his men, who now received a lesson in Roman siege methods. Vespasian sent cavalry to blockade the town, then moved up his infantry and artillery; while the defenders were cleared off the ramparts by a barrage of arrows, sling-stones and catapult-bolts he set his men to building an access ramp. When this reached a practical height, shielded battering rams were wheeled up to pound the walls; when the defenders dangled fenders on ropes down the face of the wall to cushion the impacts, the Romans cut them free with sickles on long poles. Even when the garrison managed to break a ram by dropping a boulder, and set its housing alight, Vespasian's engineers had it back in action by nightfall. After his assault on the first breach failed, Vespasian had three iron-sheathed siege towers built, from which his missile weapons dominated the battlements. On the 47th day of the siege, the Romans broke into Jotapata and wiped out the garrison (except for Josephus, who managed to get himself captured alive, and gratefully changed sides).

Vespasian advanced inexorably, accepting the surrender of some towns, storming and sacking others. The garrisons of Mount Tabor and Gischala abandoned these fortresses and fled to Jerusalem, where the Zealot leader John of Gischala accused the leading citizens of Roman sympathies and responsibility for the loss of Galilee. He occupied the Temple Mount and unleashed bloody purges throughout the city; when attacked by a mob he called in 20,000 supporters from Idumaea in the far south, and the subsequent reign of terror drove many citizens to flee. Meanwhile, Vespasian was marching ever closer; in the summer of 68 Legio V was at Emmaus, cutting Jerusalem off from the west, and Legio X at Jericho, controlling access from the east. Beyond all expectation, however, the city was then given a respite of fully 18 months.

THE YEAR OF THE FOUR EMPERORS

In the autumn of 68 Nero died without any obvious successor, and the armies of rival generals contested his throne throughout the following year. Vespasian, the furthest from Italy, had to stall his main operations until the situation clarified, although in summer 69 he did march south to Idumaea to crush a new rising led by Simon Bar-Giora. The only fortresses left in rebel hands were now Jerusalem; Herodium, south of the city; Masada, west of the Dead Sea; and Machaerus, east of it. The rebels took little useful advantage of their breathing space. The citizens of Jerusalem, driven frantic by the continuing violence, appealed to Simon Bar-Giora to rid them of John of Gischala, but soon found themselves at the mercy of two rival fanatics. When Simon attacked the Temple Mount the Zealots built four new towers to defend it; then the Zealots themselves split into two factions – one, led by Eleazar, held the Temple's inner court, while John of Gischala's men in the outer precinct were caught between them and Bar-Giora's fighters in the city. Each party tried to destroy the others' food supplies, and the warehoused corn gathered to withstand a Roman siege went up in flames.

THE RENEWED ROMAN OFFENSIVE

Nero's first opportunist successor, Galba, was overthrown by Otho, who was defeated in his turn by Vitellius. In response, Vespasian's troops in the East proclaimed their own general as emperor in July 69. His allies from the Danube legions defeated the Vitellians at Cremona, and Vespasian sailed for Rome to take the throne. He left his son Titus the task of finally crushing the Jewish Revolt with four legions: as well as his V Macedonica, X Fretensis and XV Appolinaris, Titus received XII Fulminata from Syria. Chaotic Jerusalem would now receive the undivided attention of a strong Roman army led by a general who, for obvious political reasons, needed a clear-cut victory.

In April 70, Titus marched on the city from the north, collecting Legio V on his way. He occupied Mount Scopus on the northeast of Jerusalem; when Legio X arrived from Jericho it camped on the Mount of Olives east of the city. Titus then levelled the ground between Mount

TITUS (41 – 81)

After Titus Flavius Sabinus Vespasianus had served as a junior officer in Germany and Britain, his father gave him command of Legio XXII in 67. Although only 26, he performed creditably; he was said to be highly literate, judicious in command and personally brave. As commander-in-chief during the siege of Jerusalem he went into the front lines, and showed himself to be a skilful archer. He became unpopular in Rome during his years as a young prince, but when he succeeded Vespasian as emperor in 79 he proved to be a worthy heir to his respected father. However, he died – apparently of natural causes – after only two years, to be succeeded by his less admirable brother Domitian (51–96).

Scopus and the city walls; he moved part of his army into two new camps about 400 metres (1310 ft) from the western defences, just out of catapult range – one on the northwest and the other, for Legio V, facing the citadel of Herod's palace on the western side; Legio X stayed on the Mount of Olives. With their auxiliaries and allies, the Romans numbered anything up to 70,000 troops. The defenders had perhaps 23,000 men in all: Simon Bar-Giora, with some 15,000, manned the northern and western defences including the citadel, while about 8400 Zealots led by Eleazar and John of Gischala held the Temple sector in the east.

The Temple was a superb feat of engineering. A huge stone platform capped a sloping rock hilltop, its eastern wall rising perhaps 46 metres (150 ft) from the Kidron Valley. Along the inside of tall, blank-faced walls a rectangle of pillared porticoes edged an outer courtyard measuring about 480 by 300 metres (1575 x 985 ft), with a massive range of buildings closing its south side and the Antonia fortress glowering over the northwest corner. In the centre rose the Temple itself, enclosed with its inner courtyard by another rectangle of high walls. The character of the whole complex was massive and forbidding, with only a few restricted entrances.

THE ROMAN ASSAULTS

The Jews made an early sortie towards the Roman camps, inflicting significant casualties, and rejected an offer of terms carried by Josephus (who claims that they then started fighting among themselves again). In May, Titus launched his first attack – in the west, on the newly built 'third wall' just north of Herod's citadel; here the legionaries worked to raise a ramp, while X Fretensis kept the Zealots occupied by bombarding the Temple Mount from the Mount of Olives. The

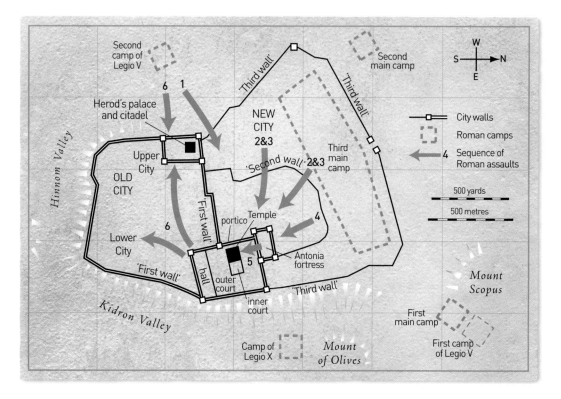

ROMAN ARTILLERY IN JUDEA

The Romans had acquired not only heavy siege catapults but also, by the time of Julius Caesar's campaigns in the 50s BC, improved 'field artillery'. These light catapults accompanied the infantry, to provide supporting 'firepower' for assaults alongside the archers, slingers and javelineers; an early 20th-century reconstruction of a light *catapulta* achieved ranges of around 274 metres (300 yards). It is believed that by the time of Vespasian each infantry legion – comprising ten cohorts, each of six centuries – was allocated one arrow-shooting catapulta per century, and one stone-throwing ballista per cohort, thus giving the legion 60 light and ten heavy artillery pieces.

Josephus writes that 160 machines were present at the siege of Jotapata in 67, including some shooting incendiary arrows, and heavy 1-talent (26kg/57lb) stone-throwers; the heaviest employed at Jerusalem three years later were apparently the 1-talent pieces of Legio X Fretensis. The great majority of the stone balls recovered from Israeli archaeological sites are much lighter, in the range of 0.9 kilograms (2 lbs) to 4.1 kilograms (9lbs); but they include a few up to 26 kilograms (57 lbs), and a single massive example from Machaerus weighs 90 kilograms (198 lbs). Josephus claimed a range of 400 metres (1310 ft) for a 1-talent ballista; a reconstruction tested in 2002 achieved only 100 metres (330 ft), but many details of the construction were, unavoidably, only educated guesswork.

heavy stone balls did a great deal of damage; Josephus tells us that when the Romans noticed that the defenders were learning to dodge their slow flight by spotting their light colour against the background of olive trees, they painted them dark to camouflage them.

When the western ramp was completed, battering rams were wheeled up under cover of light artillery, and began their work; then iron-sheathed siege towers were rolled up the ramp in their turn, to sweep the battlements with missiles. The Jewish defenders tried to wreck and burn the siege engines, with their own missiles and by making sorties, but were driven back. On the 15th day of the siege the western wall was breached; the citadel stood firm, but Bar-Giora's men abandoned the New City in the north – into which Titus immediately moved part of his troops – and withdrew within the 'second wall'.

Although siege engines made a narrow breach in this after five days, an initial advance beyond it was driven back after difficult fighting in the narrow streets. Four more days' pounding created a second breach, and subsequent assaults captured the whole length of the 'second wall', which was

Map of Jerusalem, showing the sequence of Roman assaults on the city between April and September AD 70.

then demolished. The northern half of the Temple Mount and the Antonia fortress were now exposed to attack, but Titus, well aware of the probable cost of direct assaults, rested his men while he applied psychological pressure. For four days they held highly visible pay parades in full dress uniform, and Josephus was sent again to summon the garrison to surrender.

Four new siege towers were built near the Antonia, where XII Fulminata and V Macedonica began building a ramp against the northern wall; meanwhile X Fretensis and XV Appolinaris started raising another against Herod's citadel. The erection of the Antonia ramp took 17 days, giving the Zealots time to dig a tunnel under the walls to undermine it; this was filled with inflammable materials and set on fire, and the wooden foundations of the ramp burned and collapsed. Meanwhile a sortie to the west by Simon Bar-Giora's men succeeded, at great cost in lives, in burning the siege engines and ramp outside the citadel.

The Romans, dreadfully patient, were undismayed by these setbacks. Titus ordered the complete investment of the city by the building of a circumvallation – a continuous palisade all round the outside of the east, south and west perimeters. With his huge labour force this took only three days; the wall, nearly 5 miles (8 km) long, was linked to the camps inside the New City, on the Mount of Olives and west of the citadel, and incorporated 13 forts for auxiliary units.

So far, parties of defenders had still been able to slip out through hidden passages to forage for food and mount hit-and-run attacks; now Jerusalem was finally cut off. The food shortage was soon causing serious hunger; fighting broke out over the remaining supplies, and when the public storehouses were empty the followers of John of Gischala and Simon Bar-Giora began to loot and brutalize the citizens. When the Romans caught anyone trying to creep through the perimeter in search of food they crucified them before the walls, but famine still drove deserters out to surrender.

The legions were now concentrated against the Antonia fortress. The countryside for miles around was scoured for timber, and in three weeks a ramp had been rebuilt, bridging the valley

MASADA

A final siege of Herod's clifftop fortress of Masada, overlooking the western shore of the Dead Sea and held by several hundred rebels under Eleazar ben Ya'ir, was carried out in 72–3 by Flavius Silva with Legio X and auxiliary troops. Since Masada was well provisioned and watered (with large cisterns cut into the rock) the siege lasted for seven months. Labouring in punishing desert conditions, the Romans built a circumvallation to cut off all escape, and patiently piled up a huge ramp against the 91-metre (300-ft)-high western cliff. When they finally got a siege tower up to the wall around the plateau, they found nearly 1000 corpses – the garrison had killed their families and committed suicide when defeat became inevitable. This act of desperation seemed to symbolize the conclusion that there was ultimately no refuge that was proof against Roman military engineering.

from the Bethesda hill and reaching high enough up the walls for siege engines to batter them above their solid stone foundations. The Zealots tried to fire the ramp, but were driven back; the Roman rams at first made little impression on the massive masonry, but then a subsidence in the original Jewish mine brought a section of it down. A secondary wall had been built inside, but three nights later this was captured by auxiliaries in a surprise attack, which confused the defenders into retreating from the Antonia to the Temple platform. Roman troops followed them into the outer court; although driven back in heavy fighting, they established an outpost at the northeast corner.

THE FINAL EFFORT

The Roman assault now entered its last, most exhausting and bloodiest phase. While fighting continued along the northern edge of the Temple complex, the Romans undertook the enormous task of demolishing the Antonia fortress – except for its southeast tower, kept as an observation post – and used its rubble to extend their ramp down into the northwest corner of the Temple court, where the fortress had stood some 23 metres (75 ft) above the platform. Meanwhile, fighting raged for days along the portico leading south down the west side of the courtyard, where access limited the numbers of men who could advance together. Finally, the Jews withdrew to lure Roman troops into advancing down the roof before firing the building, burning many of them to death.

As the rubble of the Antonia extended the ramp both forwards and sideways, more and more Roman troops and siege engines could be brought forward, and after about six days they were able to attack down onto the platform – even cavalry was brought over. The huge empty expanse of the outer court was perfect for Roman close-combat tactics, and they soon drove the last defenders back into the inner Temple complex. The gates into the inner court were burned down; the starving Zealots made a desperate sortie, only to be caught in the open by Roman cavalry; the survivors withdrew inside, and the final assault went in. Supposedly by accident, the sanctuary was set on fire, and the last Zealots died in the blazing Temple.

The sanctuary fell in mid-August, but it was to be three more weeks before the fighting ceased. From the Temple the Romans patiently cleared first the Lower, then the Upper City. It took 18 days to raise ramps against the citadel, but when the Romans broke in the surviving defenders were so weak with starvation that they offered little resistance. It has been calculated that the city finally fell on 7 September, after five months; it was completely sacked and partially razed. Untold thousands died, and many of the survivors were sold into slavery; any active defenders captured alive were sent to the amphitheatres, or to Rome for display in Vespasian's and Titus's eventual triumph, where Simon Bar-Giora was executed; John of Gischala spent the rest of his life in a Roman dungeon. Surviving parts of the citadel were incorporated into a new fortress for Legio X Fretensis, which remained to garrison Judea.

Stalemate – the besieger besieged ACRE

27 August 1189 – 12 July 1191

'I take pleasure in seeing archers near the loopholes,

When the stone-throwers shoot and the wall loses its parapet,

And when the army grows in numbers,

And forms ordered ranks in many an orchard ...'

FRENCH TROUBADOUR BERNAT ARNAUT DE MONCUC, 'ERCAN LI ROZIER' (*c.*1212)

The wars that took place from the 11th to the 13th century in Outremer – the transplanted Crusader state in Palestine – witnessed many sieges, and it was to the Byzantine and Muslim worlds that Western Europe owed the preservation during the European 'Dark Ages' of siegecraft from the classical world. One of the longest and most famous of these struggles took place at Acre, in territory over which both Alexander and Vespasian had marched more than 1000 years before. However, for much of its nearly two-year course this siege was essentially an exercise in frustration. The resources available to armies of the day were not up to the standards of those earlier conquerors, and the typical siege tactics were rather more lethargic; but the siege of Acre is also a telling example of what happened when a besieger was hampered by repeated outside interference.

THE CRUSADES

In 1095, Pope Urban II (1042–99) summoned the kings and nobles of Europe to co-operate in a great expedition to recover the Holy Land from its Muslim conquerors, promising all who died in the attempt a heavenly reward. His appeal drew a remarkable response, and in July 1099 the soldiers of this First Crusade (1096–9) captured Jerusalem (and celebrated their victory with a pitiless massacre of innocents). Thereafter many of the Western European knights and commoners remained in Palestine, establishing a feudal Christian 'kingdom of Jerusalem'.

The town of Acre (Tel e-Fukhar) lies on a promontory at the northern end of what is now called Haifa Bay, sheltering a deep-water harbour. It was captured in May 1104, and new walls and a breakwater were built; as its traffic increased Acre became more strategically important than Jerusalem itself, some 75 miles (120 km) to the south. It would be held continuously by the Crusaders throughout the almost 200-year history of their state, excepting only the years 1187–91.

The ruling nobility of the kingdom imported the envious rivalries of Norman Europe; their quarrels over the worldly rewards of the East cost them much of their support from Western

Assault on a walled city by trebuchets, as depicted in a 13th-century manuscript illumination. Saladin's engineer al-Tarsusi mentions the use of such siege engines at Acre.

TIMELINE

1174 Saladin becomes sultan of Egypt

1185 Guy of Lusignan ascends the throne of Jerusalem

1187 Christian armies routed by Saladin at the Battle of the Horns of Hattin; Jerusalem besieged and captured

1188 Christian monarchs of Europe promise forces for the Third Crusade (1189–92)

1189 (August) Beginning of 23-month-long siege of port of Acre (modern Akko)

1190 (June) Death of Holy Roman Emperor Frederick Barbarossa as he crosses Asia Minor on Crusade

1191 (July) Siege of Acre ends with surrender of Saracen garrison

1193 Death of Saladin in Damascus

Christendom, although their military dominance was bolstered by the foundation of the stern orders of soldier-monks – the Hospitallers (Knights of the Order of St John of Jerusalem) and Templars (Poor Fellow-Soldiers of Christ and of the Temple of Solomon). In 1185 the throne of Jerusalem was acquired under dubious circumstances by Guy of Lusignan (c.1150–94). Two years later he led an army of nearly 20,000 men to disastrous defeat at the Battle of the Horns of Hattin at the hands of the Muslim sultan of Egypt and Syria, the brilliant Kurdish-born ruler Salah al-Din Yussuf ibn Ayyub (1137–99), commonly known in the West as Saladin. Guy and many of his knights were captured, and Saladin's armies swept over the Crusader kingdom, capturing – among other towns – both Acre and Jerusalem.

At the shocking news of the loss of the Holy City, Pope Gregory VIII (c.1100–87) started negotiating with Christian monarchs to assemble what became the Third Crusade (1189–92). In January 1188 the kings of England and France pledged themselves, followed in March by Emperor Frederick I Barbarossa of Germany (r. 1154–90); but it would be many months before their armies could hope to arrive in the Middle East.

THE SURVIVING ENCLAVES

The port of Tripoli held out, thanks to the timely arrival of the energetic Conrad of Montferrat (c.1145–92); so did Tyre, reinforced from Sicily by a Pisan fleet. (These harbours were respectively some 110 miles [177 km] and 25 miles [40 km] north of Acre.) In July 1188, Saladin released Guy of Lusignan in return for an oath never to fight him again. Humiliated, and widely blamed for the loss of Jerusalem, Guy made his way to Tyre to pick up the pieces of his weakened and disunited kingdom – only to be turned away by Conrad, who now ruled there in his place. Guy came back at the head of an army in April 1189 and tried to blockade Conrad into making concessions, but he lacked the necessary strength. (Meanwhile, far away in Europe, Barbarossa began an epic overland march for the Holy Land, leading some 30,000 men – a huge army for the 12th century – across Hungary towards the Balkans and Anatolia.)

After four months the frustrated Guy of Lusignan raised his siege of Tyre, and turned south; desperate for any success to restore his prestige, he broke his parole to Saladin and blockaded Acre instead. Guy had perhaps 400 mounted knights and 7000 infantry spearmen and crossbowmen; he also had a fleet from Pisa, although this was as yet only strong enough to mount a partial blockade of the sea lanes. Nevertheless, on 27 August, 1189, Guy began to entrench his army around the city.

ACRE'S DEFENCES

The port was protected by the Mediterranean on the west and south. The fortified area was shaped roughly like an 'L' turned to the right through 90°, enclosing the harbour in its angle. Its defences had been strengthened by Saladin since 1187, but are not known in detail, due to 13th-century and Ottoman rebuilding. It is believed that the northern walls ran for about 1400 metres (4600 ft) inland from the coast, ending in the powerful Maledicta ('Accursed') Tower at the northeast corner. From there the walls dropped south and then southwest in two runs of about 350 metres (1150 ft) each, reaching the southern shore east of the harbour. On the west side, the walls ran some 650 metres (2130 ft) north–south; so the enclosed land area and harbour together may have covered about 5.3 hectares (13 acres). The size of the garrison installed by Saladin is unrecorded, but judging from the perimeter of around 1.85 miles (3 km) it must have numbered 3000 at the very least.

The Crusaders built a 'fishhook' circuit of ditched palisades perhaps 2 miles (3.2 km) long, following the line of the walls. Various reinforcements arrived from Tyre and Europe, on uncertain dates; at some stage the army included French, Flemish, Germans (under Ludwig of Thuringia), Danes, Italians and a contingent led – grudgingly – by Conrad of Montferrat. The Knights Templar were stationed nearest to the sea north of Acre; next to them were Ludwig's Germans, then Conrad, then Guy's main multinational force, hooking round to the east and southeast of the city; a division led by Guy's brother Geoffrey of Lusignan was placed in a second line in the centre, closest to the northern city walls. The Pisan ships interdicted Muslim access to the harbour to some degree, but vessels carrying supplies and reinforcements from Saladin did slip past them periodically; a true investment of the city was not achieved before the spring of 1191.

TORSION-POWERED ARTILLERY

Both attackers and defenders at Acre employed similar siege engines of varying sizes. *Al-Tabsira*, a technical manual written for Saladin by Murda al-Tarsusi, describes several classes of weapon, of which one was torsion powered. Like those of ancient Greece and Rome, these machines had arms passing through springs of twisted cords. Al-Tarsusi describes a two-armed type used at Acre, which resembled what Europeans called an espringal. This had two vertical springs holding bow-arms moving in the horizontal plane; mounted inside a timber frame, it shot either large arrows or incendiaries. The single-armed torsion catapult resembled the late Roman onager or 'kicking mule'; this had a horizontal spring powering a long arm swinging in the vertical plane.

SALADIN'S REACTION

When Guy made his lunge south, much of Saladin's army was occupied in the siege of Beaufort far to the north. He did not move immediately; presumably confident in his garrison, and in its sea links with his Egyptian and other ports, he waited while he called up further Syrian vassals. When he finally arrived in mid-September 1189, he established his rear base at Saffuriya some miles southeast of Acre; then he stationed his troops outside and mirroring the crusader siege lines – in places only a few hundred yards from them, in others more than 2 miles (3.2 km) back, but always threatening to close in. Again, we have some information about his dispositions. The troops facing the Templars were led by his nephew Taqi al-Din, and included élite Mamluks from Damascus. On their left was the Mosul contingent; then the divisions of two of Saladin's sons, al-Afdal and az-Zahir. The sultan's field headquarters lay south of the Saffuriya road, behind the Kurdish contingent forming the centre of his army; to the left of them were more Mamluk troops.

It is impossible to guess the numbers of fighting men on either side; during the siege both received periodic reinforcements, and Muslim contingents – mostly of Turks, Turcomen, Kurds and Arabs, but some from as far afield as Sudan and the Sahara – arrived and departed at various stages. Early accounts of warfare notoriously exaggerate all numbers, sometimes grossly. We can say that in those days an army of 10,000 actually brought to battle was considered respectably large, and we may guess that the totals on either side in Palestine probably never exceeded the low tens of thousands. The Muslim lines were fluid and far from continuous; their army must presumably have outnumbered the Crusaders at some stages, but probably not by any extreme margin. The essential point, however, was that before spring 1191 at the earliest the Muslim field army was sufficiently strong to threaten the Crusader force dangerously, obliging it to divide its efforts between two fronts: facing both the city and the plain, it was never strong enough to carry the walls. This imbalance would frustrate the besiegers for nearly two years – and, in a place and time of lethal endemic diseases and rudimentary hygiene, it would condemn them to a constant haemorrhage of deaths in their overcrowded camps.

THE FIGHTING BEGINS

After some preliminary skirmishing, in mid-September 1189 a strong force under Taqi al-Din cut a path into the city for provisions, reinforcements and for Saladin himself, who entered and inspected the defences. After this setback the Crusaders improved their line of circumvallation, and on 4 October they launched a major attack on Saladin's army. Guy did not enjoy unquestioned authority; it was anyway in the nature of Norman barons to lead their divisions independently, and lack of central control now cost them dearly. At first the Templars forced Taqi's right wing back by the weight of their charge, and Saladin moved troops across from his centre to shore up that flank. Noting this, the Crusaders facing the centre attacked in their turn, and by good co-operation between infantry and cavalry beat the Mosul troops from the field. But instead of wheeling to destroy one of the Saracen wings, these Crusaders now advanced into the gap – some said, to loot the Muslim camps – and gave Saladin time to regroup and counter-attack; at some stage the city

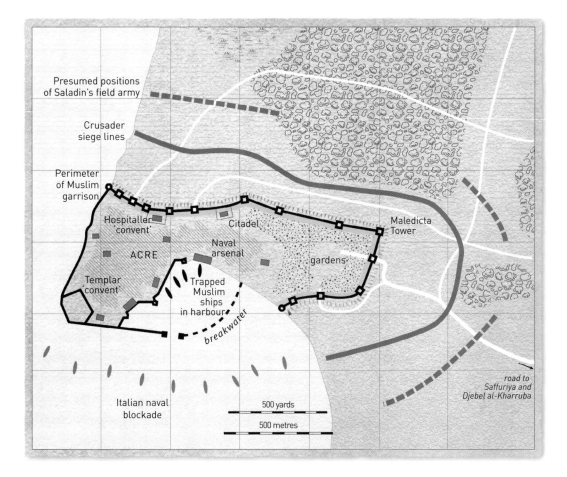

Map showing the circumvallation of Acre by Crusader forces and the deployment of Muslim forces.

garrison also sortied and caught the Templars in the flank. Crusader losses were heavy, including the Grand Master of the Templars. However, they had done enough damage to prevent Saladin exploiting his success fully; both sides duly withdrew to overwinter in their camps.

More Crusaders arrived in November 1189; Conrad sailed for Tyre to gather supplies, and returned in March 1190. Between the end of October and the beginning of February two separate Saracen convoys got into the harbour with men and provisions; Saladin also sent in his engineer Baha al-Din Qaragush, an Armenian eunuch, to strengthen the fortifications. At news of the progress of Barbarossa's army the sultan also had to send troops north to guard those approaches.

A YEAR OF PROFITLESS SACRIFICES

In spring 1190 the Crusaders took the initiative again. They had cut down much of the local woodland for palisades and winter fuel, and before building large siege engines they had to await Conrad's return from northern Lebanon with timber. In March they built three large, wheeled siege towers; a Muslim source described these as holding 500 men each, with stone-throwing mangonels on the top decks, and protected from fire-arrows by soaked hides. In April–May 1190 the Crusaders mounted determined attacks supported by catapults; they started to fill in parts of the dry moat in order to bring the siege towers up to the walls (and, by some reports, began to undermine them). However, the garrison sortied and managed to burn the towers – perhaps using the flame-thrower weapon called 'Greek fire' that Muslim armies had inherited from Byzantium. Then Saladin launched a series of attacks on the Crusader rear over eight full days; these successfully drew them off from the city, but were finally indecisive. This suggests that since Saladin's transfer of troops to the north the two armies at Acre were now of roughly equal size, and that this stalemate was cutting both ways.

In June 1190 strong reinforcements arrived under Henry of Troyes, who took command of the actual siege operations; he had some heavy new battering rams built, and reportedly spent a huge sum on constructing one great stone-throwing mangonel. News came that in July the Crusader armies of King Richard I 'the Lionheart' of England (r. 1189–99) and Philip II Augustus of France (r. 1180–1223) had finally got on the march south from central France. They would have to winter in Sicily to await the return of good sailing weather, and even then their progress would be leisurely – Richard would make a diversion to capture the lucrative prize of Cyprus. The long-awaited word of the kings' departure would soon be overshadowed by another message, however: that summer, in southern Anatolia, the emperor Frederick Barbarossa died while crossing the Saleph river, and his demoralized army – already thinned by its punishing 15-month march – began to unravel.

On 25 July the siege army made a major outwards attack on Saladin's right wing. They succeeded in striking deeply into the Muslim camps, but then discipline broke down in looting; the Saracen centre swung up, and defeated them with heavy losses. Skirmishing continued during late summer and autumn 1190, but the besiegers concentrated on the city. Mangonels and a large iron-headed ram battered its walls; but no breach was made, attacks using scaling-ladders were repulsed, and Qaraqush sent out raiders to destroy some of the mangonels. Meanwhile more contingents arrived from Europe, including 500 men led by the Archbishop of Canterbury, but these must have barely made up for the losses in battle and to camp-fever; the army was never strengthened to the point where it could either drive Saladin away, or storm the hungry city.

In October 1190 the remnant of Barbarossa's army straggled in, led by his son Frederick of Swabia. After the emperor's death it had been further weakened by desertions, and had had to fight its way past Saracen blocking forces; one estimate puts its final strength on arrival at little more than 1000 soldiers. Anxious to make his mark, the younger Frederick now urged an all-out attack on Saladin, and this was made in November. At a high cost in casualties, it succeeded in forcing the sultan to withdraw some 3 miles (4.8 km) to the south, into a much shorter north-facing line between the coastal dunes and the village of Ain el-Bass, with a new rear base at the Djebel el-Kharruba.

This actually eased Saladin's supply problems during the winter, and the arrival of troops no longer needed in the north also allowed him to rotate some of his divisions to rest. However, his army was worn down by disease and discouraged by this apparently endless campaign, and his headstrong nephew Taqi withdrew his command for several months to pursue his own ends in Turkey. (A medieval prince – even such a charismatic one as Saladin – could never count on the obedience of his subordinate nobility.) To set against this, the Muslims broke through the siege lines again on 13 February 1191, taking in badly-needed supplies and a new commander for the

Mangonels

The mangonel, used for centuries everywhere from China to Western Europe, was a 'beam-sling' weapon. A springy, tapering wooden arm, swinging in the vertical plane, was pivoted on an axle mounted across the top of a pyramid-shaped frame. A sling-pocket was hooked to the thinner rear end of the beam to hold missiles – modern experiments suggest weights of up to 60 kilograms (130 lbs). At the forward end of the beam was a crosspiece, to which 10–12 ropes were attached. While the sling end was anchored down, a team of men (perhaps two to each rope) pulled downwards against the tension of the flexing beam; when this was released it whipped upwards and the sling hurled the missile, fast enough to carry about 120 metres (400 ft). Al-Tarsusi mentions mangonels being used by both sides at Acre, including some mounted in wall- and siege towers. They were often grouped in large batteries, and medieval sources suggest that teams of men working in shifts could reach rates of up to one shot every 7 seconds from each catapult.

garrison; and the defenders beat off two major assaults during the winter, despite the collapse of a section of wall. For their part, the Crusaders went hungry, as winter gales kept supply ships away; disease was also stalking their camps, and was no respecter of rank – Frederick of Swabia was among the dead (the duke of Burgundy would also fall victim the following summer). In the spring Duke Leopold of Austria arrived with a small following, and took over command of the survivors of Barbarossa's army.

The Coming of the Kings

In March 1191 the first French ship arrived at last, carrying both badly-needed corn and the news that Philip II Augustus was not far behind. The king finally anchored with his first six ships on 21 April, in the 20th month of the siege; his vanguard was small, but it included engineers, who set to work building new siege engines and laying out zig-zagging trenches to get the besiegers closer to the walls. Like the count of Troyes before him, the duke of Burgundy now paid for a massive new stone-throwing machine. Philip Augustus delayed operations while he waited for Richard of England, whose first 25 ships arrived on 8 June. The balance between the two sides had finally reached a tipping-point.

Richard resisted Philip's urging of an immediate assault until the bulk of his army and some specialized equipment for building siege engines arrived; he fell ill, but had himself carried around the siege lines in a litter, occasionally shooting a crossbow at Muslims on the ramparts. By late June the new machines were ready, including a tall siege tower in which he had such faith that he named it Mategriffin – 'Checkmate'. Richard focused on a single tower, bombarding and undermining it until it fell, and then offered a bounty to any soldiers who would creep up to remove more stones from the wall. Moreover, the Crusaders now had the support of a Genoese fleet; not only did they complete an absolute sea blockade of the now-starving city, but they provided crossbowmen and engineers for the army ashore. Although two assaults by the English and French failed, the plight of the Acre garrison had now become critical.

On 2–3 July, Saladin's army attacked the siege lines, which had been greatly strengthened; despite a crisis on the Crusaders' left wing they held him off, and inflicted heavy losses (which argues that the two armies were again of closely comparable size).

SURRENDER

After this setback the garrison and leading citizens of Acre finally despaired of relief, and began to negotiate terms of surrender. They concluded an agreement which committed Saladin to damaging concessions (of which he only learned afterwards); and on 12 July 1191 they opened the gates and marched out, leaving about 2600 hostages against the honouring of the agreed payments and prisoner exchanges.

Apart from a watching force, Saladin pulled his army several miles back towards Saffuriya. A first exchange of prisoners and cash took place on 24 July; and on 31 July Philip Augustus sailed away, though leaving most of his men under the duke of Burgundy's command. Richard, who had quarrelled violently with all the other leaders, now wielded his authority as the only king present. When a dispute prevented the completion of the agreed exchanges, on 21 August he had all the hostages slaughtered in full view of the Saracen outposts. The number of deaths from combat and sickness during the two-year siege are impossible to estimate, but among the Christian soldiers and their many camp-followers they must have run into the tens of thousands.

On 22 August, Richard moved south down the coast from Acre, with the ultimate objective of Jerusalem. Saladin shadowed his progress, and on 7 September the two armies fought a pitched battle at Arsuf. Despite the potentially fatal disadvantage of having his army strung out in line of march, Richard achieved a great tactical success. Coming so soon after the loss of Acre, this defeat was a considerable blow to Saladin's prestige. Both he and Richard were suffering from illness; their countermarching and skirmishing continued indecisively for the next year, but the Crusaders never reached Jerusalem. On 2 September 1192 the king and the sultan agreed a limited peace treaty, which left the Holy City in Muslim hands but conceded visiting rights for Christian pilgrims. Acre remained the capital of the so-called Kingdom of Jerusalem and the main port for trade and pilgrimage, until the final Muslim victory in 1291 brought the crusading era to a close.

View of the castle ruins at Château-Gaillard, showing its formidable defensive position on top of a ridge overlooking the River Seine.

The failure of an expensively purpose-built castle
CHÂTEAU-GAILLARD

AUGUST 1203–6 MARCH 1204

'Behold, what a beautiful daughter I have, after only one year!'

ATTRIBUTED TO KING RICHARD I OF ENGLAND, 'COEUR DE LION',
ON SEEING THE FIRST YEAR'S BUILDING WORK AT CHÂTEAU-GAILLARD (1197)

The same siege techniques that were used to take cities were employed in more concentrated form against purpose-built castles; these formidable fortifications are the most obvious surviving gift to our landscape from the Normans. A famous example, built by Richard I of England (r. 1189–99), was Château-Gaillard in the Vexin borderlands of Normandy. He sited it with care, incorporated advanced features in its design, spent vast sums on its construction, and had such confidence in it that he declared he could have held it *'even if it had been made of butter'*. He was dead before his boast came to proof; but when it did, the limitations of technology, and the importance of simple human factors, were underlined.

WARS WITHOUT CEASE

Through multiple inheritance, Richard I of England was also ruler of more territory in what is now France than that country's nominal king, his fellow-Crusader and deadly rival Philip II Augustus (r. 1180–1223), whose realm surrounded Paris. Their endlessly quarrelsome barons were enmeshed in complex networks of often contradictory feudal obligations, and Richard spent most of his reign campaigning in France. He rushed back there soon after his return from the Third Crusade in spring 1194, delayed for nearly two years by an unfortunate shipwreck and imprisonment for ransom in an Austrian castle. In the meantime, Philip Augustus had ignored the convention that absent Crusaders' lands were sacrosanct, and had seized much of Richard's territory in Normandy.

After Richard reached France, Philip abandoned several sieges rather than face 'Lionheart' in pitched battle; this was not uncommon (since battles were always unpredictable), and in this case Philip, while a more effective king, had none of Richard's military prestige. To counter Philip's earlier successes, Richard now planned a series of new castles in a defensive belt. Medieval armies were relatively small, and the annual campaigning season usually lasted only a few months due to the difficulties of keeping an army together, moving it and supplying it. A coherent belt of separate strongholds had the advantage of forcing an army either to divide against them – thus lessening the numbers of men available for the enormous labour involved in any one siege – or to attack them one by one over many months. The longer and more complex a campaign was, the greater the likelihood that one of the uncertain chances of medieval warfare might force the raising of a siege, and the onset of winter would usually bring a campaign to an end.

THE LIONHEART'S IMPUDENT DAUGHTER

The site Richard chose for the greatest of these new castles was on a loop of the River Seine, where a riverside castle would not only control the important water traffic between Rouen and Paris, but would itself be easier to supply. The terrain was highly defensible: a steep chalk spur on the right bank of the Seine rose over 91 metres (300 ft) in the angle between the river and the southern edge of a cul-de-sac lake. At the mouth of the latter lay a fortified island village, Petit Andely, while at its eastern end stood the town of Grand Andely. Petit Andely was linked by a bridge to the smaller fortified Ile de l'Andely, and thence to the left bank of the Seine. The castle was built at the northwest end of the spur, protected by steep drops which made approach almost impossible from any direction but along the ridge from the southeast.

Work began in 1194, and it has traditionally – but almost incredibly – been claimed that it took little more than a year to complete (based on a misinterpretation by a 14th-century writer of the quotation at the head of this chapter). Richard's chosen name 'Gaillard' can mean either 'impudent' or 'bold', and the total cost of this stone challenge thrown at Philip Augustus was about £11,500. The daily fee for a knight in 1195 was 12 pence, and a knight had to serve for 40 days in a year, so that was the equivalent of 2674 'knight/months' (or, at one penny per day, 19,166 'footsoldier/months'), and his new castle cost Richard about the same as paying an army of 1000 knights and 10,000 soldiers for a year's 80-day campaign season.

DEVELOPMENTS IN CASTLE DESIGN

European timber-and-earth forts began to be improved or replaced with stone during the 11th century. At first they consisted only of a walled enclosure with a single large defensive keep; the White Tower in the Tower of London (c.1076) is an example of these tall, plain rectangular blocks. The largest might be up to 27 metres (90 ft) high, measuring 21–26 metres (70–85 ft) on a side, with walls up to 3 metres (10 ft) thick; the entrance was usually on the second of the four or five floors, perhaps 6 metres (20 ft) above the ground and reached by removable timber steps. Though very strong, their flat surfaces gave these squared towers potential weak points and many 'blind spots'.

From about 1150 the keep or donjon started to become polygonal or round; this threw off missiles better, and gave all-round 'fields of fire' for archers on the battlements – there were not many loopholes, and defenders mostly manned the tops of these towers. Stone 'curtain' walls were now built to defend the outer yard ('ward' or 'bailey'), at first plain but later defended by towers; one of these enclosed the gateway, reached by some kind of lifting bridge over a moat. These castles did not yet have concentric layers of defences; once an attacker breached the curtain wall or gate tower he faced only the keep.

More elaborate and extended layouts like Château-Gaillard, with many more wall towers giving 'converging fire' on most approaches, appeared in the late 12th and early 13th centuries. Provided that the garrison had a reliable well and plentiful provisions, it could often sit out a siege until relief arrived or the attacker gave up.

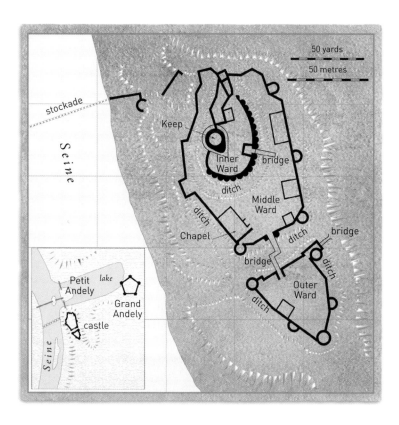

Map of Château-Gaillard, showing the triangular outer ward to the southeast, linked to the five-sided middle ward by a narrow bridge.

DESIGN OF THE CASTLE

The castle was roughly boat-shaped, the 'bow' confronting the southeastern approach with a strong tower. The 'forecastle' or outer ward was roughly triangular, with two flanking towers on its curtain walls; the latter, 9 metres (30 ft) high and 3.7 metres (12 ft) thick, were protected by deep side ditches, with access via a bridge to a gate tower at the northeast corner. Strikingly, the outer ward was cut off from the rest of the castle by a 2.4-metre (8-ft)-thick rear wall, probably with towers at each end, and by a ditch about 9 metres wide and 6 metres deep (30 ft x 20 ft), cut across the ridge through the solid chalk.

This outer ward was linked only by a narrow, crooked bridge to the straight southern wall of the 'waist and stern' of the stone boat, which was of irregular five-sided shape, with five wall towers at its angles. This middle ward contained a chapel against the southwest wall and various domestic buildings. Inside the 'stern' was the inner ward, shaped rather like a human ear; the exposed two-thirds of its perimeter was protected by another rock-cut ditch and by a wall of novel appearance. Its outer face was made up of close-set, rounded lobes, from whose upper loopholes archers thus enjoyed completely overlapping 'fields of fire'. Access to the inner ward was by a bridge over the ditch to a gatehouse on the east side.

Inside, the keep or donjon formed part of the west wall of this inner ward; its 2.4-metre (8-ft)-thick walls had a deep, solid, outward-sloping base drawn out in a solid beak at the eastern corner. (This feature of castle architecture, known as a 'talus', had several advantages: it defied mining; rocks dropped from above would ricochet outwards into the ranks of attackers; and it ensured that scaling ladders would have to be longer and set at a shallower angle – any ladder over about 9 metres [30 ft] long was liable to break under the weight of a crowd of climbing attackers; most famously, such walls were built to protect the Crusader fortress of Krak des Chevaliers in Syria.) On the side walls of the keep, buttresses fanned out as they rose; some historians believe that they united at the top in arches supporting the battlements, pierced with 'machicolations' – vertical slots, through which to shoot or drop missiles on attackers below. The facing ashlars of the keep, like some other parts of the castle, included bands of contrasting grey or pink stone against the white. Outside and down the cliff to the northwest was a round tower, from which a wall dropped steeply to the river bank. In line with this, a triple timber stockade was sunk across the bed of the Seine, to control shipping from Paris to the south.

Château-Gaillard has been termed a 'proto-concentric' design, since it lacked the true concentric defences that would be such a feature of the virtually impregnable 14th-century castles built by Edward I (r. 1272–1307) in Wales. There, an attacker piercing one layer of the shell at any point was always faced by another, higher wall from which the garrison, retreating inwards, could continue to shoot down on him. Nevertheless, the design of Château-Gaillard used the terrain with great intelligence, backing up layers of the defences wherever feasible; and the separation of the outer and middle wards condemned an attacker to successive efforts, which should have bought the garrison the time for a relief force to arrive.

The walls and towers would have been crowned with typical 'hoardings' or 'penthouses' – roofed, shuttered wooden galleries projecting outside the battlements; these gave cover to defenders,

TREBUCHETS

Saladin's expert military engineer al-Tarsusi had mentioned the use of these siege-engines at Acre (see page 37). They operated on the same 'beam-sling' principle as the mangonel, but were larger and more powerful, throwing wall-smashing stones. Instead of a springy beam being pulled down by men with ropes, a rigid beam had a heavy counterweight (al-Tarsusi mentions a net of rocks) attached to the forward end to provide the impulsion for the swinging motion. One witness claimed that part of Acre's walls was reduced to the height of a man by bombardment.

Trebuchets were the main 'siege artillery' of 13th-century Europe. An account from 1211 describes the destruction of a turret with a single shot, and many casualties being caused when stones fractured on impact. Several recovered stones are spherical, 43–50 centimetres (17–20 ins) in diameter and weighing around 40 kilograms (90 lbs). In 1989 a Danish experimental reconstruction, using a counterweight of just under 2 tons, achieved ranges of 180 metres (196 yards) with a 15-kilogram (33-lb) ball, and 91 metres (100 yards) with a 47-kilogram (103-lb) ball. The range could be adjusted slightly by altering the ballast weight, and choosing the ball-weight and the angle of the hook that held the sling-pocket proved critical for efficiency. It was obviously very laborious to traverse – to shift the aim sideways – but the reconstruction gave remarkably consistent results: all shots in a single sequence fell within a 6-metre (19-ft) square. This would have allowed attackers to concentrate a bombardment on a single section of wall until it crumbled.

and allowed them to pour water on any attempt to fire the gates, or to drop things to crush or burn anyone attacking or climbing the walls. These might include stones, quicklime or red-hot sand (the boiling oil of legend was probably rare – scalding water was cheaper and just as effective). Incendiary mixtures of pitch, resin and sulphur could also be dropped to set fire to the mantlets sheltering miners or battering rams working at the base of a wall.

THE OPPORTUNIST OF PARIS

Richard I died on 6 April 1199 from a crossbow wound suffered in a petty siege; he had no legitimate heir and the English barons preferred his younger brother John (r. 1199–1216; insultingly remembered as 'Lackland' or 'Softsword') over his 12-year-old nephew Arthur. Many of John's Normandy barons contested this choice, and he faced interminable rebellions. When Arthur was captured and murdered in 1203, many barons in Normandy formally shifted their allegiance to Philip Augustus, who (now that the Lionheart was safely dead) used this to justify a war to drive John out of his French possessions. At first neither king showed much energy, but that summer Philip marched on Château-Gaillard.

His army arrived during August 1203, but after a preliminary clash Philip limited himself to scouting and planning. We do not know the size of the garrison, but it was probably only a few dozen knights and squires and 200–300 crossbowmen and spearmen; medieval castle garrisons were not expected to man a continuous perimeter, but to concentrate opposite the points of attack. The castellan of Château-Gaillard, Roger de Lacy (c.1171–1212), was described as both brave and experienced; he must have been confident in his strong defences and in the prospect of a relief force from Rouen. If so, he misjudged his new king, and this misplaced faith now led him into the first element of 'human error': at some point during the next few weeks he allowed a large number of local civilians to come inside the castle for protection.

BLOCKADE AND INVESTMENT

Philip Augustus knew that to isolate the garrison and starve them out he first had to take control of the river. Accordingly, his troops captured the Ile de l'Andely, and swimmers somehow disabled the Seine palisades; the permanent bridges were cut and replaced by a bridge of pontoons, removable at any sign of attack on either bank. By the time John finally reacted to news of this setback the French had taken Petit and Grand Andely, and were astride both the river and the landward approaches to the castle. Philip did not let his troops disperse over the countryside in pillaging raids, which often dissipated the strength of siege armies; instead he set them to digging ditches and building palisades and guard towers to protect his camps on the west bank, and across the southeast neck of the ridge. During the autumn, with the investment of the castle complete, he settled down to wait. Roger de Lacy reduced the food rations, drove out perhaps 1000 of the civilian refugees (whom the French allowed to cross their lines), and hung on in hope of relief.

Belatedly, the lethargic King John ordered the earl of Pembroke to break through to Château-Gaillard; this would involve cutting a way through French lines on both banks of the Seine and

THE COST OF SIEGE ENGINES

Trebuchets took time, money and skilled labour to construct, and – perhaps apart from special iron fittings – were normally made on the spot. The advantages of this are clear from an account of a Welsh siege in 1288, when one machine had to be dismantled, brought across country (presumably because there were no trees big enough near the next targeted castle), repaired and rebuilt. This took four large wagons drawn by a total of up to 60 oxen, plus 120 packhorses for ammunition. The total cost of hired labour, transport and materials (timber, ropes, hides, grease and the smithing of iron fittings), plus constructing the machine and providing 480 stone balls, amounted to £180. At that time, this was roughly equivalent to a whole month's wages for 720 archers – and that was just for one machine: besieging a large castle required trebuchets grouped in batteries.

re-opening the river access. Pembroke planned a complex night operation: 70 boats carrying supplies were to row up-river (from north to south), accompanied by a force strong enough to break the blockade, while a second force attacked the French lines at the neck of the ridge. Given the difficulties of medieval command, control and communication, it is not surprising that Pembroke failed. At the onset of winter the Seine's current was too strong, delaying the river force; the overland party attacked too soon, and the French were able to beat them both in succession. John's response was to return to England to deal with troublesome barons: Roger de Lacy's hungry garrison were on their own.

At some date during the bitter weather of December 1203 or January 1204, he was forced to push another 400 civilians – the sick, the women and children – out of the castle, and shut the gates on their pleading. This time the French would not let them through, so they huddled in the ditches outside, eating grass (and worse) while they starved to death. Even in a harsh age the impact on the morale of the garrison must have been damaging: they would have been soldiers from the surrounding district, and they knew these poor wretches – perhaps they would even have been related to some of them. Eventually, Philip Augustus returned to his siege camp and ordered them to be let in and fed, but by then it was too late for most of them.

THE MINERS

In February 1204 – a full five months after arriving – the French made their first attack on the already weakened garrison. Soldiers called siege towers 'malvoisins'; now one of these 'bad neighbours' was dragged up facing the outer ward, while crossbowmen raked the battlements from behind cover. Catapults began to pound the walls at the southeast prow of the castle, and a rolling shed or 'sow' was pushed up to the outer ditch; under its cover, men laboriously filled in part of the dry moat with cartloads of gravel and earth, so that miners could get right up to the wall under

TIMELINE

1194 On his return from the Third Crusade, Richard I ('the Lionheart') of England is held captive in Germany by the Holy Roman Emperor Henry VI; his brother John ('Lackland') and Philip II Augustus of France offer money to have his imprisonment prolonged

1197–8 Richard builds the castle of Château-Gaillard on the Seine in his duchy of Normandy

1199 Richard is killed while besieging the castle of Chalus-Chabrol in Haute-Vienne, France; succeeded by King John

1203 (August) Philip II Augustus begins siege of Château-Gaillard

1204 (March) Final defenders of Château-Gaillard surrender

1216 Death of King John

1223 Death of Philip II

cover of its armoured roof. After bombardment with trebuchets – including a monster that the French named 'Cabulus' – a possible breach was identified in the wall east of the apex tower. The miners climbed ladders to get above the solid rock of the ditch and reach the masonry courses; then they prised away the outer stones until they could pick a cave in the rubble infill of the 3.7-metre (12-ft)-thick wall, shoring it up with timbers as they worked. When they had penetrated far enough into the wall, they filled in the recess with brushwood and pitch, and set fire to it, whereupon the props burned away, the wall above collapsed into the ditch, and soldiers scrambled up this rough ramp into the outer ward. After a spell of fierce fighting the defenders abandoned the outer ward and fell back across the bridge into the middle ward.

It must have taken immense labour to get siege engines up through the enlarged breach, but eventually catapults and towers were dragged inside. Judging from the fragmentary ruins, the attackers dismantled the northern wall of the outer ward so as to expose the southern wall of the middle ward to their artillery. This time the miners struggled in vain to make an impression on the masonry above the 6-metre (20-ft)-deep ditch dividing the two walled courtyards; they drove daggers into the chalk face as climbing-pegs and rigged makeshift ladders, but once up them they had no space to wield their picks and crowbars. It was at this point that the 'human factor' came into play for a second time.

THE OVERLOOKED LATRINE

A French soldier in the ditch spotted the outflow of a latrine chute which passed down through the west wall of the middle ward, outside the chapel; carelessly, the castle builders had made the outflow low enough to climb up to, and far above it the soldier could see that a chapel window was unbarred. The shaft was wide enough to accommodate a man: he took a coil of rope, somehow braced himself all the way up the stinking, slimy chimney, reached the chapel unseen, and let down his rope from the window so that a few comrades could climb up. The exact sequence of events is unclear, but reportedly they and a group outside set up confusing commotions that distracted the defenders; part of the chapel was set on fire; the chapel party somehow managed to open a gate for the troops outside; and in the face of the resulting assault the defenders abandoned the middle ward and fell back yet again.

The inner ward still presented a daunting obstacle, with its multi-faceted walls from which bowmen could sweep the courtyard, but the French doggedly repeated their combination of techniques. Catapults smashed the timber hoardings to kindling-wood and broke the merlons off the battlements, while a storm of crossbow bolts kept the defenders away from the parapet above the eastern entrance bridge. Meanwhile, beneath the bridge, the miners set to work once again. This time they drove a tunnel under the wall; Lacy's men detected this and sunk a countermine to meet them. This weakened the wall above still further; Cabulus hurled its heavy stones at the subsiding masonry and eventually it collapsed. The survivors of the garrison, weak with starvation, did not even try to defend their last redoubt in the keep, and some tried in vain to flee through a postern gate. On 6 March 1204, the last 20 knights and 120 soldiers laid down their weapons.

Philip Augustus led his army deep into Normandy, and the garrisons of other castles and towns asked for 40 days' grace to await relief – a normal medieval agreement, in order to avoid the great cost to both sides of siege and assault. King John feared treachery too much to leave England, however, and his remaining Norman vassals duly made terms and opened their gates to Philip. John Lackland's other possessions in France would soon go the same way.

'*Were its walls made of iron, yet would I take it!*'

ATTRIBUTED TO KING PHILIP II OF FRANCE REGARDING THE SIEGE OF CHÂTEAU-GAILLARD

'God forbid that I should live as an emperor without an empire. As my city falls, I will fall with it. Whosoever wishes to escape, let him save himself if he can, and whoever is ready to face death, let him follow me.'

<small>REPORTED WORDS OF CONSTANTINE XI PALAEOLOGOS, LAST EMPEROR OF BYZANTIUM, UPON REFUSING THE FINAL OTTOMAN SURRENDER TERMS (24 MAY 1453)</small>

Although cannon were at least 120 years old by the 1450s, and had reduced many castles and towns, Constantinople was their ultimate test. The development of efficient European gunpowder artillery was slow but steady; despite the perfection of concentric defensive architecture in the 14th century, by the beginning of the next the tall, relatively thin curtain walls were falling to gunpowder in every campaign. Every prince in Christendom wanted these new weapons, and only princes could afford them – they were the 'nuclear deterrent' of their age. The first cannon founders often hired themselves out to both make and operate weapons, and found they could name their price for their skills. Henry V of England (r. 1413–22) employed 75 Flemish gunners for the 1415 Agincourt campaign – they made the breach at Harfleur into which Shakespeare has him urging his Englishmen *'once more'*; and the great Turkish guns that eventually smashed gaps in the walls of Constantinople 40 years later were made and aimed by a Hungarian freelance gun founder. Nevertheless, this siege also demonstrated that strong defences could still be held for many weeks by even an outnumbered garrison of brave and highly motivated men.

THE DYING EMPIRE

Its final confrontation with the vigorous new power of the Ottoman Turks found Constantinople – the capital of the eastern Roman and later Byzantine empires for 1100 years – virtually moribund. The empire had never recovered from two great defeats: in 1071 at Manzikert, at the hands of the Muslim Seljuk Turks (and Byzantine traitors); and in 1204, at the hands of the Fourth Crusade, which led to 57 years of occupation punctuated by civil war. By the mid-15th century its territory had been reduced to little more than the city itself, and the treasury was so reduced that emperors could no longer raise mercenary armies.

The Ottoman advance into Europe had bypassed Constantinople; their sultans already styled themselves 'rulers of the Romans', since they saw that as their destiny, and Sultan Mehmet II's headquarters at Edirne in the Balkans was 100 miles (160 km) west of Constantinople. Mehmet's last major European land enemy was Hungary; but Constantinople's unrivalled strategic position astride the narrow channel between the Black and Mediterranean seas offered a valuable base for

Book illumination (1455, from the workshop of Jean Mielot) depicting the Turkish army encamped outside Constantinople during the siege of the city.

TIMELINE

330 Inauguration of Constantinople as a 'New Rome' (Nova Roma) by Roman emperor Constantine I ('the Great')

408–50 Emperor Theodosius II constructs massive new landward defences for Constantinople, a wall stretching from the Sea of Marmara to the suburb of Blachernae

1204 Constantinople sacked during the Fourth Crusade; 'Latin empire' established there until 1261

1448 Constantine XI Paleologus ascends the throne of the moribund Byzantine empire

1451 Mehmet II becomes Ottoman sultan

1452 Sultan Mehmet builds the fortress of Rumelihisari on the shore of the Bosphorus; Hungarian cannon founder Orban casts a series of huge bronze siege cannon for his Ottoman paymasters

1453 (May) Constantinople falls to the besieging Ottoman Turks; Constantine XI and 4000 of his compatriots are killed trying to defend the city

1481 Death of Mehmet II

future operations against Italian maritime powers. Despite its weakness it also still enjoyed great symbolic prestige, and its capture was politically necessary: the 21-year-old Mehmet was not yet secure on his throne, and had embarassing failures to wipe out.

The Byzantine emperor Constantine XI considered Mehmet an inexperienced boy, but feared his strength and aggressiveness. In 1452, Mehmet had a new fortress – Rumelihisari – built on the European shore of the Bosphorus where it narrowed to less than 100 metres (330 ft), thus dominating the passage from the Black Sea. Constantine's pleas for help from Europe were frustrated by Ottoman diplomacy and by the innate hostility between the Roman Catholic West and Greek Orthodox Byzantium. In November 1452 the guns of Rumelihisari sank a Venetian ship returning from the Black Sea, and Venice promised the emperor ships, men and supplies. They never came; but in January 1453 a Genoese squadron did arrive with some 700 soldiers. Among them was an experienced professional captain, Giovanni Giustiniani Longo, who was soon put in command of the city's land defences.

THE WALLS OF CONSTANTINOPLE

Its uniquely strong defences had enabled the city to withstand seven previous sieges since the seventh century. Constantinople was built on the end of a promontory facing southeast, at the junction of the Bosphorus and the Sea of Marmara. Its defended area was triangular; the strongest walls ran for c.2 miles (3.2 km) across the neck of the peninsula, linked to sea defences following the shores of the Sea of Marmara and the Golden Horn inlet. Originally built in the fifth century, they were extended at the northeast corner in the seventh century to enclose the Blachernae suburb, and further improved in the ninth and 12th centuries. The land walls were the strongest; from the outside inwards they presented an enemy with three obstacles, each higher and more formidable than the last.

The moat was more than 18 metres wide and 6 metres deep (60 x 20 ft), lined on both sides with masonry, its inside wall rising 1.8–2.1 metres (6–7 ft) above the ground. Next came a clear terrace about 18 metres (60 ft) wide, in front of the outer wall proper. The latter – where most of the fighting took place in 1453 – was 8 metres (27 ft) high on the outside, and 2 metres (6 ft 6 ins) thick. It had a battlemented wall-walk along the top, above arched rear chambers where men could shelter; close-set towers, 9–11 metres (30–35 ft) high, projected 5 metres (16 ft) to allow enfilading (sideways) fire along the front face. Behind it was another terrace for troop movements, in front of the inner wall. This rose higher still – today, about 9 metres (30 ft) above the outer terrace, plus the crenellations; its thickness tapers from more than 4.6 metres (15 ft) at the base to 4 metres (13 ft)-plus at the top. Originally it had 96 square and polygonal towers spaced roughly 55 metres (180 ft) apart, in the intervals of the towers on the outer wall; they were nearly 18 metres (60 ft) high, projecting 5.5–10 metres (18–34 ft) externally. At ground level each had a large chamber for stores; above this was an upper chamber, windowed for defensive weapons, which was accessible only from the battlements (reached by flights of steps slanting up the wall's rear face). From this chamber steps led up to the battlemented fighting and weapon platform on the roof of the tower.

The walls' faces were built of squared masonry bonded with very strong lime/aggregate mortar, with rubble infill. At regular intervals brick courses from front to rear tied the structure together, and these red stripes originally gave the white walls an imposingly regular appearance. There were ten main gates protected by large flanking towers, and a few small posterns. In the later Blachernae sector the wall was single, but more massive than elsewhere, with nine higher, more closely spaced towers. Since they were so difficult for an invader to reach, the seaward walls on the other two sides of the promontory were also of single construction; powerful currents off the Marmara shore made

THE FIRST 100 YEARS OF CANNON

The first documentary mention of guns is in Florence in 1326. Early gun founders soon learned how to cast bronze guns of any size, including the largest pieces needed for smashing down walls – 'bombards'; but they could not yet cast these reliably in cheaper iron. Iron guns were therefore of the inherently weaker 'stave-and-hoop' construction, hammer-forged around a cylindrical pattern from strips of iron; one 450-pounder recorded in Burgundy in 1378 took a master craftsman and eight other smiths 61 days to complete. The surviving 'Ghent bombard' of c.1382 was made of 32 lengthways iron staves, with 41 hoops heated and then shrunk on to the outside; 5.5 metres (18 ft) long, it had a calibre of about 63 centimetres (25 ins), took a powder charge of 64 kilograms (140 lbs), and fired a ball weighing 272 kilograms (600 lbs). While many smaller cannon had removable breech chambers for the powder and shot, loaded separately and then wedged in place at the base of the barrel, bombards were muzzle-loading: the gas seal of a breech-loader was too approximate for such powerful cannon.

OPERATING 15TH-CENTURY BOMBARDS

Castle-breaching cannon were the ultimate weapon for kings defied by rebellious barons, since their manufacture, transport and use required the sort of wealth only available to a monarch. Competitive princes went deep into debt to acquire this war-winning technology, but early cannon were technically immature and often unreliable. In October 1409, Duke John the Fearless of Burgundy besieged the castle of Vellexon with his cannon; his recorded difficulties are typical of those still faced by Mehmet II in 1453.

Large bombards were too heavy for a timber carriage, so they were taken on campaign in wagons and emplaced by means of cranes, in up-sloping trenches dug opposite the chosen length of wall. Several massive blocks of wood wedged in behind the breech were supposed to absorb the recoil forces, and the barrel was held steady with strong timber stakes hammered into the ground along each side. At Vellexon, many of the guns soon burst due to the gunners' inexperience (presumably they were over-charged with powder); two large bombards had to be sent 40 miles (64 km) to Auxerre for repairs. Although 200 men were needed to lift the largest – which fired 385-kilogram (850-lb) balls – remarkably, both were back in place in three weeks.

The jolting of the wagons had separated the pre-mixed gunpowder into its ingredients, so Duke John had to send to Paris for 227 kilograms (500 lbs) each of saltpetre and sulphur to be mixed on the spot (with local charcoal). To make stone cannonballs to fit the barrels kept 18 masons busy for 90 days, at a production rate of about one ball per mason per day. The shock of firing shifted the bombards in their trenches, so they needed frequent and laborious repositioning with levers and cranes; it also repeatedly split the wooden packing behind the breeches, so new blocks had to be made with iron strapping. When the castle of Vellexon finally fell on 22 January 1410, it was to old-fashioned mining under the walls; the phenomenally expensive wonder-weapons had demolished the buildings inside, but made only small and quickly-repaired breaches in the castle's outer walls.

any landing almost impossible, and a huge chain boom on wooden floats could be drawn across the entrance to the Golden Horn at will.

THE OTTOMAN ARMY

In the winter of 1452–3, Mehmet gathered in contingents of provincial vassal troops for his multi-ethnic army. This included not only conscripts from conquered and transplanted Christian populations, but also willing Christian auxiliaries; at least half were Slavs and Albanians ('Rumelians'), the rest Anatolian Turks. Alongside irregular light infantry and archers the provinces provided many permanently formed regiments. The hard core were the Kapi-Kulu or palace regiments: paid, well armed, well trained and disciplined soldiers, mostly conscripted as boys from the families of Christian slaves or prisoners. The élite of this élite were the Janissary corps, probably about 5000 strong in 1453, who were among those troops issued with matchlock handguns.

Artillery had been used since the late 14th century; although the quality of the Turkish guns lagged behind the best in Europe, the sultans had also imported guns from Italy and the Balkans. In 1452 a Hungarian named Orban (Urbanus) supposedly offered his services to Constantinople; when his price proved too high he turned to Mehmet, who was happy to pay even more than he had asked. Orban cast several gigantic siege bombards, throwing 450-kilogram (1000-lb) stone balls up to a mile; they were enormously difficult and costly to transport, and could fire only about ten times a day, but Mehmet knew that they were the only feasible key to Constantinople.

The total combined strength of Mehmet's forces in 1453 is estimated at *c*.80,000–100,000 fighting men, with that many again of ancillary non-combatants. The Ottoman army was known for its high standards of hygiene, so its camps were unusually free from disease; its campaigns were carefully planned in every respect, and the logistics were administered by a sophisticated bureaucracy.

The Garrison

The Byzantines ('Greeks') did not have to worry about provisions, since the area enclosed within their walls was well watered and included plentiful open ground for crops and cattle; Constantine's problem was assembling enough men to hold the walls. A balance of various accounts suggests that he had 6000–7000 trained soldiers, and perhaps three times that many second-line militia. Lacking the money to hire mercenaries, he relied on foreign volunteers, mainly Italians from Venice and Genoa – although in his hour of need the walled Genoese merchant district of Galata, facing the city across the Golden Horn, chose (notoriously) to remain neutral. Most of the soldiers and sailors were infantry, armed – like their adversaries – with swords, spears and other pole-arms, bows, crossbows and matchlock firearms; they also included a small number of heavily armoured knights.

The city's cannon were smaller than Mehmet's, and were handicapped by a lack of prepared emplacements in the defences. Constantine did have the mysterious 'Greek fire' flame weapon (an early form of napalm), supposedly supervised by a Scots-German engineer named Johannes Grant, but it was not much used. We are also told that up to 500 unspecified 'siege engines' were mounted in the towers. The small defensive fleet harboured in the Golden Horn was largely Italian.

Approach and First Assaults

Despite his numerical strength, Mehmet was not assured of a quick victory or of the absolute loyalty of his senior officers. He was in a hurry, since Western Europe might stir itself to relieve the city. He therefore had to use his guns to minimize his casualties, limit the length of the siege and husband his army's morale. Constantine, by contrast, needed to hold out as long as he could, to shame Europe into mounting a rescue operation. His general, Giustiniani, planned to defend the outermost land wall stubbornly, hoping that its great strength would cancel out Mehmet's numerical advantage – huge numbers were of limited value when only relatively few at a time could physically reach the enemy.

By the time Mehmet himself arrived on 2 April, and the drawing of the Byzantine boom across the Golden Horn signalled the start of the siege, the Ottoman army were in place in assembly camps, and his fleet had anchored at Diplokionion Bay just up the Bosphorus. Mehmet had about 69 guns emplaced in some 15 batteries, the majority facing Blachernae, the Charisius Gate, the St Romanus Gate and the Pege Gate; most batteries had one or more heavy bombards and several lighter pieces. The 'giants' – of which the biggest supposedly fired half-ton balls – faced Blachernae and St Romanus. (The Turks also had about a dozen trebuchets, but these were not significant.)

On 6 April the Turks moved up to entrenched siege lines, with the Rumelians on the left, the Anatolians on the right, reserves behind, and a detached division on the north side of the Golden Horn. The garrison manned their walls, in most places very thinly, with only a handful of soldiers in each tower; but the emperor and Giustiniani held the St Romanus sector with about 2000 Greeks and Italians. Sailors manned the Golden Horn walls, and the Greek general Loukas Notaras had some mobile cannon in reserve in the Petrion quarter.

The opening bombardment of 6 and 7 April brought down part of the moat wall near the Charisius Gate; but opposite Blachernae the second-largest bombard – the Basiliske, firing 363-kilogram (800-lb balls) – overheated, and on 11 April it would crack. During the first days of counter-battery fire the largest Byzantine gun also burst, and thereafter their cannon were used for anti-personnel work with grapeshot. The first assault, probably on 7 April, was repulsed from the moat wall fairly easily, and the damaged section was repaired. The defenders made several sorties, but after a few days Giustiniani decided that the losses were not worth the gain, and pulled his men back from the rear wall of the moat to the outer wall proper. (During this period the first of several unsuccessful Turkish naval attacks was made on the boom.)

The Turks paused to reposition several batteries; the bombardment resumed on 11 April, and was fairly continuous thereafter, at a rate of 100 to 150 shots a day. Orban advised the gunners to fire three medium-weight shots to hit the wall in a rough triangle, and then one from a heavy bombard between them at the weakened area. Most of the stone cannonballs fractured on impact, but men were sent forward with nets to recover those that fell intact outside the walls.

On the night of 17–18 April an assault on the walls between the St Romanus and Charisius gates was beaten off, while on the 20th morale soared when four ships fought their way through the blockade of smaller Turkish galleys and entered the Golden Horn, bringing supplies and Genoese soldiers. The Ottoman admiral was dismissed for this failure, and there was some muttering in Mehmet's headquarters; his Grand Vizier, Candarli Halil, argued for an offer to lift the siege in return for political and financial tribute, but was outnumbered by more bellicose advisers such as the Albanian general Zaganos Pasha.

THE GOLDEN HORN BREACHED

The Ottomans now showed ingenuity and engineering skill of a high order: they built an overland slipway – a trench lined with greased planks – right across the hill behind Galata, from the Bosphorus to the Valley of the Springs on the north shore of the Golden Horn. This was used to drag many of the smaller Turkish vessels across country; the first was launched into the inlet on 22 April, and eventually 72 craft, including 30 galleys, would contest the waterway with the Byzantine fleet on a daily basis. More defenders now had to be transferred from the landward to the seaward walls to shore up the defences there.

On 28 April a fireship sortie against Ottoman ships in the Bosphorus failed; and on 3 May a small, disguised Byzantine vessel slipped out of the Golden Horn to sail in search of the promised Venetian fleet. Soon only the ships guarding the boom itself could be manned, and the other crews landed to help garrison Blachernae (which was once again under fire from the repaired Basiliske).

On 6 May a breach was blown in the outer wall near St Romanus, but it was so narrow that assaults on it failed. Another was made near the Caligaria Gate by 11 May, and a night assault on the 12th got into the Blachernae Palace before being driven out. The Ottomans set Serbian miners to dig a tunnel in the same sector, but Johannes Grant's countermine broke into it on 16 May. This underground war went on for nearly ten days, but the defending engineers were finally successful,

The old city of Constantinople: the landward walls formed a daunting defensive barrier.

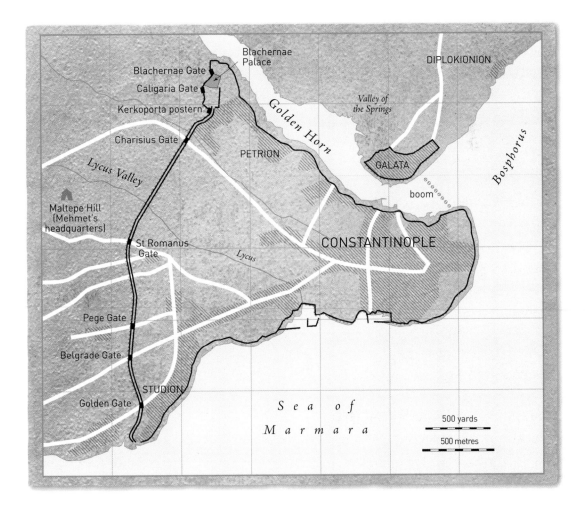

either flooding or smoking out the Ottoman miners. The Turks had also built static siege towers outside the walls, but Grant's engineers countered these with incendiaries and gunpowder charges.

THE FINAL DAYS

Breaches in the vulnerable Lycus Valley sector were getting increasingly difficult to repair or barricade under fire, and although some assaults were taken in the flank by cavalry sorties through the Kerkoporta postern, ammunition and morale were both running low. The bitterest blow fell on 23 May, when the scout boat returned with no news of a Venetian fleet. The next day the Turks sent a final embassy to demand surrender, which Constantine rejected with resigned dignity.

On 27 May the Ottoman camps were told to prepare for a final push on the 29th; feasts were provided, rewards promised, and on the 28th most troops were rested. Ships' crews and troops from the north shore augmented the assault forces. On the evening of 28 April guns were dragged forward, and work continued to fill in the moat. In the most threatened St Romanus sector, Giustiniani had about 400 Italian and 2600 Greek soldiers; the Venetian ambassador Minotto commanded at Blachernae, and Loukas Notaras at both Petrion and the sea wall on the Golden Horn.

Three hours before dawn on 29 May a bombardment heralded a massed assault by irregulars around St Romanus, but after two hours this was hurled back with huge losses. After a renewed cannonade Anatolians attacked the same sector; these more disciplined troops could be trusted to withdraw periodically to allow the artillery a clear field of fire, and then resume their attacks. After two incursions were repulsed, Mehmet finally committed his palace troops, including 3000 Janissaries, whom he led forward in person as far as the filled moat. They attacked the main St Romanus breach in the outer wall yet again, and, after an hour's fighting, about 50 men on their far left flank managed to get through the Kerkoporta postern and up to the wall-walk, where they waved flags.

At this moment Giustiniani, on a wooden parapet inside the main breach, was wounded by a bullet (mortally, as it later turned out), and had to be taken to the rear through the inner wall gate. Seeing this, his men wavered; panic spread, and some tried to follow him. Janissaries rushed forwards on their heels, and at great cost in lives captured this section of the third line of defence. Their success proved fatal for the city. In confused fighting the Blachernae sector was also lost; a general flight ensued back to the city (and, by foreigners, for their ships), and Mehmet's columns flooded across the open country behind the walls. The emperor Constantine XI died fighting; some 4000 of his people had died with him by the time resistance – and looting – came to an end.

At about noon on 29 May, Mehmet II rode in through the Charisius Gate. He was notably protective of his new conquest, which – as Istanbul – would become the capital of his increasingly powerful and centralized state.

A contemporary miniature by Lienzo of Tlascala shows Cortés and his conquistadors storming the Great Temple (*teocalli*) at Tenochtitlán at the head of his Tlaxcalan allies.

Cortés's destruction of the Aztec empire
MEXICO (TENOCHTITLÁN)

yeꝗrla ti tvtzavitl
yn mal ques.

'*When the news spread through all the distant provinces that Mexico was destroyed, [they] sent their chieftains to congratulate Cortés on his victories ... and to see for themselves if the city ... which they had so dreaded really was razed to the ground.*'

BERNAL DIAZ DEL CASTILLO, *HISTORIA VERDADERA DE LA CONQUISTA DE LA NUEVA ESPAÑA* ('*TRUE HISTORY OF THE CONQUEST OF NEW SPAIN*'; c.1565)

The storming of the capital city of Aztec Mexico is these days seen mainly as an iconic episode in European colonial history – the violent irruption of white colonizers into the Americas and their destruction of an indigenous culture. Since only a relative handful of Spaniards were involved, their victory is popularly ascribed to the supposedly great advantages bestowed by horses, steel armour and gunpowder weapons. In fact these seem to have played a relatively small part in a battle fought overwhelmingly by Cortés's local Tlaxcala allies, whose material and military culture was identical to that of the Mexica defenders. However, the directing intelligence was European, and wide differences in attitudes to warfare were certainly decisive.

THE LAWYER FROM EXTREMADURA

In October 1518 the Spanish governor of Cuba, Don Diego Velásquez, agreed to sponsor (as a minority shareholder) a third voyage of exploration to the Mexican coast. Since spring 1517 two captains had gone ashore at various points in the Yucatán and Campeche, reporting both hostile and friendly contacts – and, intriguingly, the existence of a great empire of enormous wealth overland to the west. Velásquez had already sent to Spain to request appointment as governor of any new territory acquired on the mainland, but he needed the investment of private individuals to outfit such an expedition.

The man he commissioned to lead it was the 34-year-old Hernán Cortés (1485–1547), a well-to-do lawyer and landowner on Santo Domingo. Born and raised in the bleak far western Spanish upland province of Extremadura, Cortés had the self-reliant determination of a man bred in Castile's historic borderland with the Moorish territories that Spain had only reconquered within living memory. Since he left Spain for the new colonies at the age of 19 he had prospered, but had also become a political opponent of the governor. So purposefully did Cortés prepare and recruit that Velásquez changed his mind, and tried to replace him with a more pliable representative; but Cortés forestalled him by sailing from Santiago de Cuba on 18 November before his little squadron was ready, completing its fitting out and loading at another port.

He sailed for Mexico on 10 February 1519, taking 530 Europeans, 16 horses, 6 small cannon and several hundred slaves for labouring work. They touched during March and April at various points on the Yucatán coast, and took the town of Potonchán in Tabasco, whose people were unhappy vassals of the Aztec empire. There he acquired useful information and an invaluable female interpreter, before sailing up the coast to land at modern Veracruz on 22 April. This brought his first contact with Mexican imperial officials, with whom he exchanged gifts and fenced diplomatically for an opportunity to visit their emperor.

AN EMPIRE OF GOLD AND BLOOD

After a century of local dominance the city of Mexico had conquered a large empire from which it extracted rich tribute in gold, crops and all other kinds of material wealth – and also in human beings, handed over for sacrifice in the temples of its terrifying gods. It was hardly surprising that the Spaniards encountered many groups among the empire's provincial subjects and neighbours who – after some initial skirmishing – were happy to ally themselves with these formidable strangers, in the hope of throwing off the Mexican yoke. With a plausible vision of conquest, Cortés formally founded the township of Villa Rica de la Vera Cruz; he then sent in his resignation from Velásquez's commission, and a request direct to Spain for recognition as governor of a separate colony under the crown. While awaiting a reply – which would inevitably take many months – he marched inland on 16 August, having first secured his grip on the troops by hanging a mutinous supporter of the Cuban governor, and dismantling his own ships.

THE AZTEC EMPIRE

During the 13th century AD, as the great Toltec civilization declined, one of the wandering tribes from the north who arrived in the central valley of Mexico were the Aztecs ('people from Aztlan'), who settled the west banks of Lake Texcoco and (according to tradition, in 1325) established the town of Tenochtitlán on a muddy island off shore. In about 1428 they rose against their original Tepanec overlords, and by the late 15th century their conquests extended from the Atlantic to the Pacific coasts and south as far as modern Guatemala. At some point they gave up the names 'Aztec' and 'Tenochtitlán' for 'Mexica' and 'Mexico'.

Expansion extended not only their trade routes but also their 'tax base' for tribute from subject peoples, and this included quotas of victims for human sacrifice. The Aztecs' religion was darkly fatalistic: they believed that the sun would inevitably die, and that the end of the world could only be postponed by feeding it with blood. Huge numbers of men and women died on their altars, their living hearts ripped out with obsidian knives – on special occasions many thousands were sacrificed in a single day. The insatiable hunger for sacrificial victims fuelled the whole Aztec ethos of warfare and imperial domination, which made them feared and hated among their subjects. The only two neighbouring peoples who successfully resisted conquest were the Tarascans to the west and the Tlaxcalans in the hills to the east.

TIMELINE

1485 Hernán Cortés born in Extremadura, Spain

1502 Moctezuma II becomes ruler of the Aztec empire

1519 Cortés leads an expedition from Cuba to the central American mainland; landing in March, the Spaniards enter Tenochtitlán peacefully in November

1520 Death of Moctezuma; Spaniards flee Tenochtitlán on the Night of Sorrows

1521 Siege of Tenochtitlán begins in May and lasts for over two months; fall of the city marks the end of the Aztec empire

1522 Cortés appointed governor of New Spain

1547 Cortés dies in Spain

In August–September he was at first resisted and then welcomed by the people of Tlaxcala, who had long been sworn enemies of Mexico. Along the way various messages were exchanged with envoys of the Mexican emperor, Moctezuma II, whose true attitude was hard for Westerners to fathom: in the face of recent heavenly portents of universal doom, the emperor professed to welcome the newcomers while also plotting to ambush them. He set a rendezvous for his ambassadors at Cholula; the Tlaxcalans warned Cortés that Mexican warriors were gathering there, and so on 18 October Cortés struck first, massacring all men of military age. This impressed both his allies and Moctezuma, who greeted the Spanish in his capital on 8 November 1519.

THE CITY ON THE LAKE

By this date Mexico (as the former Aztec capital Tenochtitlán was then known) covered an island some 2 miles (3.2 km) from north to south and just under the same distance wide. Its densely packed streets, divided into districts by many canals and dominated by two great pyramid temples, were home to *c*.200,000 people. The northern Tlatelolco district was the commercial centre of the whole empire, with a vast open plaza capable of holding 40,000 people on market days. The Spaniards were astonished by the size and richness of the city, into which they marched along the southern causeway; this, and the canoes clustered around it, were crammed with exotic onlookers, as were the streets along which they were led to quarters in the Axyacatl palace in the Great Temple precincts. The lavish costumes of nobles and priests, the monumental architecture and the gold artefacts spoke of a sophisticated and hugely wealthy culture.

The stinking, blood-encrusted shrines to the war and rain gods at the top of the Great Temple, which the Spaniards were also shown, told another story. Two of the conquistadors calculated that the racks outside held the skulls of no fewer than 136,000 sacrificial victims. With remarkably tactless courage Cortés declared to Moctezuma his detestation of these devilish rites, and proclaimed the truth of the Christian Gospel. Late in November news of a Mexican attack back on the east coast, and the death of two Spaniards, prompted Cortés to take Moctezuma hostage, and thereafter he tried to manipulate events through the mouth of the emperor. Moctezuma's responses were confused, as two utterly alien mindsets grappled with one another; for some months his people remained obedient to him, but outraged members of the nobility plotted against the white men.

On 20 April 1520 a force led by Pánfilo Narváez arrived off Veracruz, sent from Cuba by Governor Velásquez to snatch the credit and wealth of this new prize. Cortés seduced many of the newcomers with proof of the huge potential plunder; by the time he arrived back on the coast with 250 men to confront his rival most of Narváez's men were ready to change sides, and the skirmish at Cempoala on 27 May was brief. In his absence he had left Pedro de Alvarado in command in Mexico, and on 16 May that officer had fired on a crowd during a religious festival to which he objected, killing many in the temple precinct. The city rose in fury, and when Cortés returned on 24 June, with 1100 Spaniards and several thousand Tlaxcalans, he found his men besieged in the palace.

Moctezuma tricked him into freeing the emperor's brother Cuitlhuac as a gesture of reconciliation, but the resistance party promptly elected Cuitlhuac emperor in the captive Moctezuma's stead, and tried to storm the palace. Cannon and crossbows held them back for a while; Cortés had Moctezuma address the crowd from the roof in an attempt to calm them, but the emperor was struck on the head by a sling-stone and died three days later. A sally was clearly the Spaniards' only chance. On the dark, rainy night of 30 June they tried to sneak out of the city , but were spotted as they neared the Tacuba causeway; soon Mexicans swarmed after the heavily laden column.

The Night of Sorrows

The causeway, 7.3 metres (8 yds) wide and more than a mile (1.6 km) long, had been breached in eight places. Cortés had brought a portable bridge made from beams from the palace; while this was

MEXICAN WARRIORS

Although they had no metal weapons, the Mexicans – alone among the 'Indian' peoples encountered by the conquistadors – were a formally organized military force. They fought in units enlisted in particular districts of the city or in subject communities, and experienced and younger warriors were mixed together in the ranks. Mexico had two training schools, one for nobles and one for commoners, where officers and veterans instructed in the use of shields and weapons – bows, javelins, blow-guns, slings, thrusting spears and wooden swords edged with razor-sharp blades of glass-like obsidian. Warriors wore quilted cotton armour proof against arrows and javelins; ranking individuals or groups had decorative over-suits fashioned to resemble jaguar-hide or eagle feathers, and animal-totem helmets of wood and bone.

The object of combat was not to kill, but to capture prisoners for sacrifice, and the number captured determined a warrior's prestige. This mindset, and the highly ritualistic nature of Aztec life, meant that the warriors were nonplussed when they first encountered the entirely pragmatic Spanish soldiers, who were fighting for their lives against great odds and had no interest in ritual displays or in taking prisoners. This psychological gulf was more decisive in battle than the guns, steel armour and horses of the hugely outnumbered handful of Europeans.

placed over a gap by several hundred men the others held off the pursuers, before crossing it and changing places with the carrying party. Thus the Spaniards proceeded from gap to gap; but it was a slow business, and most of them never reached the end of the causeway. In hand-to-hand fighting in the dark their muskets and crossbows gave little advantage, and for once the Mexicans seemed more intent on killing than capturing (at one gap Alvarado only escaped by vaulting across using a pike as a pole). The rearguard escorting the baggage and cannon were cut off; they fell back towards the palace, but were overrun, while the Mexicans' looting – or rather, repossession – of the baggage bought the rest a little time. Swept with arrows from canoes alongside, many of the Spanish and their allies fell into the lake, where some (particularly among Narváez's inexperienced newcomers) were drowned by the weight of their armour – and of the gold they were carrying.

The total number of men that Cortés lost on that 'Noche Triste' is disputed in the sources; the most probable figure seems to be around 700 Europeans and at least 2000 Tlaxcalans, in addition to the cannon and two-thirds of the 68 horses. It was with only a few hundred exhausted survivors that Cortés reached Tacuba on 1 July; they then faced a march of some 150 miles (240 km) – up the western edge of Lake Texcoco, right around the north of Lake Zumpango, and down southeast to the uncertain refuge of Tlaxcala. They were pursued for a week, losing more men to harassing attacks and unhealed wounds, before Cuitlhuac made the mistake of fighting a pitched battle, at Otumba on 7 July. Although his many thousands of warriors greatly outnumbered the fugitives, Cuitlhuac had only seen the Spaniards fight in cramped streets, and had no idea of the potential of their horses (or 'stags', as the baffled Aztecs called them) in the open field. In desperately hard fighting Cortés led his tiny handful of lancers in a charge right at the Mexican command group, and the impaling of a senior Aztec general began a collapse of morale. Having lost another 72 Spaniards since 1 July, on the 10th the column staggered into Tlaxcala, where they were reassured of their allies' loyalty – although the Tlaxcalans prudently charged them for supplies from now on, and wished to discuss certain future concessions. (The Tlaxcalans would remain loyal to Spain for 300 years; the Spanish crown, for its part, reneged on Cortés's undertakings to them.)

PREPARING FOR RETURN

Over the next five months Cortés proved his remarkable resilience and determination by rebuilding a small army and a strong alliance to retake the capital. He knew that his defiance of the governor of Cuba would cost him everything unless he could give his king a lucrative victory. He established and stockpiled a new forward base – Segura de la Frontera – about 100 miles (160 km) southeast of Mexico, near Tempeaca. He cajoled and bullied reluctant conquistadors, enforcing a stern military and religious discipline. He sent to Hispaniola for men, horses, guns and ammunition, requisitioned others sent from Cuba for Narváez (in ignorance of the new situation)and received the first encouraging contributions directly from Spain. He had his Basque shipwright Martin Lopéz build 13 large boats ('brigantines') powered by sails and sweeps, to be carried in parts overland to Lake Texcoco. By patient diplomacy he restored the confidence of allied tribes; and by the time he marched from Segura on 26 December 1520 he had 10,000 Tlaxcalans and the promise of many more.

THE CONQUISTADORS

Although many had previous formal military experience, the Spanish soldiers were essentially individual adventurers or leaders of small bands, who had to provide their own gear and pay for a share in the expedition, hoping to profit from its plunder and from land grants in conquered territory. Leading such men into the unknown, against huge numbers of enemies that they sincerely believed were devil-worshippers, took captains of remarkable strength and personality. Much has been made of the advantage they enjoyed from having steel armour, firearms and horses, but only very few had any of these. In 1521 the whole army had fewer than 100 cavalry; only the better-off captains and nobles could afford steel armour, most soldiers making do with a helmet and a leather jerkin or locally acquired quilted armour; and the sources mention only between 120 and 160 crossbowmen and musketeers together. Their matchlock arquebuses took more than half a minute to load even under perfect circumstances, were prone to repeated misfires, and were too inaccurate to hit a man-sized target reliably at more than about 30 metres (100 ft). Their effect in European warfare depended entirely upon massed use, and the conquistadors never had anything approaching the numbers to achieve this; while their few cannon were valuable shock-weapons, their victories were overwhelmingly won with cold steel – swords, pikes and halberds.

In the meantime, a smallpox epidemic – a new and lethal disease for Mexicans – had ravaged the city for two months. Among the many thousands to die was the emperor Cuitlhuac; he was succeeded by his 25-year-old kinsman Cuauhtémoc, who tried to rally his shocked and weakened people to defend their city.

Cortés sent columns to take the towns around the lake shore – many of which joined him willingly – and on 28 April 1521 his reassembled boats were launched. While they began a blockade of water traffic to the city, he sent messengers to summon all his promised native auxiliaries, and Tlaxcala alone sent about 50,000. His little force of 850-odd Europeans (including only about 160 crossbowmen and musketeers at most, with three large and five small cannon) was soon dwarfed by an army of some 75,000 local warriors, whom he divided into three main commands, from west to south (the northern Tepeyac causeway was left open, in the hope that the defenders would retreat along it):

* Pedro de Alvarado would attack across the Tacuba causeway, with 25,000 Tlaxcalans headed by 30 Spanish cavalry, 18 crossbowmen and 150 other European infantry.
* Cristobál de Olid would lead 20,000 auxiliaries from Coyoacán, with a spearhead of 33 cavalry, 18 crossbowen and 160 infantry.
* Gonzalo de Sandoval would attack across the Iztapalapa causeway with 30,000 auxiliaries, 24 Spanish cavalry, 13 crossbowmen, 4 musketeers and 150 other infantry.

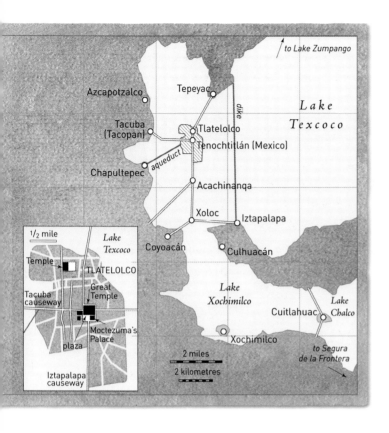

Map of Tenochtitlán, showing the causeways across Lake Texcoco that linked the island city with the mainland. Control of these was key to Spanish success in taking the city.

We do not know how many warriors Cuauhtémoc had in the city; some sources claim that smallpox had wiped out as many as 40 percent of the inhabitants, but even if this is an exaggeration it seems unlikely that a population of less than 200,000 could field more than about 50,000 fighters even including boys and older men. They would have the besieged garrison's age-old advantage of being able to meet their attackers on a few narrow fronts; but Aztec sources speak of dissent and even killings among the leadership.

Progress along the causeways would be almost impossible if the Mexicans could attack the columns from the water as well as resisting them on the narrow banks. To counter this threat Cortés himself commanded the flotilla of 13 brigantines, each carrying a captain, 6 crossbowmen or musketeers and 12 oarsmen; he may even have mounted some of his small cannon in the boats' bows.

THE ASSAULT

The siege proper began on 26 May, when the aqueduct carrying fresh water into the city from Chapultepec was cut. On 31 May, Sandoval moved to capture the Iztapalapa causeway. Some 500 canoes laden with warriors gathered to tear at his flanks; but as morning brought a wind, Cortés and his boats sailed into the midst of them, ramming and firing left and right. Many were sunk with their crews and the rest scattered. While small numbers would continue to harass the advance, they never again risked concentrating in the face of the Spanish brigantines.

A detailed calendar of the fighting does not survive; but we know that it lasted for ten weeks, and its nature is recorded vividly in several memoirs. The causeway gaps were now too wide for hasty bridging in the presence of the defenders, but anecdotes suggest that the depth of water in them must have varied considerably. On one occasion Spanish boats were able to sail right through one and fire from the flanks to support a frontal assault. On another, Alvarado led his knot of riders into the water and up the other side, only to be cut off when lurking canoes paddled into the gap behind him before his infantry could start filling it with their earth-baskets. Logic suggests that the Spanish boats could have been used to ferry men around the breaks, but in this particular action they were held back by palisades of logs carefully positioned just beneath the surface.

On that occasion Alvarado only cut his way free after five of his men had been taken alive – the fate of more than 50 before the fighting was over, and the one that all the conquistadors feared far more than death in battle. Every day the booming of the great drum and the moaning of conch-shell trumpets would tell the appalled attackers that captured comrades were about to be butchered alive on the temple pyramid; in the later stages of the fighting they could actually witness the grisly spectacle, while the Mexicans tried to sap their morale by hurling body-parts into their ranks.

Once they reached the south of the island the attackers found themselves checked and then thrown back in confused street-fighting among the canals and alleyways. In July, Cortés had to ratchet down his advance apart from limited raids into the city to keep the enemy in contact; he sent envoys around the allied towns to summon further help, and it has been said that when he resumed the all-out attack late that month he had as many as 150,000 auxiliaries. These included many warriors from communities around the lake who were now making daily independent attacks by canoe, taking a terrible revenge on the Mexicans for their many years of tyranny, and these distractions forced Cuauhtémoc to divide his dwindling strength.

In the final couple of weeks many among the hungry, thirsty, disease-weakened population simply gave themselves up to the Spaniards – who claimed that they tried to save them from massacre by their allies, but with little success. With nothing to lose, those who were still strong enough fought back from every rooftop and canal bank, and the only way to maintain progress northwards was to raze the cleared houses to the ground and use the rubble for ramps across the smaller canals. During the first week in August perhaps 15,000 remaining Mexicans were penned into an area around and east of the Tlatelolco marketplace; Spanish boats could now penetrate some of the wider waterways and fire directly into the houses, but the soldiers had to fight for every yard gained through the blazing streets. The last stand was around the Amaxac road in the northeast.

On 13 August, Cuauhtémoc and some of his people tried to escape from the island in canoes; the city they abandoned was a burning, half-destroyed charnel house, where starving ghosts crept among the ruins and the thousands of unburied corpses. The Spanish brigantines hunted among them, and the young emperor's canoe was recognized by its elaborate decorations. He was taken alive before Cortés, whom he invited to stab him dead; the conquistador declined. His veteran soldier Bernal Diaz del Castillo would end his account of the siege with the words: '*Cuauhtémoc and his captains were apprehended on the thirteenth day of August, at the hour of vespers ... in the year one thousand five hundred and twenty-one. Thanks to Our Lord Jesus Christ, and to Our Lady the Holy Virgin Mary, His blessed mother. Amen.*'

On 15 October 1522, Hernán Cortés was appointed by King Charles V as governor and captain-general of New Spain.

the myth of Ottoman
invincibility

MALTA

21 May – 8 September 1565

'I will not withdraw so long as those banners still wave in the wind.

I am seventy-one years old; how could a man of my age die more

gloriously than among my friends and brothers, in the service of God?'

REPORTED WORDS OF JEAN PARISOT DE LA VALETTE (18 AUGUST 1565)

The brave words of the old Grand Master of the Knights of St John may seem to echo those spoken by the doomed Constantine XI when facing another Turkish siege a century before; but La Valette commanded the first garrison yet described in this book to defend itself successfully. It was highly motivated and adequately provisioned; its besiegers never managed to cut it off from all outside contact; they did not enjoy either a numerical or a technological superiority sufficient to crush the defenders; and they operated under the threat – eventually justified – of outside relief. Nevertheless, the defenders of the Maltese forts earned their survival by their own extraordinary courage and determination, and at a heavy price.

THE TURKISH TIDE

After the fall of the Crusader kingdom in the Holy Land in 1291, the Knights of St John of the Hospital of Jerusalem ('Hospitallers') were soon the only one of the old military-religious orders still effectively resisting the rising tide of Muslim conquest. In 1309 the order captured the Greek island of Rhodes; they built this up as a strongly fortified naval base, and for 250 years pursued a vigorous and successful maritime war that brought them great prestige and riches. In command of slave-rowed galleys the Knights became master sea-captains, and in 1522 their 'holy piracy' provoked a determined attack by the 28-year-old Ottoman sultan Suleiman I (r. 1520–66). They lost Rhodes, but not before their stubborn six-month defence had so impressed Suleiman that he eventually offered them generous terms, allowing the survivors to sail away under arms.

In 1530 the Holy Roman Emperor Charles V (r. 1519–56) granted the Order the Maltese islands – a barren home, but one in an unrivalled strategic position. Set in the narrows between Sicily and North Africa, Malta was a perfect base for denying Ottoman shipping access to the western Mediterranean waters that the sultan dreamed of dominating. The Knights set about fortifying a superb natural harbour, and renewed their aggressive campaign against Turkish warships and commerce. By 1564 the all-conquering Suleiman – by now called 'the Magnificent'– had long and bitterly regretted the generosity of his youth, and determined to remove this costly obstacle once and for all.

The Ottoman siege of Malta, pictured in an engraving from a painting (1575–81) by Mateo Pérez de Aleccio.

'THIS NEST OF VIPERS'

Malta has no important anchorages on its west coast; at its southern tip is the large, exposed Marsasirocco Bay; but what is now Grand Harbour, on the southeast coast, is far more sheltered, and inside it the Knights had built their base around several finger-like inlets. Pointing roughly northwestward from the southern shore of the main channel are the peninsulas of Senglea, between French Creek and Galley Creek, and close to the east of it Birgu, between Galley Creek and Kalkara Creek. Senglea, sparsely populated, was entirely bounded by a defensive wall, with Fort St Michael at its base; the township of Birgu had Fort St Angelo, defended by a moat, at its seaward tip, and bastioned walls across its landward end. Facing these on the northern side of Grand Harbour was the peninsula of Mount Sciberras, separating it from Marsamxett inlet to the north again. Following a dangerous Muslim raid by the corsair admiral Dragut in 1551, the Knights built the new star-shaped Fort St Elmo at its eastern tip; they also tried to improve the fortifications of the old inland capital, Mdina, in the hills about 6 miles (10 km) to the northwest.

By the mid-16th century the principles of defence against gunpowder artillery had been well understood for 150 years. In simple terms, earth ramparts faced with masonry were made thick and low to resist cannonballs; to compensate for their squat height above ground, they were protected against infantry attack by formidable external ditches. The inner wall of the ditch rose high enough above its floor to present an obstacle to scaling, and triangular bastions protruded forward, their gun positions allowing mutually supporting enfilade fire along the ditch and the face of the wall. The ground outside the ditch was also built up towards its lip into a smooth upwards slope or 'glacis' which could be swept by the defenders' guns mounted slightly higher. This system protected the defences from the direct fire of an attacker's batteries, while exposing attacking infantry at any point to fire from the walls and bastions.

Throughout the 16th to 18th centuries this basic plan would be elaborated across Europe into thick successive belts of concentric defences, but in 1565 the Maltese forts were still fairly rudimentary. At St Elmo, in particular, hasty construction had required the use of relatively weak sandstone as well as limestone; the harbour's southern forts and walls were only partly completed, and Mdina's defences were still essentially mediaeval. Malta's natural resources were so poor that when, in 1557, the new Grand Master La Valette constructed additional outworks of timber and earth, both materials had to be shipped over from Sicily. Moreover, while the harbour was magnificent for its purpose, it was dangerously overlooked: Senglea and Birgu from higher ground to the south, and St Elmo from Mount Sciberras to the west.

FOUR OLD MEN

The adversaries in 1565 were led by men whose unusual longevity proved their remarkable powers of endurance, and spoke of deep experience. Suleiman I was now 70 years old; he would not lead his army to Malta in person, but appointed as general another man of 70 – Mustapha Pasha, a fiercely determined and brutal veteran of many campaigns (including Rhodes). He would be supported by Dragut Rais of Tripoli in North Africa, the most successful corsair of his day, who may have been as old as 80 in 1565. Dragut's mission was to advise and mediate between Mustapha and the only young commander involved: the sultan's admiral Piali, an officer of not yet 40, who was married to one of Suleiman's granddaughters. Piali's fleet of some 185 ships would carry to Malta a force perhaps 40,000 strong, including 6300 élite Janissaries. They, and many of the 13,000 *sipahis* and *ialyars* from Anatolia and the Balkans, carried matchlock muskets as well as bows, swords, pikes and halberds, and were backed by several thousand levies of more variable value. Excluding sailors and support troops, Mustapha probably had at least 25,000 fighting men; the exact number of cannon is unknown, but since 80,000 roundshot were shipped his artillery presumably had at least 100 guns, including a number of massive bombards.

Awaiting them on the island, and warned by his efficient spy network, was Grand Master Jean Parisot de la Valette. This sternly devout 71-year-old sea-soldier had devoted his life to the order, and had ascended through its ranks steadily until elected to supreme authority in 1557. (He and Dragut had met: both had previously been captured in sea-battles, and had spent hellish months as galley-slaves before being released in prisoner-exchanges.) His knights and sergeants on Malta numbered about 700, backed by some 8500 local Maltese troops and foreign volunteers; they were concentrated around the harbour, apart from a modest cavalry force that La Valette based at Mdina. The European soldiers of this period fought in full- or half-suits of plate armour, with matchlock firearms and a wide range of blade and pole weapons.

The Maltese forts were well supplied with cannon, crewed by highly skilled gunners; they also had sufficient supplies, provisions and water. As for the hope of relief, La Valette had summoned

SULEIMAN I KANUNI (1494 – 1566)

The sultan known to Turks as *Kanuni* ['the Lawgiver'] and to Christians as 'the Magnificent' not only presided over, but to a great extent shaped the greatest years of the Ottoman empire. His father Selim I Yavuz (r. 1512–20) had been the greatest general of all the sultans, almost doubling the size of the empire by victories in Persia, Syria and Egypt during his brief reign, and acquiring the foundation of a powerful navy. His son first used his inheritance to challenge the Christians; Suleiman captured Belgrade in 1521, Rhodes in 1522 and Buda in 1526. He failed before Vienna in 1529–30, but forced the Habsburg emperor to accept his peace terms. Then he turned east again, and in 1534–5 he gained Persian territory in Mesopotamia. In 1538 his victory of Preveza won for the Sublime Porte the naval initiative in the Mediterranean for 30 years afterwards, during which his galleys terrorized the coasts of southern Europe. In 1541 he finally annexed Hungary into his empire, and in 1555 he forced Persia to give up much of the Caucasus. Baulked at Malta in 1565, he was at the head of another great invasion of Austria when he died, aged 72, on the night of 5–6 September, 1566, during the final stage of the siege of Szigetvár; his army were not told of his death until they had taken the fortress two days later.

THE ORDER OF ST JOHN OF THE HOSPITAL OF JERUSALEM

Originating in a hospice for pilgrims set up in Jerusalem in around 1070 by a group of Italian merchants from Amalfi, this community of monks became an independent order in 1113, and soon extended its charitable work into providing military escorts for pilgrims between the ports of the Holy Land and Jerusalem. By the 1140s these soldier-monks were a recognized multi-national military élite, following a strong discipline and garrisoning some of the most important fortresses in the Crusader kingdom. After the fall of Acre in 1291 – when the Hospitallers in the garrison died to a man – the order took to the sea in a small way from a new base on Cyprus. Their capture of Rhodes in 1309 marked their transformation into an essentially naval power, and their 250-year war against the Turks brought this increasingly rich and aristocratic order great prestige. After their victory on Malta they survived (though in increasingly degenerate form) until the French Revolution, and finally surrendered Malta to Napoleon Bonaparte in 1798. Today they visibly survive in their original role as a medical charity in Britain, sponsoring the St John Ambulance Brigade.

members of the order from across Europe to gather in Sicily, and had appealed for timely help to that island's Spanish viceroy, Don Garcea de Toledo. The Grand Master knew far too much history to place much reliance on such outside assistance; but he could hope for naval interference with the Turks' long lines of supply by some of the order's galleys based in other ports.

The Turkish fleet was sighted to the east on 18 May 1565, but immediately betrayed a lack of single-minded command. It sailed south and west right around Malta, anchored that night in a northwestern bay – and then sailed back again to Marsasirocco in the far south. It finally disembarked the army there on 20 May, and the Knights' cavalry skirmished and reported as the Turks marched north. It has been said that Mustapha Pasha wanted to capture Mdina first, then to occupy the north of the island, and to establish a naval blockade off Grand Harbour before attacking it from the land. He was defied by Piali (Dragut Rais had not yet arrived to control these squabbling commanders): the young admiral believed the fleet to be too exposed in the open roadstead of Marsasirocco, and insisted on priority being given to Fort St Elmo, to clear the way for him to sail into the shelter of Marsamxett inlet. Given the certainty of supporting fire from St Angelo, this meant that the Turks would be obliged to divide their resources between attacks on the harbour forts.

THE MARTYRDOM OF ST ELMO
The fort was initially held by about 600 men led by the Chevaliers Luigi Broglia and Pierre de Massuez. Turkish batteries emplaced on the heights of Mount Sciberras opened fire on 24 May;

the outer walls soon showed damage, and Turkish marksmen crept close enough to pick off defenders. By the end of the month entrenchments on the lower ground were making such good progress that Mustapha resited some of his artillery to reply to the fire from St Angelo. However, St Elmo's defence proved unexpectedly stubborn: a sortie on 29 May did much damage, and each night boats brought supplies and reinforcements across the harbour and evacuated the wounded.

On 30 May old Dragut arrived from Tripoli; he sited new guns at Gallows Point and Tigné to harass the night-time boat traffic, and these opened fire on 3 June. On 6 June the Turks took an important outwork; they could now start filling in the ditch and bringing guns closer, but assaults that day and the next were beaten off with heavy loss. The defenders used not only firearms but fearsome incendiary weapons, including burning hoops thrown from the battlements, which tangled up several men at a time and set their clothing ablaze. Heavy bombardment continued; but when

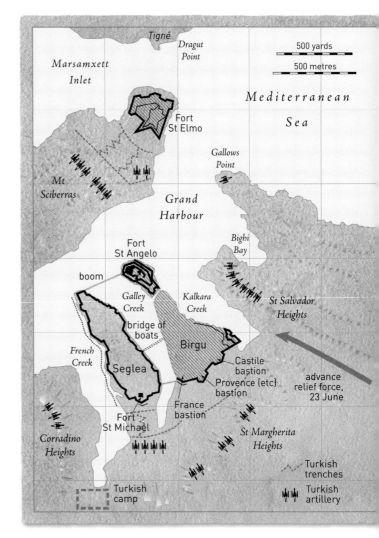

Map showing the configuration of the defences on Malta during the Great Siege of 1565.

Chevalier de Medran slipped across to ask La Valette if the garrison could withdraw to the southern forts, the Grand Master revealed that a message from Sicily had warned him that Don Garcea could not arrive before 20 June, and would not land unless St Elmo was still holding out. Despite this virtual death sentence, volunteers crossed back to the fort with Medran.

After intense bombardments, further Turkish assaults on the nights of 10 and 16 June were again repulsed with heavy casualties. On 18 June Dragut himself was mortally wounded and the *aga* (leader) of the Janissaries killed by a cannon shot, and the next day Mustapha's artillery commander also fell to fire from St Elmo. The blow to Turkish morale was aggravated by their fleet's inability to keep Christian scouting galleys off the horizon; however, the nightly boat link between Birgu and St Elmo was becoming increasingly difficult and costly in lives. On 21 June

TIMELINE

1522 Ottoman sultan Suleiman I ('the Magnificent') expels the Knights Hospitaller from the island of Rhodes

1530 Holy Roman emperor Charles V grants control over the island of Malta in the western Mediterranean to the Hospitallers

1557 Hospitallers' Grand Master La Valette strengthens the defences of Grand Harbour on Malta

1565 (August–September) Ottoman forces undertake their unsuccessful siege of Malta

1566 Suleiman I dies besieging the city of Szigetvár in Hungary

1568 Death of Jean Parisot de la Valette, aged 74

1571 Defeat of an Ottoman naval force at the Battle of Lepanto by the Holy League alliance of Venice, the papacy, Genoa, Spain, the Knights Hospitaller and others

another important outwork fell, and the next day an assault was only barely beaten back from the breach. The garrison of St Elmo made confession, and the chapel bell began a funereal tolling. On 23 June the fort was overrun; five Maltese soldiers managed to swim across the harbour, bringing word that only nine Knights had lived to be taken prisoner. The next day the defenders' heads were displayed on the walls, while their bodies, nailed to crosses, were floated across to the southern shore. La Valette replied by executing Turkish prisoners and firing their heads back from his cannon.

St Elmo had cost the Knights perhaps 1500 men by the end; it had cost the Turks some 8000, and a whole month – the expected length of the entire Malta operation, for which they had had to bring their own supplies to this barren island. Dysentery had begun to ravage their camps, and the cavalry from Mdina made a series of damaging raids on their rear lines. Moreover, while Mustapha laboriously dragged his artillery to surround Senglea and Birgu, an advance relief force of 67 Knights and volunteers and 600 Spanish infantry from Sicily got ashore and slipped into the Christian lines by night via Kalkara Creek. Piali's galleys were proving no match for their opponents, and further out to sea Turkish supply ships were being intercepted; neither did Mustapha ever manage to cut La Valette's communications with Mdina, and thence by small boat to Sicily. When Mustapha heard the cheering that greeted the reinforcements he offered La Valette the same terms given to his predecessor on Rhodes; the old man replied that the only ground he would give the Turks was the ditch in front of his walls, if they chose to fill it with dead Janissaries.

ST MICHAEL AND ST ANGELO

In an echo of Contantinople, Mustapha now had boats portaged overland to Grand Harbour. La Valette argued that boats could not live in Kalkara Creek under the guns of St Angelo; a chain boom between Senglea point and St Angelo denied them Galley Creek; therefore they must plan to attack Senglea from French Creek. He had strong chained palisades driven into the seabed just off this shoreline, and Turkish attempts to destroy them by means of swimmers and windlasses failed.

On 15 June boats carried Turkish troops newly arrived from Algiers across from the Sciberras Peninsula; some struggled ashore through gaps in the palisades, but were slaughtered at the walls. Simultaneously others attacked St Michael from the landward side; when the explosion of a powder magazine blew a breach they made a penetration, but La Valette met the crisis with troops sent across a bridge of boats from Birgu. When Mustapha sent 1000 Janissaries in boats to land at the northeastern tip of Senglea, these were almost annihilated by an unsuspected battery at St Angelo.

On 2 and 7 August, Mustapha launched massed assaults against Fort St Michael and the landward bastions of Birgu after heavy artillery preparation. A dangerous penetration threatened the loss of St Michael on the 7th, but at the perfect moment the Chevalier de Lugny brought all his cavalry from Mdina and ravaged the Turkish rear camps, causing enough confusion to buy vital time for the defenders. Toledo was now promising a relief landing by 16,000 men for the end of August, but La Valette was wise not believe him: despite the furious entreaties of the Knights on Sicily the Spanish viceroy made repeated excuses not to commit his master's troops to a cause he believed was already lost.

In mid-August, Mustapha tried old-fashioned siege tactics for the first time, building assault towers and digging mines at the Castile bastion. He planned another massed attack on St Michael to draw the Christian reserves over from Birgu, and then to blow a mine under the bastion and send his own reserves in through the dust. When the attack struck St Michael on 18 August, La Valette spotted the secondary force waiting outside Birgu and kept his reserves intact. When Mustapha lost patience and blew the mine anyway, the Grand Master led a successful counter-attack into the breach in person, pike in hand. His nephew was killed during a sortie, and the fighting continued into the next day. When a siege tower was trundled forward La Valette had a hole picked low in a wall opposite it, and brought up a cannon which toppled it by blasting its lower supports with chain-shot.

By 20 August there was open dispute between Mustapha and Piali. Unless Malta fell to them by mid-September the autumn winds would trap the fleet in harbour for months, and without spares or repair facilities it was simply not equipped for overwintering. The troops were tired and ill; supplies were running low; Christian naval superiority meant that resupply could not be counted upon, and there was a real threat of a strong relief expedition.

The Knights, too, were facing stark choices; the cannonades and mining had badly weakened the walls, and they were only holding the Turks at bay by making desperate sorties. On 23 August some of La Valette's councillors argued for giving up Senglea and concentrating the survivors inside St Angelo for a last stand. The Grand Master pointed out that this would deny St Angelo the vital supporting fire of the western batteries, and allow the enemy to concentrate on a single objective; and also that St Angelo could not accommodate, or water, all the loyal Maltese soldiers, whom he refused to abandon. He emphasized his arguments by pulling all except the artillerymen out of St Angelo and destroying the drawbridge: the rest of them now had no choice but to fight where they stood.

A sign of sinking Turkish resolve came when a belated advance on Mdina was turned back without even an attempt on its impressive-looking but crumbling walls. Don Mesquita had them visibly manned by a mass of 'soldiers' from among the civilian refugees inside, and made a confident show by firing off some of his in fact very scant cannon ammunition; at this the Turks, remembering their costly overconfidence at St Elmo, simply marched away. After a pause from 24 August until 1 September, yet more assaults on Senglea and Birgu showed a noticeable lack of determination.

DON GARCEA'S BELATED ARRIVAL

On 6 September, Don Garcea de Toledo – finally driven into action by the 200 Knights gathered in Sicily – dropped anchor in Mellieha Bay on the northeast coast. The next day he began landing some 9000 men; this figure was exaggerated by La Valette in misinformation that he planted with the Turks, prompting Mustapha to order evacuation. Piali once again missed his opportunity when Don Garcea's ships, leaving to pick up another 4000 troops, insolently sailed past Grand Harbour and fired a salute to the defenders.

On 8 September, Don Ascanio de la Corna's scouts sighted the harbour forts, whose defenders had already emerged to find the Turkish camps abandoned. Mustapha only learned the true size of the relief force when he was already embarking his men; he ordered them landed once again, but Piali would only wait to put about 9000 ashore. At Naxxar Hill these were swept aside by a furious rush of Knights from the harbour and Mdina, and the rearguard only saved Mustapha himself with

'*We saw the mines of the Turks which had made so great breaches, one in the bastion of Leb and the other in that of the palace, each about six fathoms long from bottom to top: There were also five mines under the Courtin, which would have been ready to spring in two days, when they designed a general assault; which would have been dangerous, as well for the greatness of the breach, as the diminution of the strength of the besieged.*'

A TRUE AND EXACT RELATION OF THE RAISING OF THE SIEGE OF VIENNA AND THE VICTORY OBTAINED OVER THE OTTOMAN ARMY (LONDON, 1683)

VIENNA, 1683 – THE OTTOMANS' FINAL LUNGE INTO EUROPE

The persistent Ottoman threat to Western Europe was finally ended outside the walls of Vienna on 12 September 1683. The lethargic Sultan Mehmet IV had left command of an army of perhaps 200,000 men to his grand vizier, Kara Mustapha, who advanced late in 1682 to exploit a Hungarian revolt against the Holy Roman Emperor Leopold I. The imperial general Charles of Lorraine put an 11,000-strong garrison under Count Ernst Rüdiger von Starhemberg (1638–1701) inside Vienna, while he sought to assemble a multi-national relief army led by the Polish king Jan III Sobieski (r. 1674–96). The Turks established siege lines from 14 July 1683; their guns made little impression on the ramparts, and Starhemberg conducted a vigorous defence, supported by some 5000 civilian volunteers. Assaults on various minor breaches were driven back, and Kara Mustapha put his faith in mining and starvation. On 11 September a 70,000-strong army of Austrians, Germans, Swedes and Poles under Sobieski and Charles of Lorraine appeared northwest of Vienna; the next day Sobieski led 20,000 allied cavalry in a charge that smashed through the Turkish lines, while Starhemberg led a sortie against their rear. The Ottoman army was routed, abandoning its artillery amid its 10,000–15,000 dead, and Sobieski's pursuit drove it right out of Hungary. Kara Mustapha, who had boasted that he would stable his horses in St Peter's Basilica in Rome, was executed for his failure. This imperial victory not only restricted future Turkish influence in Europe to the Balkans, but also checkmated the hostile conspiracies of Louis XIV of France.

difficulty. The last Turks scrambled aboard ship in St Paul's Bay, pursued into the very water by the Christians, and rowed away on the night of 8 September.

Turkish casualties during the siege may have reached 20,000; the defenders had lost perhaps 5000 of their original number of around 10,000. For the remaining three years of his life La Valette was a hero to all Christendom, and a new city built on Mount Sciberras would be named after him – Valetta. He outlived Suleiman by two years; and in 1571 the crushing naval defeat at Lepanto would end forever the Ottoman dream of making the whole Mediteranean a Turkish lake.

war elephants and mass suicide

CHITTOR GARH

21 October 1567 – 23 February 1568

'This wonderful animal is in bulk and strength like a mountain, and in courage and ferocity like a lion ... Experienced men judge the value of a good elephant as equal to 500 horses, and believe that when it is guided by a few bold men armed with matchlocks such an elephant is worth twice that number.'

FROM THE *AIN-I AKBARI* (LATER 16TH CENTURY)

Although we do not have an account of this siege as detailed as those found in European and Turkish histories, nor even a map of its progress, it is still an interesting example of a tradition of warfare contemporary with, but differing from, that which gave rise to the siege of Malta. The third siege of Chittor Garh, a great Rajput hill fortress in Rajasthan, north-west India, was – like that of Constantinople – a relentless attack on the fortified political capital of a state in order to end its independence, launched by a Muslim army with gunpowder artillery. Its differences lay firstly in the employment of one non-European weapon – the war elephant; and, secondly and most obviously, in its revelation of a wholly alien attitude – the preference for mass suicide over inevitable capture.

THE MUSLIM INVASIONS

By around AD 1000, turmoil among the Hindu kingdoms of northern India left them vulnerable at first to massive raids, and later to conquest, by Muslim-Turkic peoples from Central Asia. In the late 12th century Muhammad of Ghur swept down from the northern passes, and in 1207 his successor founded the first of the five Muslim dynasties collectively known as the sultanate of Delhi. In the 13th century these rulers were themselves preoccupied by fighting off Mongol attacks; but the sultan Ala-ud-din Khalji (r. 1296–1316) beat off the last of these in 1308. By his death this sultan – who styled himself *Sikander Sani*, 'the second Alexander the Great' – had extended Delhi's rule or suzerainty as far south as the Deccan, excepting only Bengal to the east.

In 1398 Delhi was utterly destroyed by the Tartar conqueror Timur the Lame, and it took a century for various kingdoms to grow again out of the devastation. The territories of the restored Delhi sultans of the 15th century had shrunk by 1500 to Delhi itself, the Punjab and part of the Ganges Valley. From 1518 a new conqueror out of Central Asia – Babur of Ferghana (1482–1530)

Mughal miniature of the assault on Chittor Garh. The Mughal commander Akbar stands at the top of the siege tower, after shooting the Rajput prince Jaimal (top left).

– raided south almost every year; and in April 1526, at the first Battle of Panipat, he finally swept away the last sultan of the Lodi dynasty.

THE MUGHAL EMPIRE

Unlike his reputed ancestor Timur, Babur was far from being a mere butcher; he was a literate and constructive ruler who established an empire that would last more than 200 years. Babur called himself a Turk, but since he was of Turco-Mongol stock his empire was known by the Arabic-Persian term for Mongol – Mughal. (In fact, long before his time much of the aristocracy of northern India was already of mixed Indian, Afghan, Persian, Turkish and Mongol ancestry.) Babur's son Humayun was deposed by a rival, but returned in 1555 with his teenage son Jalal-ud-din Muhammad, who recaptured the throne. In 1560, taking the name Akbar, this grandson of Babur embarked on a 45-year career of conquest. He was probably the greatest of the Mughal rulers, being tolerant of other religions and an energetic administrator. Among other innovations he built up an army with a core of permanently employed royal troops, around which larger field armies could be assembled from provincial levies of all ethnic groups and religions. He consolidated his power as much by diplomacy as by force, and won over many of the Rajput ruling houses to his service.

INDIAN CASTLES

The Rajput suffix *garh* is usually translated as 'fort', but 'castles' is probably the more accurate term for most fortified Indian sites of these centuries; they were a combination of military strongholds, feudal rulers' palaces and walled towns. Terrain dictated the design of their defences, but these were conventional enough. Where the site allowed they were usually surrounded by dry ditches or a wet moat (the latter sometimes stocked with crocodiles or poisonous water-snakes). Sites that incorporated a flat-topped hill, like Chittor, usually made external moats and ditches difficult to dig but also unnecessary. The natural rock of the steep hillside was reshaped and the lower courses of the masonry walls were built flush against it; this reduced the labour necessary, made the lower walls impervious to mining and stone-throwing

TIMELINE

1526 Babur of Ferghana defeats Shah Ibrahim Lodi of the sultanate of Delhi at the Battle of Panipat and founds the Mughal empire

1556 Babur's grandson Akbar becomes Mughal emperor and beats off an invasion of Suri Afghans from Bihar, again at Panipat

1567 (October) Mughal forces under Akbar begin their siege of the Rajput fortress of Chittor Garh

1568 (February) Chittor Garh captured, as the defenders commit mass suicide

1569 Rajput fortress at Ranthambhor falls to the Mughals

1572 Conquest of Gujarat gives the Mughal empire a vital outlet to the sea

1576 Mughals secure control over Bengal

1605 Death of Akbar

THE ARMY OF AKBAR

Akbar's reforms for his standing army were remarkably sophisticated, but arguably over-complex and bureaucratic. Different pay scales, promotion procedures and rotation of units through various duties were all specified, but it seems that many regulations were unpopular and only patchily observed. A hierarchy of no fewer than 33 officer ranks was created, from leaders of 10,000 men down to leaders of 10, and one 'modern' feature was the requirement that officers should work their way up through these grades by merit. Nevertheless, a man's wealth still governed the particular rank he could aspire to – a general of 5000 men had to own 340 horses, 90 elephants, 80 camels, 200 mules and 160 carts; a junior rank leading ten men had to have four horses (it was very largely a cavalry army). Apart from royal troops, Mughal armies also consisted of thousands of much less well-organized and equipped levies and auxiliaries, raised through the administrative machinery of provinces and districts.

The total strength of the Mughal army is not known, but is thought to have reached perhaps 20,000 in Babur's time, so may well have been twice as large under Akbar; it included many ethnic types apart from native Indians – Central Asians, Afghans and Turks were numerous. The strength of a particular field army must have varied considerably; Akbar had wide territories to safeguard and could not risk taking his whole household force on a single campaign.

engines, and also made them taller on the outside than on the inside – at Chittor the wall-walk is only some 1.8 to 2.7 metres (6–9 ft) above the ground inside, and five or six times that height outside.

The curtain walls long preceded the appearance of gunpowder (Chittor was founded in the eighth century), so were relatively tall and thin – typically, 9 to 14 metres (30–45 ft) high; they were conventionally built, of ashlar faces with rubble infill. The tops had wall-walks and crenellated parapets, and were loopholed for archers (and later, hand-gunners and light cannon); most loopholes at Chittor are about 0.9 metre (3 ft) high by 10 centimetres (4 in) wide, some pointing straight ahead for long-range shooting, alternating with others splayed and angled down at the bottom for shooting at closer attackers. Sometimes a gallery ran around in the thickness of the wall, opened on the inside into separate arched chambers which helped to localize any breaches.

Towers along the walls were usually of D-section, not projecting far in front, squat in shape and little (if at all) higher than the wall. On hilltop sites like Chittor they were unevenly spaced – closer where the wall was vulnerable, and at wider intervals where natural drops protected the approach. Towers were often solid half way up, leaving only one loopholed chamber below the fighting platform at the top. When cannon began to appear in India some castles received additional raised gun-platforms inside the walls. Concentric double wall systems are seen at some sites, but not at Chittor, where the curtain runs around the edge of a precipitous hilltop.

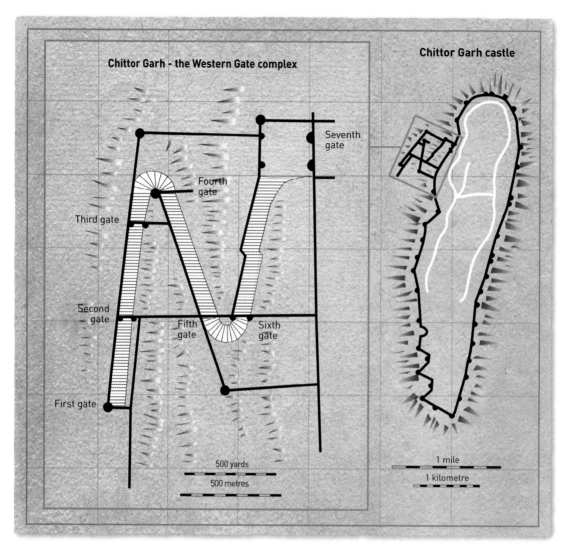

Map of Chittor Garh, showing the general layout of the castle's curtain walls and a detailed plan of the Western Gate complex.

ELEPHANTS AND GATE DESIGN

The gateways of Indian castles were usually pierced directly through the curtain wall and flanked by towers, rather than being built through a gate tower. They measured about 3.7 to 5 metres (12–16 ft) wide, by up to 7.3 metres (24 ft) high – they had to accommodate the passage of elephants with howdahs. Since they were the natural focus of attack they also had to withstand the charge of an elephant – the usual method. Some were designed with narrowly confined or angled approach-ways, so that an elephant could not get up speed in a charge, though this feature seems to have been absent at Chittor. The gates themselves were made of timber about 15 centimetres (6 in) thick, strengthened with additional beams inside and iron plates on the outside. A striking feature was that the outsides were thickly studded with iron spikes every few inches, to deter elephants – some over the whole surface, some only at elephant-head height. (Those at Chittor were of an elaborate design, forged with a hook below the spike, in the shape of an elephant-driver's ankus goad.) War elephants were therefore armoured on the head, and sometimes over the whole body.

CHITTOR

This capital of the Mewar principality, about 70 miles (112 km) northeast of the later city of Udaipur, crowned a long, narrow hilltop plateau, rising sharply some 150 metres (500 ft) above the surrounding valleys. The curtain walls following the clifftops enclosed an area about 1190 metres (1300 yds) wide by 3.3 miles (5.3 km) long. The main building complexes were three palaces: one named for the renowned 14th-century queen Padmini, one for her prince (rana) Rattan Singh II, and one for Rana Kumbha. Such palaces, walled and gated, typically enclosed courtyards with ornamental fountains, separate men's and women's quarters (at Chittor the *zenana* was a three-storey block), a large public audience hall, kitchens and other service buildings, a temple, previous rulers' tombs and elephant stables. Other public buildings, such as a library, were set among lakes and gardens. The northern part of Chittor hilltop was partly divided off, level with the west gate complex and the palace of Rana Kumbha, by the makeshift transverse Wall of Banbeer, hastily and incompletely built in 1534–5.

Castles usually included important constructions connected with wells and reservoirs; Chittor has a large swimming pool-like tank of water on a hillside shelf outside the main wall but enclosed by an outer wall. Barracks around the walls accommodated the garrison, and there were large storehouses for food, oil, firewood and all other necessities for withstanding a long siege – castles in India, as elsewhere, usually fell to bribed treachery, but blockades of well over a year were not unknown. At Chittor two ornamental towers also rose above the roofs, the taller being the nine-storey Tower of Victory, at 37 metres (122 ft). The town stretched southwards along the hilltop; its population is unknown – one source mentions 40,000, and this is not intrinsically impossible for a site of about 57 square kilometres (22 sq mi), but ancient figures should always be treated with some caution.

THE WESTERN GATE

There were three entrances to the castle (apart from a small postern at the southern tip, specifically for throwing criminals down the cliff), but only one practical approach for an army – the great Western Gate complex, built all the way up the hillside near the northern end. Like most of the fortifications, this dated mainly from the 13th century. It fulfilled the Rajput ideal of being a sevenfold construction: seven separate defended gates were spaced at intervals up a Z-shaped stepped road leading from the foot to the hilltop, and the whole climb was dominated by walls both flanking and cutting across it at intervals, allowing the defenders to bring continuous crossfires down on attackers.

The bottom gate (the Padal Pol, built in 1100) was guarded by a curtain wall on the right, and a strong tower on the left. Once through it the road climbed between walls on both sides to the second gate (Bhairon Pol). The climb from this to the third gate (Hanuman Pol) was dominated from above and right by the slanting central wall of the 'Z', linked by a transverse run to the towers defending the third gate. Once past this the attacker had to make a hairpin turn to the right, faced by towered walls on the left front and right, and – once he had turned to attack the fourth gate (Ganesh Pol) – also from behind. The long climb from that to the fifth gate (Jorla Pol) was dominated from both sides and in front; beyond that it made a left hairpin to the sixth gate (Lakshman Pol), set in the same transverse wall as the fifth, and dominated from all four sides. The long final climb was slightly crooked, and again covered from all sides. At the top was the five-towered platform in front of the seventh gate (the Ram Pol, built in 1459); attacking the gate involved turning 90 degrees to the right, under fire on three sides from walls, towers and a guardhouse.

THE THIRD SIEGE

The rana of Chittor in 1567 was Udai Singh II, leader of the powerful Sessodi clan, who stubbornly resisted making submission to the emperor Akbar and fomented unrest among other Rajput rulers. Akbar decided to lance this boil, and on 20 October he arrived in the valley below Chittor with part of his army. One source puts its strength at only 9000 including basically non-combatant troops such as engineers. This seems a modest force, given that Chittor's military garrison was supposedly 8000 strong even without thousands of townsmen; perhaps the 9000 excludes provincial auxiliaries and counts only paid royal units? The army was well and efficiently equipped by state factories and depots, and its gear and supplies were transported by a large train of mule carts, Bactrian camels, oxen and elephants.

The élite of the siege army were drawn from Akbar's 12,000-strong corps of matchlock musketeers – *banduqchis* – from Bengal and the lower Ganges; these assault troops also had clay explosive or incendiary grenades, thrown by hand or from slings. The bulk of the household troops were cavalry, but they prided themselves on their prowess in foot combat; they were equipped with steel helmets, mail and lamellar armour, bows, long straight swords and round shields. For siege work there were probably large numbers of Hindu light infantry armed with bows, spears, swords and shields. Akbar is also said to have taken 300 elephants to Chittor.

We do not know how many cannon Akbar took with him, but the Mughal artillery had been a separate and favoured arm of the household troops since the time of his grandfather, with Ottoman and Arab master-gunners supervising some very large battering-pieces. The best guns were bronze, the majority probably of iron; there were two distinct types of field guns towed by bullocks, heavy siege pieces drawn by elephants, and light two-man rampart or elephant-back guns. Akbar was enthusiastic and knowledgeable; he had established new gun foundries, tested new pieces himself, and is credited with having personally devised several types, including a 17-barrel volley gun. Mortars were available for lobbing solid and incendiary projectiles over walls; Akbar was also interested in rockets (although we can presume that these wildly inaccurate missiles were largely of psychological value).

INDIAN SIEGE WARFARE

The Muslims brought to the subcontinent the broad legacy of military influences which their far-flung campaigns and literate culture had allowed them to gather and disseminate, from sources as far apart as Hungary and China. Man-powered beam-sling mangonels were probably in use in the north by both attackers and defenders from at least the 13th century, as were a wide range of incendiary projectiles – these are described in the treatise *Adab al-Harb* written for a regional Muslim ruler by Fakhr al-Din. Mangonels are mentioned at the Rajput fortress of Ranthambhor, where in 1290–1 the besieging Jalal-ud-din Khalji failed in an attempt to build raised platforms for them. Counter-weight trebuchets were also known by about 1300, when one Muslim general mounted them on river rafts. The Delhi sultans employed rolling mantlets to get men close to the walls of besieged places, and sometimes undermined these – collapsing the tunnels first by burning the props, and later with gunpowder; in 1495 Babur employed counter-mining, both smoking-out and flooding-out enemy tunnellers. Movable siege towers were hardly ever used, and nor were Western-style battering rams – elephants were always preferred. Cannon played no part in pre-Mughal warfare in India; despite their introduction, Babur is thought to have employed them alongside missile-throwers based on the old 'giant crossbow' principle.

When Akbar arrived before Chittor, Udai Singh fled immediately into the countryside, leaving the defence to two teenage princes, Jaimal and Patta. The castle was well provisioned and watered, and the garrison supposedly had more matchlocks and cannon than the Mughal force. On 21 October some of Akbar's troops reportedly made an unauthorized assault on the outer defences and were driven off with heavy loss, after which he settled down to a blockade. A discontinuous ring of outposts was set up around the hill, its intervals patrolled by cavalry. It seems unlikely that Akbar had any serious fear of Udai Singh raising a relieving army, and the blockade concentrated on preventing any escape from the castle hill; fires were kept blazing at night to light up no-man's-land, and patrolling was constant.

Although mangonels were still in use at this time, cannon took the lion's share of siege work; we are told that Akbar set his up in three batteries, personally siting the strongest opposite the western gates. A large mortar firing 18-kilogram (40-lb) projectiles was reportedly actually cast *in situ* on a neighbouring hill, so that it did not have to be dragged up there.

GRINDING UP FROM GATE TO GATE

It is frustrating that we do not have a detailed calendar or map of events during the siege, but it is clear that the main Mughal operations were conducted against the western complex, and the road

BEAUTY AND HORROR

The ghastly Rajput rite of mass suicide that ended the siege of 1567–8 was simply a repetition of events in 1303, when Chittor had been besieged by Ala-ud-din Khalji. Legend has it that his attack was partly provoked by tales of the great beauty of Padmini, the queen of its ruler Rana Rattan Singh. After months of weary siege warfare the sultan sent word that he would withdraw his army if he could but see her unveiled face; he was eventually allowed into the castle, to glimpse her image in the last of a series of aligned mirrors. As he was escorted out he signalled his retainers to seize Rattan Singh, who was dragged outside, and the sultan demanded Padmini in return for his release. The queen agreed; but when her train of hundreds of curtained litters arrived in his camp they proved to contain not ladies-in-waiting but soldiers, and extra weapons for the litter-bearers. Rattan was rescued, but most of his best men died protecting his escape to the castle.

The furious Ala-ud-din swore a terrible revenge; and when the weakened garrison faced final defeat, Padmini led their wives and children in committing *jauhar* in underground chambers of the palace. When the doors had been closed on the terrible fires, Rattan Singh led his remaining men out in the suicidal *shaka* charge. The funeral pyres are believed to have been lit in caverns under what was later called Rana Kumbha's Palace; these are still sealed.

The Rajputs recaptured the castle from the Delhi sultanate about ten years later, and in fact repeated the *jauhar* twice: at a siege by the sultan of Gujarat in 1435, and again in 1568.

zig-zagging uphill must have been taken gate by gate. Apart from bombardment, the methods available included elephants with armoured head-pieces charging the gates; these could do great damage, not only to timber but also to brickwork and light masonry, and pin-pricking them with arrows or musket-balls only increased their destructive rage. More prosaically, heavy mantlets were used to cover approaches to the walls; timber towers and platforms of sandbags were raised to overlook or over-shoot them; and escalading troops were equipped with a range of normal and especially wide scaling ladders.

The most striking aspect mentioned at Chittor is the digging of a very wide and deep sap – *sabat* – to take assault troops forward under cover, with loopholed side parapets raised above ground level, and a roof of heavy planks protected from fire with wet hides. This is described as being wide enough for ten riders abreast, and tall enough to conceal an elephant; if we can believe this, then it must have been dug up to the first gate at the foot of the hill, to deliver sappers and perhaps elephants to it under cover.

We are also told that in mid-December two mines were ready for blowing – again, the first gate would seem the only practical place for these. One made a breach and the assault troops rushed forwards, only for the second to explode late, killing many men of both sides; the Rajputs recovered first, and were able to repair the breach. The first gate was taken later, and one of the best-known episodes of the battle took place at the second gate when Akbar, taking aim at the head of his troops with his personal matchlock 'Sangram', shot and killed the Rajput commander Prince Jaimal.

Losses must have been heavy during the slow advance up the zig-zag road, to arrows, javelins and musket-fire from the parapets on all sides; Rajput tactics also included stockpiling boulders on the wall-walks for dropping, chipped roughly spherical or oval so that they could easily be rolled from one part of the wall to another. Incendiary grenades were also used by the defenders, and probably both light guns loaded with grapeshot and stone-throwing mangonels; both new and old weapons would have been deadly when trained down a fixed line of approach, and the transverse walls prevented the attackers from outflanking any of the gates. It may be significant that the second, fourth and fifth gates today show major signs of later rebuilding. Progress must have been steady, since at one point Rajput envoys were sent out to offer their fealty to Akbar; but his price was the handing-over of Udai Singh – and since the rana had abandoned his people, the garrison could not comply.

It is said that on the evening of 22 February 1568, after four months' fighting, the Mughals saw the light of huge fires glowing inside the castle, and noticed the remaining defenders pulling back from the perimeter they still held. That night explosives breached another wall, and a final assault led by elephants penetrated the last defences and raged through the town, while the sinister fires lit up the palaces. Rather than face capture the defenders had chosen to commit *jauhar* – the self-immolation of the women on funeral pyres. The last warriors then performed the *shaka*: after ritual ablutions and painting themselves with sacred red signs, they put on saffron robes and *mor* wedding turbans, and then made a final suicidal charge into the Mughal ranks with axes and trident spears, having sworn to die at the enemy's or their own hands.

On the morning of Tuesday 23 February, Akbar rode into the devastated castle on an elephant. Supposedly some 30,000 Rajput soldiers and townsfolk died in the siege and assault; it was the only occasion on which Akbar let his troops kill and sack unchecked. Some Rajput musketeers apparently declined to join in the grisly ritual of *jauhar* and *shaka*; disguising themselves – not difficult, given the multi-ethnic composition of the Mughal army – they escaped, escorting their families as if they were prisoners. The faithless Udai Singh himself evaded capture, and later established a new capital at Udaipur.

Tokugawa's Samurai
live up to the warrior code

NAGASHINO

16–28 JUNE 1575

'*We should not confuse the romantic illusion with reality ... A close reading of the historical sources proves that for samurai to choose to fight to the death was a rather unusual event; they may have aspired to the unbending code of bushido, but in reality they often failed to live up to it.*'

DR MITSUO KURE, *SAMURAI* (2001)

The constant struggles between rival regional baronies in 15th- and 16th-century Japan saw many sieges, but the particular cultural and material context produced – even more strikingly than in India – great contrasts with practice in contemporary Europe. The siege of Osaka by the Tokugawa army in 1614–15 is often cited as an example of Japanese siege warfare, but in some respects it was atypical, and a much more modest episode perhaps conveys a more Japanese flavour. The defence of the castle of Nagashino lasted for only 12 days; but it was the catalyst for one of the decisive battles of this Sengoku period, won by the armies of the conqueror Oda Nobunaga and his junior ally, Tokugawa Ieyasu – to whom the castle belonged. Propaganda since the 1930s has certainly distorted the true nature of the *bushido* code attributed to the samurai (the lords' armed vassals or retainers); however, the siege of Nagashino provides at least one impressive example of its being honoured unto death.

ODA, HIDEYOSHI AND TOKUGAWA

The immensely complex and bloody history of late medieval Japan may be very briefly summarized as follows. Since the 12th century the emperors had been cloistered in a purely ceremonial role, and real power was wielded by the shogun, a hereditary military dictator presiding over a parallel court. From the outbreak in 1467 of the so-called Onin War, central control by the shogunate steadily broke down, and the country descended into chaos as families of *daimyo* – regional barons – vied for territory in the provinces. From 1560 a series of three great politico-military leaders – Oda Nobunaga (1534–82), Toyotomi Hideyoshi (1536–98) and Tokugawa Ieyasu (1542–1616) – set about extending and consolidating their conquests and alliances, thus gradually reducing the number of players at the board.

The Battle of Nagashino, sparked by the siege, effectively removed the great Takeda clan of Kai province from an active part in the equation, and by the time of his murder in 1582 Oda controlled

The Battle of Nagashino, which followed the siege of the castle there, depicted in inks on a 17th-century six-fold screen.

TIMELINE

1542 First Portuguese traders arrive in Japan, introducing firearms

1568 Oda Nobunaga, the first warlord to attempt the unification of Japan, captures the imperial capital Kyoto

1575 Nobunaga's ally Tokugawa Ieyasu orders castellan Okudaira Sadamasa to defend Nagashino Castle against siege by Takeda Katsuyori of Kai; the garrison holds out and is relieved by an army commmanded by Ieyasu

1582 Death of Nobunaga; succeeded by his former general Toyotomi Hideyoshi, who rules most of central Japan in alliance with his rival Tokugawa Ieyasu

1600 Tokugawa Ieyasu succeeds Hideyoshi after failed attempts to invade Korea

1615 Tokugawa Ieyasu successfully brings 150 years of civil war to an end, establishing a shogunate that would rule Japan for more than two centuries

much of central Honshu (the main island of Japan). His general Hideyoshi avenged him, and continued his centralizing conquests until his death in 1598, although latterly distracted by a profitless invasion of Korea. The struggle to succeed Hideyoshi was won by Oda's former ally Tokugawa; by 1615 he had brought 150 years of chronic civil war to a triumphant close, ensuring the rule of the Tokugawa shogunate for 250 years to come.

SIEGE WARFARE IN JAPAN

Before the mid-16th century, the main stronghold (*honjo*) of a *daimyo* was normally in hill country, and was built by scarping – and scalping – natural features cleared of their forest cover. The hilltops were palisaded or walled to make a series of baileys, enclosing timber buildings; the gulleys and hollows were shaped into ditches, and sometimes into moats filled by diverted streams. The lord usually lived in a mansion on the plains, only retreating to the *honjo* when threatened by invasion; this redoubt therefore did not have to be either large or luxurious. It has been estimated that in the mid-15th century there were at least 30,000 of these hill fortresses in Japan, in addition to the networks of secondary castles (*shijo*) held by the barons' trusted retainers, and even smaller forts and stockades.

However, although the blockading and assaulting of such positions was common, the technology of siege warfare developed in the Middle East and Europe played virtually no part in Japanese campaigns. Starvation, fire (to which the timber construction was always vulnerable), assault and (where feasible) flooding were the usual methods of reducing strongholds when threats or treachery failed. There are a few mentions of long folding scaling ladders, movable mantlets and man-powered mangonels, and static observation and sniping platforms were often built to overtop the walls. There is a reference from 1468 to mangonels throwing paper-wrapped gunpowder charges; but these had no fragmentation effect, and so can only have been useful as incendiaries or blast bombs, without much killing-power unless they landed in a crowd of soldiers. 'Cannon' made from hollowed tree-trunks were used to some extent for throwing incendiaries into defended places, and

FIREARMS IN JAPAN

Portuguese traders first brought matchlock arquebuses to Japan in 1542, and they were first used in battle in significant numbers in 1548-9. They were soon copied locally, and played an increasingly important part in Japanese warfare. Oda Nobunaga was one general who understood their potential, and 1000 matchlock musketeers were crucial to his victory at Nagashino on 28 June 1575. The previous year Oda had employed light ship-mounted cannon at Nagashima; nevertheless, despite contacts with Ming dynasty China (where cannon were being cast from the 1350s), and the acquisition of a few guns from European ships, the use of artillery for siege warfare was simply never pursued seriously in Japan until very late in the Sengoku wars. Encounters with Korean and Chinese artillery during Hideyoshi's Korean war in the 1590s came as a shock, but only a few *daimyo* seem to have brought home any enthusiasm for cannon. One was Tokugawa Ieyasu, who assembled all the guns he could for his siege of Osaka in 1614-15, but after his death artillery was again neglected.

perhaps fired a kind of anti-personnel grapeshot, but they were far too weak to take the size of charge needed for stone or iron balls to breach walls.

Metal gun-founding in Japan was at least 100 years behind that in China and Korea, and so was the tactical application of artillery. Even the few cannon acquired from Portuguese and English ships, and the smaller imitations cast by local gun-founders, were employed as a sort of heavy sniping weapon rather than being massed to batter castle walls. Perhaps the explanation for this neglect – not only of guns, but of siegecraft in general – lies in the samurai mentality: for these warriors it was close combat that brought honour, rather than the scientific application of technology. As in Europe, a garrison without hope of the arrival of relief was expected to negotiate terms to save their lives.

However, from the mid-16th century the footsoldiers raised from the barons' peasant farmers were increasingly provided with matchlock arquebuses as an easily taught supplement to archery, to sweep the parapets of castles in the attack or their approaches in defence.

'Swift as the wind, quiet as the forest, conquer like the fire, steady as the mountain.'

MOTTO OF THE *DAIMYO* TAKEDA SHINGEN OF KAI (1521-73; FROM *THE ART OF WAR* BY CHINESE MILITARY STRATEGIST SUN TZU)

JAPANESE CASTLE DESIGN

The classic image known today from pictures and reconstructions – a white-painted tower keep rising in tapering tiers, adorned with windowed gables and upswept roof eaves – only appeared in the last 50 years of the Sengoku wars. Before the mid-16th century most strongholds were built by landscaping natural ridges and hollows into mounds and moats, improved with walls and palisades. The clearing of the forest cover from slopes and the frequent heavy rains made the foundations of these *yamashiro* unstable; three storeys was the (infrequent) maximum possible height for buildings, and look-out towers had to be skeletal frameworks.

This led to the development of great stone base platforms, to support heavier structures, during the later 16th century. Natural or man-made earth mounds were faced with massive, dry-laid stones; the outward taper of the base was not to throw off projectiles, but to accommodate the stresses of the great tower keeps which began to appear simultaneously. The first of the classic tower keeps is believed to have been built at Tamon for Matsunaga Hisahide in 1567; and a seven-storey tower was built for Oda Nobunaga at Azuchi in 1576, the year after Nagashino.

THE ROADS TO NAGASHINO

In 1572, although the strongest leader in Japan, Oda Nobunaga still ruled only a limited area around the capital, Kyoto; one of his allies was Tokugawa Ieyasu, ruler of Mikawa province to the east, and one of his rivals was the great Takeda Shingen of Kai to the northeast. That year, Takeda moved against Tokugawa and defeated him at the Battle of Mikata-ga-hara. Encouraged, Takeda invaded again the following year, but was killed by a sniper's bullet while besieging Noda Castle. His son Takeda Katsuyori returned in 1575 at the head of 15,000 men (of whom some 4250 were cavalry), thrusting southwest into Mikawa; but his plan to take the Tokugawa capital at Okazaki misfired and had to be aborted. He then tried to take Yoshida Castle, but the garrison was too strong. Frustrated, and aware that some were muttering that he was not the man his mighty father had been, Katsuyori turned impatiently on another small Tokugawa castle at Nagashino. On about 16 June, 1575, his troops began to deploy around its perimeter defences.

The castellan sent riders to warn both his overlord Tokugawa at Okazaki, and Oda Nobunaga at Gifu. Oda decided to take some 30,000 of his men to Tokugawa's aid, marching to link up with Tokugawa's 8000 at Okazaki on 21 June; but the combined army made no further immediate moves, and if any reassuring message was sent to the garrison, it never arrived.

NAGASHINO CASTLE

This strategically sited stronghold, astride the north–south Toyokawa river valley through Mikawa province, had been built in 1508. It occupied a rocky headland in the angle of the 'Y'-shaped confluence of two rivers, the Takigawa and Onagawa, which united there to flow south as the Toyokawa. At that date the cliffs and bluffs rose to about 46 metres (150 ft) above the rivers, which were 46–55 metres (50–60 yds) wide. From boggy ground to the north of the 'Y', slopes ran up into woodland on the southern side of Daitsujiyama Hill.

Nagashino was far from the popular image of a classic Japanese castle, with a high tower rising in gabled tiers; it was simply a series of enclosures defended by ditches, walls and palisaded earth ramparts. At its heart was the inner bailey (*Hon maru*), a diamond-shaped yard measuring about 114 metres (125 yds) in both directions, containing sturdy but simple timber buildings and thatched sheds; probably only the main house rose to two or three storeys high, to give a view of the surroundings. The bailey was walled with the usual materials: dry-stone foundations and lower courses, surmounted by walls of a sort of strong wattle-and-daub construction. Vertical wooden posts at intervals of about 1.8 metres (6 ft) were linked by bamboo frames built up with bundles of lashed bamboo; this structure was plastered over with a mixture of clay and crushed stone, and protected from rain by thatching along the top. The whitewashed walls were pierced with loopholes for archers and hand-gunners; they were braced along the inside with a strong framework of vertical and horizontal beams, over which planks could be laid as a firing-step when the garrison needed to shoot over the top. At Nagashino only the *Hon maru* was protected by these stone-based walls; all the other enclosures were surrounded by earth ramparts topped with palisades of thick bamboo stakes and planking.

Down the west side of this inner bailey a mountain stream ran from the north into the Takigawa river. A bridge over the stream outside the northwest corner of the *Hon maru* led to an enclosure built on the west bank; this *Danjo-guruwa* contained a number of storehouses and other buildings. Adjoining the east wall of the *Hon maru*, on a terrace stretching nearly to the edge of the bluff dropping to the Onogawa river, was another palisaded enclosure, the *Yagyu-guruwa*. The whole defended core of Nagashino, comprising these three areas, measured about 300 metres (330 yds) from east to west and 230 metres (250 yds) from north to south.

To the northeast, outside the dry ditch defending the inner bailey and *Yagyu-guruwa*, were two further defended areas: the second bailey, protected by a dry ditch and partially by a rampart and palisade; and outside this the third bailey, with a palisade covering the whole arc between the stream to the west and the Onogawa bluffs to the east.

Finally, there were two much larger outermost areas. West of the mountain stream and surrounding the *Danjo-guruwa* was a field called the *Hattori-guruwa*; roughly 183 by 274 metres (200 x 300 yds), this had a western rampart and, at the northwest corner, a gated section of palisade, whose line was continued (probably only by earthworks) up into the woods on the slopes of Daitsujiyama. Beyond the third bailey, to the north and northeast between the mountain stream and the Onogawa bluffs, lay the *Fukube maru*, an area of some 320 by 457 metres (350 x 500 yds). Its eastern edge was protected by a second stream running into the Onogawa river, with a palisade built along the near bank; this line, too, was continued in some form right up into the woods on Daitsujiyama Hill.

A DETERMINED YOUNG COMMANDER

Early in April 1575 the defence of Nagashino had been entrusted by Tokugawa to Okudaira Sadamasa, a samurai not yet 30 years old. The Okudaira family had been vassals of the Tokugawa, but after the latter's defeat in 1572 they had been forced to serve old Takeda Shingen; to ensure their obedience he had taken Sadamasa's wife and younger brother to his court as hostages. When Shingen died in 1573, Sadamasa had renounced his forced fealty and marched his men home – whereupon the new Takeda lord, Shingen's son Katsuyori, had had his family crucified. Tokugawa could hardly have chosen a more motivated castellan. The samurai who officered the garrison under his leadership wore the striking and complex armour of the period, and were expected to be expert with all bladed weapons, from the bow and the legendary sword to spears and pole-arms. Firearms were despised as un-knightly weapons, fit only for commoners; the bow was noble, but the samurai's ideal was to close with his enemy and fight to the death face-to-face, preferably with swords – and for the victor to present the loser's severed head to his lord.

The garrison led by these warriors was only 500 strong; they included 200 matchlock musketeers, the other *ashigaru* footsoldiers being armed with bows, long pikes and various other pole-arms, and protected by steel war-hats and less elaborate armour. (While the Japanese class system was rigid, it was not impenetrable – Toyotomi Hideyoshi himself had begun as a humble *ashigaru*, being promoted steadily in his lord's service for conspicuous courage and intelligence.) Okudaira's garrison also had at least one metal cannon; we know nothing about this gun, but it was probably of cast bronze, of a calibre between 7.6 and 12.7 centimetres (3–5 in) and firing a ball of between 2.3 and 3.1 kilograms (5–7 lbs) weight.

THE ASSAULTS

Takeda Katsuyori divided his army into eight detachments to surround Nagashino. He occupied the wooded hills north of the castle with three divisions totalling 8000 men. On the east bank of the Takigawa, west of the enclosures, he stationed 2500 troops, and another 3000 northeast of the castle. South of the Takigawa river, facing the castle across its deep canyon, he placed 1500 men, presumably strong in missile weapons; on their left flank were a 1000-strong reserve. Finally, 1000 men were kept on the Tobigasuyama Hill, well back from the east bank of the Tokoyama.

The rough sequence of the assaults is recorded, although throwing up tantalizing questions. The general pattern of the first five days was of successive assaults by the northwest and northeast Takeda divisions, supported by fire across the Takigawa river from the detachment facing the castle from the south. In the manner of that time, much of the fighting took place on open ground outside the various defences. One of the obvious puzzles is how smaller detachments from a garrison of only 500, presumably rushed from sector to sector, managed to survive such encounters against immediate odds of at least ten to one.

On 17 June a probing attack was made on the northwestern gate into the *Hattori-guruwa*. The following day, Takeda Katsuyori ordered an all-out attack on the same front; this was held off, and a counter-attack set fire to the bamboo mantlets carried by the attackers, while arrows and

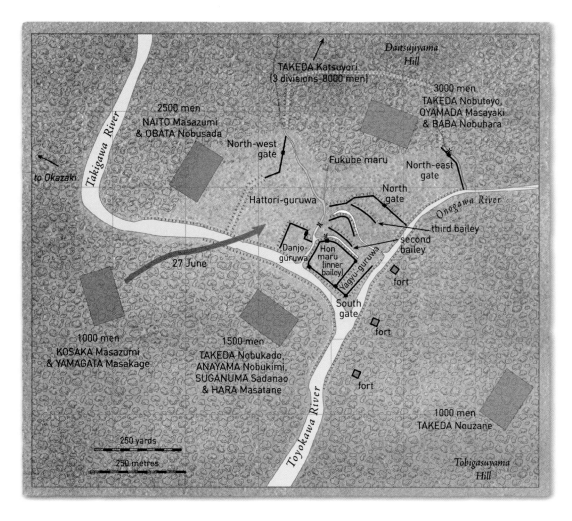

Map showing the deployments of the besieging force and the enclosures comprising Nagashino Castle in 1575.

bullets from the wall of the *Danjo-guruwa* reportedly thinned their close-packed ranks at ranges of between 91 and 183 metres (100–200 yds). On 19 June, Takeda soldiers were floated down the Onogawa on a raft to attempt a landing at the foot of a path up the bluffs to the south gate. The raft was spotted, raked with arrows and bullets before it could land, and finally sunk with dropped rocks.

On the dark, cloudy night of 20–21 June attacks were pressed home from both northeast and northwest. The first got over the palisade defending the northeast of the *Fukube maru* by means of ropes and grapnels, and eventually pushed the outnumbered defenders back into the third bailey. At the same time the northwest gate finally fell, and the *Hattori-guruwa* also had to be abandoned. Before sunrise on the 21st, Takeda Katsuyori had a rough timber siege tower built under cover of mantlets in the now-occupied *Fukube maru*; but at dawn the defenders' single cannon promptly knocked this to pieces with well-aimed fire.

THE SURVIVAL OF JAPANESE CASTLES

Since only the base platforms of castles were faced with stone, and all the built structure was of timber, the damage caused by time and weather required frequent repair and replacement. Although many stone foundations can still be seen, nearly all the keeps were completely destroyed by earthquakes, fire (sometimes accidental, sometimes deliberate), and finally on the orders of the 19th-century Meiji regime. The original interior structures of only three survived this final slighting: Himeji, Hikone and Matsumoto, of which only the last is on its original site. All the others visible today are complete reconstructions; for instance, Osaka Castle has been burned to the ground three times since it was first begun for Hideyoshi in 1583, on the site of the great Ishiyama Honganji fortified temple of the Ikko-Ikki sect, which had defied Oda for ten years before he finally destroyed it in 1580.

During 21 June the assaults were relentless. The third bailey was attacked in the early morning, but the Takeda troops were driven back by a sortie. However, Takeda's skilled tunnellers managed to undermine and bring down a section of wall at the western corner of the defences. That day saw the most intense fighting, and by nightfall on the 21st Okudaira Sadamasa's garrison had lost both the *Danjo maru* on the west bank of the stream (and with it their storehouses), and the northern third bailey. After five days and nights Okudaira's men were tired out by constant alerts and fighting, while their attackers could be rotated to rest.

On 22 June, although he had penned the garrison into the inner and second baileys and the *Yagyu-guruwa*, Takeda Katsuyori slackened off his assaults; he too had lost many men, and he believed that without their storehouses the garrison must soon starve and surrender, under continuing harrassment by his archers and musketeers. It was only now, apparently, that Takeda ordered the building of a palisade of his own – a circumvallation along roughly the line of the third bailey and *Danjo-guruwa* perimeter walls – to blockade the castle tightly; perhaps he had been overconfident of success before this point? On this and the next day several of the defending samurai were killed by musket-balls, and a revered 79-year-old veteran died of natural causes.

THE SACRIFICE OF TORII SUNE'EMON

On 23 June an Okudaira retainer named Torii Sune'emon, who knew the region well, volunteered to slip out the south gate and try to bring help. The Takeda had strung rope nets fitted with noise-making clappers across the rivers, but, on the night of 23–24 June, Torii succeeded in cutting his way through these under water. He lit a pre-arranged beacon signal on a hilltop, then began the 16-mile (26-km) run to Okazaki. There he reported to Tokugawa Ieyasu that the castle had only three days' rations left; when they were gone, Okudaira proposed to commit suicide himself so as to allow his surviving men to save their lives by surrendering. Tokugawa and Oda promised to march to Nagashino's relief the next day, 25 June, and Torii returned to the castle.

On his hilltop he lit the three fires that signalled that relief was on the way; then, for some reason, he tried to slip back into the perimeter – but since his escape metal bells had been added to the nets, and he was captured. Taken before Takeda Katsuyori, he was offered his life if he would call across to his comrades that no relief could be expected. He agreed; but when dragged to the top of the southern bluff he shouted to them to hold out – rescue was on the way. Takeda had him crucified on the spot; the garrison determined that he should not die in vain, and Torii's self-sacrificing courage became legendary throughout Japan.

THE BATTLE AND BREAK-OUT

Faced with a much stronger relieving army, Takeda Katsuyori nevertheless ignored his veteran generals' advice and determined to take about 12,000 of his men to fight Oda and Tokugawa in the open field, leaving only 3000 to watch the castle; his reserve crossed the Takigawa for this purpose. By the evening of 27 June the allies were deploying their 35,000-strong army on the plain of Shidarahara about 3 miles (5 km) west of the castle, with musketeers emplaced behind palisades to break the impact of the strong Takeda cavalry. The battle that followed on the 28th was much longer and more complex than suggested by Japanese director Akira Kurosawa's famous film *Kagemusha*, but after ten hours it still ended in disastrous defeat for the Takeda army.

Nobunaga also sent a detachment in a southern hook to hit the forts Takeda had left on the east bank of the Toyokawa river and on Tobigasuyama Hill; this was a complete success, and when he saw smoke rising from the forts Okudaira Sadamasa led the survivors of his garrison out in a charge on the nearest enemy troops, inflicting hundreds of casualties. The garrison's resistance, against great odds, had created the conditions for a victory with strategic consequences.

Choices with unpredictable consequences

LONDONDERRY

18 April–31 July 1689

'I have the idea that when a man plays his last stake he ought to play it himself, on the spot. The King of England seems to be in this condition. His last stake is Ireland.'

SÉBASTIEN LE PRESTRE DE VAUBAN (1689)

The king to whom the renowned French fortress builder Vauban was referring was the deposed James II (1633–1701), and he would lose his gamble – at Londonderry and on other fields, culminating in his final defeat at the Battle of the Boyne on 1 July, 1690. Although chiefly remembered for its political importance to the Protestant community of Northern Ireland, militarily this siege was an example of an attacking army too small and too distracted by a number of objectives to be truly successful anywhere. Londonderry also calls to mind the choices that always faced towns during the uncertainties of war. Most of the townsfolk were determined to defy James's approaching army, but not all of them. Those who had most to lose faced a choice based on guesswork – about the chances of outside relief, and the simple question of which side was likely to win the war. Moreover, this choice had to be made at a time when many elderly people could remember all too clearly the ghastly massacres committed in Ireland during the 1640s.

THE BIRTH OF THE JACOBITE CAUSE

The events that led to the siege began with Charles Stuart's restoration to the throne of Protestant England as King Charles II in 1660, after the nine-year Puritan dictatorship of Oliver Cromwell. Popular though the Restoration was, it was always vulnerable to the Stuarts' warmth towards the Catholic King Louis XIV of France. Louis' aggressive expansion had polarized Europe into pro- and anti-French factions, and Charles II had the wit to avoid an open confrontation with his people. However, like their beheaded father Charles I, Charles II's openly Catholic younger brother James did not; and when Charles's death without a legitimate heir brought him to the throne in 1685 as James II, suspicion of his pro-French leanings soon threatened his authority. When the birth of his son in 1688 opened the prospect of a continuing Catholic dynasty, powerful interests secretly invited his son-in-law (and a grandson of Charles I), the anti-French Dutch Protestant champion Prince William of Orange, to accept the throne of England in explicit partnership with his wife, James's daughter Mary.

William's unopposed landing in November, followed by the defection of part of James's army, prompted James to flee to France; this was presented by his enemies as *de facto* abdication, and

The relief of Londonderry in July 1689, after a long siege by Jacobite forces, is shown in this contemporary painting.

TIMELINE

William III and Mary were crowned as joint sovereigns in February 1689. However, the Jacobite cause (from the Latin Jacobus, meaning 'James') still had many supporters in Scotland and Ireland, who offered him a possible path back to the throne. Since his accession King James had encouraged his governor in Ireland, the earl of Tyrconnell, to raise troops there led by Catholic gentry; before William III was firmly established in England, Tyrconnell urged James to join him at the head of this force of (at first) about 7000 men. Success in Ireland would allow James to cross the water to reinforce the Jacobites led by 'Bonny Dundee' in Scotland, for a march on England. Provided by Louis XIV with arms, advisers and some French troops, James landed in Ireland on 12 March 1689.

FROM DERRY TO LONDONDERRY

Derry was a small settlement a few miles up the navigable River Foyle from the deep-water inlet of Lough Foyle on the northern Irish coast. After the English crushed Irish resistance in 1603, confiscated estates in Ulster had been 'planted' with Protestant English and Scottish settlers. In 1613 the land around Derry was granted to the City of London for colonization and development, under the name of Londonderry, and a new walled town was later built on the riverbank.

During the bloody Catholic rebellion of 1641–2, Londonderry remained a safe Protestant refuge. During the English Civil Wars the town, like its parent city, supported Parliament; in 1649 it held out against a Royalist blockade lasting 20 weeks. After Cromwell's ruthless stamping out of the Irish Royalists in 1649–50 the dominance of the Protestant settlers increased; but from James II's accession they felt threatened by Tyrconnell's intentions. The declaration of a war between James Stuart and 'Dutch William', before the arrival of William's army from England, presented local leaders with a dilemma. Which king represented legitimate authority; which was likeliest to win; and what was the balance of risk and reward in making a choice between them?

ROBERT LUNDY AND THE CITIZENS' CHOICE

In November 1688 a group of townsmen – hailed ever after as the 'Apprentice Boys' – slammed the gates of Londonderry in the face of Tyrconnell's attempt to install a Catholic regiment as its garrison. Lieutenant-Colonel Robert Lundy was allowed in with two companies of Protestant soldiers, and he began strengthening the defences in case of a future siege. The active merchants of the town hastened to raise militia companies and order a shipload of gunpowder.

By the time James landed in March 1689 most towns had been occupied by Tyrconnell's troops; but in Protestant Ulster 'armed associations' of militia held six towns including Londonderry, and a co-ordinating Council of the North appealed to England for help. The Protestants had no effective central command, however, and a number of their forces were defeated in detail by Tyrconnell's troops. On 14 March his subordinate General Richard Hamilton advanced into Ulster, where Protestant soldiers and refugees crowded into Londonderry – a strategic harbour that the Jacobites needed, to ensure their planned sea links with Scotland.

In April two separate forces were approaching the town: Hamilton's from the east, and a much larger army led by King James in person from the south. On 14 April, Lundy led most of the Londonderry garrison out to try to check Hamilton at Cladyford on the River Finn, where he was badly beaten. When he got back to Londonderry, with his morale shattered, he found that English ships had arrived in the lough with two regiments of troops – but instead of welcoming them, he persuaded their commander that Londonderry was indefensible, and they reluctantly sailed away again. Lundy then recommended opening negotiations with the Jacobites, and was supported by some of the leading citizens. Hamilton offered generous terms, and a promise that his troops would not approach the town while these were being considered.

On 18 April, when the decision was finely balanced, the separate army led by James arrived from the south and, unaware of Hamilton's ceasefire terms, the king in person rode up to the

A COUNTRY DIVIDED AND DEVASTATED

The Ulster campaign of 1689 took place in a country not yet recovered from appalling bloodshed and destruction throughout the 1640s, which had included the routine execution of captured garrisons. The Catholic rebels of 1641 massacred some 37,000 Protestant settlers; the refugees' tales of atrocity damned all Irish Catholics as devils in English eyes, and the troops sent to crush the rebellion repaid these murders tenfold. Many Englishmen saw Charles I's raising of Irish troops to fight against Parliament in England during the Civil Wars as the blackest treachery, and Cromwell's final crushing of the Royalist garrisons in Ireland in 1649–50 became a byword for brutality. It has been calculated that between 1641 and 1652 perhaps 600,000 Irish of both communities had died of violence, disease or want – an almost incredible 40 percent of the total population of some 1.5 million.

Bishop's Gate and called upon the town to surrender to him. At this apparent sign of treachery the apprentices' cry of *'No surrender!'* rang out again; the gates were closed, and cannon opened fire on the king's party. Lundy was expelled from the town as a suspected traitor, and the siege began.

DEFENDERS AND ATTACKERS

The town was protected on the north and east by the River Foyle, which at high tide came up to the quay outside the north wall, and on the west by a large area of bogland, crossed by a causeway to the Butcher's Gate. The walls were about 7.3 metres (24 ft) high, of 3.7-metre (12-ft)-thick earth ramparts faced with 1.8 metres (6 ft) of solid masonry; they stretched for just under a mile, with four gates and 11 bastions. Outworks had also been built – palisaded earthworks to protect the gates and keep sappers away from the walls; the most important outwork was a large triangular 'ravelin' outside the Bishop's Gate in the south. An outpost was established a few hundred yards to the southwest, in ruins on Windmill Hill.

The garrison totalled 7361 well-armed and highly motivated men: four regular companies and the rest militia, organized in eight regiments each responsible for its own sector, under overall command of Colonels Henry Baker and Adam Murray; 20 cannon were mounted in the bastions, and on the dominating tower of St Columb's Cathedral. Responsibility for the 20,000-odd civilian inhabitants and refugees was placed in the hands of the Reverend George Walker. The major worry was the shortage of provisions: with perhaps 27,000 mouths to feed, the stores held only enough for about two weeks at the original generous scale of rations.

The Jacobite force was initially only about 4000 strong; this was barely enough to draw a weak line of investment around the town, let alone prosecute a siege. At its peak the siege army would be reinforced to about 12,000 men, but James's generals were simultaneously distracted by operations against Protestant forces elsewhere, particularly in the stronghold of Enniskillen and along the important waterway of the Erne Valley. Jacobite command at Londonderry was at first given to the French General de Maumont, seconded by Generals de Pusignan and Hamilton. James's bastard son the duke of Berwick was also present for part of the siege, but was later sent to the Erne Valley.

Batteries were set up on the opposite bank of the Foyle north and south of the town, and to the southwest on high ground beyond the bogs, where an earth fort was built to command the causeway. The Jacobites had few heavy guns, and lacked suitable positions at close range to enable them to breach the walls; but they did have a number of mortars, apparently including some heavy pieces.

PENNYBURN MILL AND WINDMILL HILL

On 21 April, Murray led his horsemen about a mile north to engage Jacobites manoeuvring towards Pennyburn. General de Maumont led the Jacobite cavalry vanguard; this was engaged at Pennyburn Mill before the rest came up, and de Maumont was killed in the mêlée. Murray then retreated – by a road on which he had placed an infantry ambush, which shot the pursuing Jacobites off his heels, killing about 80 of them. On the 23rd, Murray made another sortie; another fierce clash took place around Pennyburn; and this time de Maumont's successor in command,

General de Pusignan, was mortally wounded. Command now devolved on Richard Hamilton, who made strong appeals to Dublin for more men and the materials to conduct a siege.

The duke of Berwick soon handed him a valuable prize: at the end of the month he managed, by cunning more than strength, to capture the important outlying fort at Culmore, commanding the Foyle narrows about 2 miles (3.2 km) north. Eleven guns were to be emplaced on both banks of the river, which at this point is barely 274 metres (300 yds) wide. The guns included 24-pounders heavy enough to deny the approach of ships up-river from the lough and the sea.

The Protestant position on Windmill Hill was the key to bringing guns close enough to breach the walls, and on the night of 5–6 May about 3000 men of one French and five Irish regiments attacked it. In the darkness the guns on the walls were blind, and it was only at daybreak that Colonel Baker saw that the outpost had fallen and Jacobites were digging in along an arc, from the bogs to Windmill Hill and beyond it to the river. About 1500 men went out to attack them and recapture the hill; this took fierce fighting, with the enemy losing 200 dead and more captured. Murray then constructed a line of redoubts of his own outside the south and southeast walls.

MAY: BOMBARDMENT AND HUNGER

While there were no further assaults during May, the town endured bombardment and growing hunger. Shelling by the Jacobite mortars began on 24 April and continued until 21 July; it is reckoned that 584 shells were fired in all. In the worst period, during the first half of June, between 28 and 35 fell each day. If the time-fuses were cut correctly the explosive bombs might plunge through a roof and explode deep inside a house – even inside its cellar; since most houses were of timber-framed construction many were destroyed or burned down, and many people killed. Wisely, Butler divided his powder stores between small dispersed dumps.

CANNON AND MORTARS

Unlike the 'direct' fire of a cannon, sending a cannonball at a target within sight of the gunner, 'indirect' fire was at targets beyond obstacles to sight (such as walls), and involved more calculation and judgement than visual aiming. The weapon for this was the mortar – a short, squat, large-calibre weapon that fired at a steep upwards angle, so the projectile lost momentum without travelling far and then fell beyond the obstacle. By the 17th century mortars usually threw hollow-cast iron bombs (shells or 'grenadoes') filled with gunpowder. A fuse fitted into a hole in the casing and burning at a (theoretically) predictable speed was cut to a calculated length, and lit just before the propellant powder charge in the barrel was fired. Mortars took more time and care to load than cannon, since their heavy bombs had to be lowered into the muzzle, by means of carrying chains hooked to brackets cast into the casing, with the fuse at the correct angle.

In the damp, muggy weather the health of those packed inside the small town quickly deteriorated due to bad water, disease and hunger. The active defenders were now allowed a daily ration of only 0.9 kilograms (2 lb) of flour, 2 lb of oats and 2 lb of dried, salted animal hide (to make soup); but the civilians had to make shift for themselves, buying whatever food they could afford when it was available. When there was any horsemeat to be had (for example, after the 'second battle of Windmill Hill' in early June left many Jacobite troop-horses dead within the outer perimeter), it sold for 1s 8d a pound; but often there was none to be had at any price. A dog's head cost 2s 6d – at least three days' pay for a footsoldier – while a pound of tallow (animal fat) sold for 4 shillings.

Although their food was more plentiful, the health of the soldiers in the Jacobite camps was even worse. It was a notably wet spring, sanitary discipline was lax, dysentery was habitual and medical ignorance was almost total. When typhoid fever and smallpox broke out the death toll climbed into the thousands.

JUNE: RENEWED ASSAULTS AND HOPE DEFERRED

King James sent orders for an all-out assault; and on 4 June about 12 regiments of infantry and 15 squadrons of cavalry – something between 5000 and 6000 men in all – advanced in two divisions. One hooked round to the south and attacked up the west bank of the river below Windmill Hill, and the other crossed the bogs and headed east up rising ground to the town walls. Most of the garrison fought in the earthworks outside the walls. On the riverbank only a handful of the cavalry broke into the Protestant line; most of their horses were killed and the survivors were driven out again, while the defenders held onto Windmill Hill above them. Led by grenadiers, the main western force reached and took the outworks screening the Double Bastion at the southwest corner, but Baker threw reserves into the ravelin, while wall-guns played on the attackers with case-shot, forcing them back. The Jacobites lost some 400 dead, 120 wounded and many captured; it was said that some retreated carrying their dead on their backs as protection from bullets, but Irish troops were anyway notable for the importance they attached to taking off their dead.

On 7 June the defenders were overjoyed to see ships in the distance on Lough Foyle. On the 9th an English warship, the *Greyhound*, tried to get up-river past the fort at Culmore, but was badly holed by gunfire and forced to withdraw. General Hamilton had ordered his French engineer, the Marquis de Pointis, to construct a floating boom across the river narrows to physically prevent the passage of shipping. This was made of beams from demolished buildings, clamped end-to-end with iron brackets, and held in place by a series of rope rings from a heavy cable; it was anchored at both banks, with the cable slack enough to allow it to rise and fall with the tide, and the gaps at the ends were blocked with scuttled boats full of rocks. On 11 June another probe by the frigate *Dartmouth* (36 guns) found the boom in position; the commander of the relief force, General Percy Kirke, withdrew while he awaited further orders from London. He was probably content to wait, in hope that the expected landing of another force in County Down would draw the besiegers away without further effort on his part. The ordeal of the garrison and townsfolk worsened, and no messengers

Map of Londonderry during the siege of 1689, showing the fort at Culmore and the boom across the River Foyle to prevent relief supplies to the city.

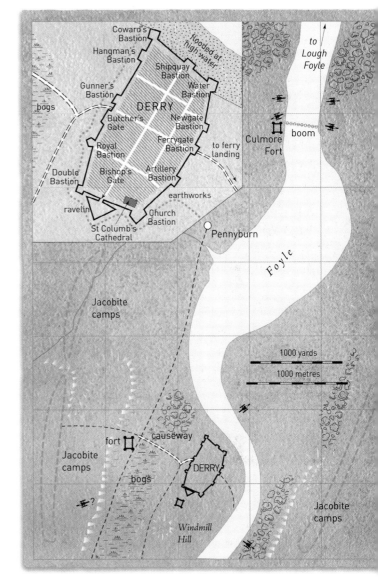

could get through between them and General Kirke.

Given his mounting losses from combat and disease, General Hamilton was minded to renew negotiations in late June; but Conrad de Rosen, a Lithuanian-born French general, arrived with another order for decisive action from the impatient king in Dublin. Royal rebukes did not make up for the lack of a strong battering-train or positions to mount it; the only method open to Hamilton was another infantry assault against the unbreached defences, from trenches pushed forward towards the Butcher's Gate in the west wall. This was duly made on the night of 28 June, by the earl of Clancarty's regiment; they captured the outlying earthworks, and sappers and miners pressed forward to the walls. Their tunnel soon broke through into a cellar close to the gate, and they began filling it with gunpowder kegs. The garrison commander Colonel Baker was by now seriously ill; but Captains Noble and Dunbar led a sortie out through the Bishop's Gate and followed the walls to the right, creeping round under the Double and Royal Bastions in the darkness until they were within point-blank range. When they opened fire on the right flank of the assault troops, cannon in the Gunner's Bastion blasted them from the left; the Jacobites were driven off at heavy cost to both sides, leaving their miners to their fate.

On 30 June, Henry Baker died; he was replaced in command by another professional soldier, Colonel John Michelburn, who hoisted a large crimson flag – the 'Bloody Flag', signifying defiance unto death. His exhausted soldiers had to spend their nights repairing artillery damage to the defences; by now it was becoming hard to find enough hands to keep up with burying the dead, and corpses were mouldering in cellars.

General de Rosen was so infuriated by this failure that he had thousands of Protestant civilians rounded up from the countryside as far as 30 miles (48 km) away. He drove them into no-man's-land beneath the town walls, and declared that they would starve there unless the garrison cared to take them in and share their rations. Michelburn responded by building a gallows on the Royal Bastion, parading his Jacobite prisoners under it, and sending out a message requesting a Catholic priest to give them the last rites. On 4 July, Rosen gave in and allowed the hostages to depart; some young men among them slipped into the town, changing places with defenders who were old or sick.

July: The Breaking of the Boom

On 13 July a lad managed to get through to the town with a concealed message from General Kirke, promising early relief; by now the garrison were losing 100 men a day, while trying to keep their strength up with repulsive pancakes made from a mixture of starch and tallow. To make matters worse, Colonel Murray was badly wounded on 26 July during a failed sortie to capture cattle. Percy Kirke was probably unmoved by the town's sufferings – he was a brutalized veteran of the Tangier garrison and the crushing of Monmouth's Rebellion – but he had now received positive orders from London. He put his troops ashore on Lough Swilly, making as if to march on Londonderry; but instead, on the evening of 28 July, he sent ships to force the Culmore boom.

Captain Leake's frigate *Dartmouth* led the way, with the supply ships *Mountjoy* and *Phoenix*. While the *Dartmouth*'s guns duelled with the Jacobite fort the *Mountjoy* went full tilt at the boom; it cracked, but did not give way. A longboat full of hands from the warship *Swallow* rowed up to the damaged length and the sailors hacked at the cable with axes; at last it parted and, under punishing cannon and musket-fire from the banks the whole way, first the *Mountjoy* and then the *Phoenix* burst through the debris and sailed up-river. At 10 p.m. that night they tied up at the quayside and, sheltered by a line of earth-filled barrels, the townsfolk began unloading the precious cargo of food.

Generous rations were doled out; bonfires were lit, bells pealed, and though the Jacobite guns fired all night the outcome was clear to all. On the night of 31 July the fires of burning huts were seen in the siege camps, and by morning Hamilton's army was marching away, leaving behind the graves of perhaps 8000 of their men. The total of the townsfolk who died from enemy fire, disease or starvation during the 105 days of the siege cannot be known; various estimates put civilian deaths anywhere between 3500 and 10,000 out of some 20,000. The garrison had lost at least half its starting strength of 7360 killed or died, and of the 4000-odd who survived 1000 were sick or otherwise disabled.

The siege of Yorktown: Washington and Rochambeau (pointing) are pictured making preparations for a final assault in this 1836 painting by Louis-Charles-Auguste Couder.

*The gentlemanly siege that won
America her independence*

YORKTOWN

29 SEPTEMBER–19 OCTOBER 1781

'The safety of the place is, therefore, so precarious that I cannot recommend that the fleet and army should run any great risk in endeavouring to save us.'

LIEUTENANT-GENERAL LORD CORNWALLIS, COMMANDING AT YORKTOWN,
TO BRITISH COMMANDER-IN-CHIEF LIEUTENANT-GENERAL SIR HENRY CLINTON
AT NEW YORK (15 OCTOBER 1781)

The late 17th and 18th centuries saw the science of fortification against gunpowder artillery, and the parallel science of siege warfare, brought to a peak of theoretical perfection. Although Italian designers had been building defences specifically to defy cannon since the beginning of the 16th century, until the 1660s siege warfare was still a haphazard affair, and fortresses were equally varied – organic growths of stone and brick, with the ideas of recent generations grafted into the worn reminders of previous centuries. Between 1667 and 1704, however, the wealth and ambitions of King Louis XIV of France allowed his brilliant engineer Marshal Sébastien de Vauban to transform France's frontier strongholds – and with them, the science of siegecraft. Vauban designed some 160 fortresses, whose plans are masterpieces of geometry in depth.

Unlike the rearing medieval castle, Vauban forts were exercises in the horizontal: wide, concentric flower-patterns of masonry provided facings for immensely thick earth banks to absorb the shock of artillery, receding in mutually supporting systems countersunk into the ground. Every angle of approach was covered by enfilading fire from cannon in projecting bastions, while 'covered ways' allowed the garrison to move around in safety. But Vauban mastered both sides of the equation, and his technical innovations in siegecraft were also enormously influential over the next two centuries.

YORKTOWN'S CLAIMS ON HISTORY

It may thus seem perverse to choose an example of an 18th-century siege that involved not the strategic defence of one of the age-old European invasion corridors, but a tiny former tobacco port on the York river in Virginia; not Vauban's great superimposed patterns of stonework, but simple earthworks and timber palisades; not months of starvation and disease, but only three weeks from the arrival of the attackers to the surrender of the garrison and their plentiful stores of food; not bloody slaughter in the breaches, but only some 300 deaths among nearly 8000 defenders.

Yorktown is significant, however, as an example of the besieged fortress as a single piece in a wider game of chess, whose fall was made inevitable by the moves of the other pieces on the board, thus persuading its commander to surrender – in the best traditions of scientific 18th-century generalship – without forcing the game to its potentially murderous conclusion. It was also important, above all, as a victory that sealed the result of a whole long war, and in the process it ensured the birth of a great nation.

A FINAL, WEARY EFFORT

By spring 1781 the American Revolutionary War had lasted six exhausting years and both sides longed for an end to it. During repeated, see-saw campaigns in New England, New York, New Jersey and Pennsylvania, General George Washington's Continental Army had slowly grown in skill and resources. In the autumn of 1777 the capture of General Burgoyne's British army, isolated at Saratoga by General Horatio Gates, had breathed new hope into the faltering revolution; it also brought the priceless alliance with France in spring 1778. Although the small French expeditionary forces that began to arrive in 1779–80 were not immediately impressive, French and Spanish operations elsewhere were a serious distraction that weakened Britain's military and naval forces in America, while French seapower threatened Britain's vital naval control of the east coast (and, indeed, of the English Channel).

From 1778 the troops available to the British commander-in-chief, General Clinton, were restricted to the vicinity of his New York base and a few coastal enclaves, and that year saw the end of major campaigning in the north. Now the British focus switched south, where they hoped for greater support from American Loyalists. In 1779–80 the redcoats overran Georgia and the Carolinas, inflicting a costly defeat at Charleston; but the Loyalist response was disappointing, and General Nathaniel Greene ably conducted a guerrilla-style campaign against the small British field army led by General Lord Cornwallis in the Carolinas. General Clinton – confident of uninterrupted British naval dominance – believed in dispersing his troops between a number of coastal hubs of operations. Cornwallis, a talented tactical commander with long campaign experience in America, believed that the weakened British forces must be concentrated. He argued

MORBUS CAMPESTRIS

Throughout history 'camp fever' haunted both garrisons and siege camps, and even during such a short siege as Yorktown the deaths from disease could quickly outstrip those in battle. The classic cause was typhoid or enteric fever, an acute bacteriological infection which, in crowded places with poor sanitation, was spread rapidly by flies and dirty hands touching food. After a two-week incubation the sufferer came down with high fever, headaches, exhaustion and bowel disorders, followed by a rash. By the fourth week the victim was emaciated and delirious; death rates, from toxemia or a variety of complications, differed widely, but there was no treatment apart from nursing care, which was often perfunctory before the late 19th century. Those who did care for the sick could catch typhoid from the blankets of those already affected.

TIMELINE

1775 The American Revolution (War of Independence) breaks out after years of tension with the British colonial power over excessive taxation and lack of parliamentary representation

1776 Declaration of Independence of the United States of America presented to the Second Continental Congress in Philadelphia

1777 Washington's Continental Army defeats and captures a British army at the two battles of Saratoga; France enters the war in support of the colonists

1780 British army under Sir Henry Clinton captures the key southern town of Charleston and its garrison of 5000 men

1781 French tactical victory in Battle of the Virginia Capes prevents Royal Navy from supplying beleaguered British forces in Yorktown; siege of the city ends in surrender of the garrison under General Cornwallis to George Washington, effectively ending the War of Independence

1783 Treaty of Paris confirms British acceptance of US independence

for a major effort in Virginia, whose navigable rivers inland from Chesapeake Bay offered tempting access; but his direct correspondence with the London government soured relations with his commander-in-chief in New York.

CORNWALLIS IN VIRGINIA

In May–July 1781 Cornwallis manoeuvred his 7000 men around Virginia against smaller forces led by Lafayette and Wayne. General Clinton was fixated on establishing a naval base in Chesapeake Bay, however, and from long distance he badgered Cornwallis with repeated changes of movement orders. On 2 August, Cornwallis was obliged (for lack of a better site) to base his force at Yorktown on the northeast coast of the York Peninsula between the York and James rivers, looking across the former towards Gloucester Point on its north bank. Here, in the sweltering heat, his men began to entrench in the sandy soil, aided by hundreds of runaway slaves. The essential nature of Yorktown was thus that of a defended coastal base to support operations inland, linked by sea with a safe rear area – New York. In this, if in nothing else, it resembled the medieval stronghold of Acre in the Holy Land (see pages 30–38).

Two weeks later, outside New York, the French commander in America, General Rochambeau, informed General Washington that an expected French fleet under Admiral de Grasse from the Caribbean could not operate north of Chesapeake Bay. The allied Franco-American army accordingly gave up plans to attack New York, and on 19 August began to march south against Cornwallis. Meanwhile, the French and British fleets had been playing hide-and-seek between the Caribbean and New York since March; but de Grasse won the game, and on 5 September, when south of Philadelphia, Washington learned of the admiral's arrival in Chesapeake Bay with more French troops.

That day, the British Admiral Graves arrived off the Virginia Capes with 19 warships, and de Grasse sailed out to meet him with 24 – armed with heavier guns, in a better state of repair and

THE BATTLE OF THE VIRGINIA CAPES

On 5 September 1781, a fleet of 19 ships under the command of Rear-Admiral Sir Thomas Graves (1725–1802), which had set sail from New York, approached the mouth of Chesapeake Bay. Graves was surprised to find 24 French ships lying at anchor there behind Cape Henry. The French squadron's commander, the Comte de Grasse (1722–88), had arrived in the bay a week earlier and disembarked three regiments of troops to aid American forces in the planned blockade of Yorktown, farther up the bay. Realizing that he must at all costs avoid being caught in the confines of the inlet, De Grasse immediately ordered his fleet to put to sea and head for open waters to engage the British.

The ensuing two-hour Battle of the Virginia Capes (also known as the Battle of the Chesapeake) was a hard-fought engagement that brought casualties to both sides. Six Royal Navy ships sustained major damage (one so seriously it later had to be scuppered), while around 300 British sailors were killed or injured. The French suffered more than 200 casualties, with four of their ships badly damaged. In sheer terms of attrition, then, the battle was a draw. However, from a tactical point of view, it represented a decisive victory for the French; de Grasse had succeeded in his primary objective of denying the British access to Chesapeake Bay, thus dashing Cornwallis's hopes of being resupplied, reinforced or evacuated.

The two fleets shadowed one another for several days following the battle before Graves eventually disengaged and headed north back to New York with his battered fleet. Naval tacticians believe that he missed a golden opportunity in failing to annihilate de Grasse's ships as they sailed in single file out of the bay before they had a chance to form a line of battle.

more recently provisioned. The British got the worst of the clash; and on 12 September, after further indecisive manoeuvring, Graves was forced to sail for New York for repairs and resupply. It was hoped that these would be completed by 5 October, and at least 5000 troops would then be embarked to sail south and relieve Yorktown. Until then the French navy would enjoy unprecedented freedom of action off the coast of Virginia, and Cornwallis's redcoats were on their own. On 29 September, Washington's and Rochambeau's armies – each some 8500 strong – drove in British skirmishers and took up position in a crescent line surrounding Yorktown.

THE BESIEGED

Cornwallis's troops numbered roughly 7800; about 5000 of these were seasoned British regulars, with some 2000 equally solid Hessian veterans, and around 700 Loyalists. These battalions occupied both a double defensive line of trenches, redoubts and batteries around Yorktown, and Gloucester Point across the river. The defensive works were competently laid out, with earth banks

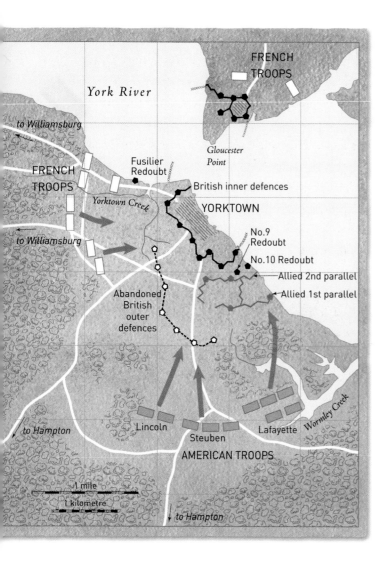

Map of the siege of Yorktown, showing the placement of American and French forces and British Redoubts Nos. 9 and 10 southeast of the town.

and ditches, earth-filled baskets (gabions), bundles of packed brushwood (fascines) and palisades of sharpened timbers, surrounded by outer entanglements of sharpened branches (the abatis). The inner defence line was anchored on ten redoubts – palisaded earthwork strongpoints; the outer arc stretched for about a mile between Yorktown Creek north of the town and Wormley Creek to the south. In the north between Yorktown Creek and the sea was the isolated Fusilier Redoubt; Nos. 9 and 10 Redoubts likewise commanded the coastal approach south of the town.

Cornwallis received a letter from Clinton promising him relief about a week into October. He knew this was a hope rather than a guarantee; his men were weakened by long summer marches, hard labour and disease; he was outnumbered well over two to one; but at least water was no problem and his storehouses were packed with food. However, his ammunition stocks were far less satisfactory.

THE BESIEGERS

The American divisions of the marquis de Lafayette, Benjamin Lincoln and Baron von Steuben held the southern part of the siege lines. The Continental Army, reduced in strength, still suffered from uncertain supplies of all kinds; the soldiers were beggared by inflation of the currency, and mutinies and desertion were not uncommon. But at least the organization worked better than in the early campaigns – as shown by the fact that most of them had marched from the Hudson river to the York Peninsula in a month, arriving together in fairly good order. Painfully accumulated experience was no longer lost by the troops disbanding at the end of each annual season, and they served in cohesive permanent brigades. The years of disappointment had burned away many incompetent officers, and real talents had emerged from the furnace. Since 1778 the regiments had been steadily trained to manoeuvre and fight along European lines; it was maturity in conventional tactics, not the legendary 'rifleman sniping from the woods', that won and lost battles (together with the inherent logistic difficulties of campaigning in sparsely populated America). The nine brigades at Yorktown were from the New England colonies, New York, New Jersey, Pennsylvania and Maryland, with one line regiment and about 3000 militia from Virginia, and 13 artillery companies. The generals present were not the most highly gifted as tacticians, but Baron von Steuben's previous experience on the Prussian general staff was to prove invaluable in this set-piece operation.

General Rochambeau, with roughly five French brigades – including marines and a volunteer 'legion' – held the northern arc of the lines; he had 11 excellent artillery companies and expert engineers. In addition, the French army (and navy) had benefited from the duc de Choiseul's reforms following the disastrous Seven Years' War (1756–63), during which British and American provincial forces had driven them out of North America; the troops were now well equipped, well trained and well led.

THE SIEGE

When the sun rose on 30 September the allies discovered that during the night the British had abandoned the outer defences, and had pulled back to Yorktown and the inner perimeter. Cornwallis had to match the length of defences that he could hold to his available manpower; the garrison was already weakened by detaching men and guns to Gloucester Point, and had nearly 1000 sick. The allies moved into the abandoned positions and began converting them to face the other way; this took four days, under a brisk British cannonade, but a system of sentries to warn of incoming shells kept the casualties down. Meanwhile heavy guns were brought down from Williamsburg.

'*The British officers in general behaved like boys who had been whipped at school. Some bit their lips, some pouted, others cried. Their round, broad-brimmed hats were well adapted to the occasion, hiding those faces they were ashamed to show.*'

ACCOUNT OF AN AMERICAN OFFICER WITNESSING THE BRITISH SURRENDER AT YORKTOWN

THE MATHEMATICS OF DEFEAT

When Yorktown fell, 7247 British soldiers and 840 sailors surrendered; 309 had died during the siege – the majority from sickness – and 4 had deserted. American and French battle casualties totalled about 200, but others had died from disease, and Washington hanged a few American deserters found in Yorktown.

The main batteries at Yorktown and Gloucester held some 65 and 20 guns respectively, and only 332 Royal and German artillerymen were listed, although guns and men landed from scuttled ships may well have doubled these figures. The booty included some 2000 rounds of artillery ammunition; on average, therefore, by that time the operational guns had enough loads for little more than an hour's firing each. The allies captured 8000 muskets with 266,000 cartridges – in other words, 33 rounds per musket, which could have been expended in half an hour.

Although six British and 16 German regimental flags were taken, those of the 23rd Royal Welch Fusiliers, who had bravely held the outlying northern redoubt, were smuggled away to safety by two officers.

After the surrender the British stores were found to hold no less than 45 tonnes (100,000 lbs) of meat, 33 tonnes (73,000 lbs) of flour, 30 tonnes (66,000 lbs) of bread, 9 tonnes (20,000 lbs) of butter and large quantities of oatmeal, peas, rice, coffee, cocoa, sugar and alcohol. This amounted to at least two weeks' full rations for 8000 men, and a good deal longer on reduced rations.

On 3 October a last British foraging sortie from Gloucester Point, led by the notorious cavalry commander Colonel Banastre Tarleton, had a sharp fight with approaching French and Virginia troops; after Tarleton had fallen back these settled down facing the British perimeter and prevented any further movement.

On the afternoon of 6 October about 1500 allied troops advanced and began digging the 'first parallel' – a line of trenches between 550 metres and 730 metres (600–800 yards) outside the British inner lines – while guarded against interference by some 2800 others. Meanwhile the Régiment Touraine made a diversionary attack on the Fusilier Redoubt on the northern coast, but the British were warned in advance by a deserter. The following day Lafayette's American troops entered the first parallel trenches; work continued on new redoubts and batteries; and on 9 October, both French and American artillery opened the bombardment. Once the first parallel was completed, the text-book prescribed that 'saps' should be dug forward from it: these were zig-zagging trenches, their diggers protected from fire by gabions, fascines and earth spoil thrown up on the threatened side of each leg. When the saps reached close enough to the defences, a 'second parallel' would strike off sideways, linking their heads in a continuous entrenchment that would act as the jumping-off place for an eventual assault.

The smooth progress of all phases of the siege owed a great deal to the detailed work of Baron von Steuben and the artillery commander Henry Knox. On 10 October more artillery was emplaced; Governor Thomas Nelson, commanding the Virginia militia, suggested his own house in Yorktown as the first target, since it was likely to be Cornwallis's headquarters (in fact it was not; and the house still stands, on Main Street). By morning on the 11th, British ships in the harbour had been either set ablaze, sunk or driven across to Gloucester, and 52 cannon, howitzers and mortars were firing (howitzers were short cannon used for firing explosive shells – a more mobile and versatile development of the mortar principle). That night work began on the 'second parallel' only 320 metres (350 yds) outside the British lines. As the artillery of both sides duelled, the allied stranglehold tightened.

Completion of the second parallel at its southern seaward end now required the capture of the outlying British strongpoints, and consequently Redoubts Nos. 9 and 10 were stormed on the night of 14–15 October. The first fell to men from the Régiments Gatenois and Deux Ponts in half an hour of fierce fighting; No. 10 was captured in ten minutes by American light infantry from Lafayette's division. Before dawn working parties had incorporated the captured redoubts into the second parallel.

Cornwallis now accepted the inevitable, but felt that a sortie had to be tried, for honour's sake. On the night of 15–16 October, Colonel Abercrombie led some 350 redcoats in a raid that succeeded in spiking guns in the second parallel, but these were back in action six hours later. On the following night, Colonel Tarleton sent boats over from Gloucester in hope of evacuating most of the garrison, but a storm put paid to the plan.

Next morning, as 100 allied guns were hammering the town, a British officer was sent out to ask for a truce to discuss terms. On the afternoon of 19 October the garrison marched out and surrendered, accompanied by bands playing a tune called 'The World Turned Upside Down'. Most of the officers were given parole and the Loyalists free passage, but the British and Hessian rankers were bound for prison camps.

On that same day in New York, the naval relief expedition finally set sail, with 7000 troops; the repairs and resupply had been much more difficult than expected, since New York had no properly equipped Royal Navy dockyard. The fleet arrived off the Capes on 24 October, and 'stood on and off' indecisively for several days before returning north.

On hearing the news of the capitulation, on 25 November, the British prime minister Lord North exclaimed 'Oh God! It is all over!' Lord Germain, Secretary of State for the Colonies, was forced to resign in February 1782, and in March the government fell. Although the final Treaty of Paris was not signed until November 1783, Yorktown marked the virtual end of active campaigning in the Revolutionary War, and the final loss of Britain's Thirteen Colonies.

The fourteenth siege of the key to the Mediterranean
GIBRALTAR
21 June 1779–3 February 1783

'Look round, my boys, and view how beautiful the Rock appears by the light of glorious fire!'

MAJOR-GENERAL WILLIAM ELIOTT, ON THE BURNING SPANISH MAGAZINES
DURING THE 'GREAT SORTIE' (26–27 NOVEMBER 1781)

The Rock had been contested and had changed hands on many earlier occasions; but the most convincing demonstration of its strength was given during the 43-month 'Great Siege' of the British and Hanoverian garrison by Spanish and French forces. The decisive factor was the Royal Navy's ability to maintain Gibraltar's sea links with the outside world, thus presenting a stark contrast with the simultaneous loss of Yorktown (see pages 105–113) on the far side of the Atlantic. Indeed, the holding of Gibraltar was a rare success during an unimpressive period for British arms.

THE PILLARS OF HERCULES

The Strait of Gibraltar – the narrow channel between the Atlantic Ocean and the western end of the Mediterranean Sea, lying between southern Spain and northern Morocco – has been recognized since ancient times as one of the most strategic links in the world. From the Spanish coast a promontory, about 3 miles (5 km) long by 1370 metres (1500 yards) at its widest, thrusts southwards on the east side of Algeciras Bay. South of its narrow, low-lying neck a jagged blade of limestone rises some 400 metres (1300 feet) above sea level, almost sheer on the north and east and sloping steeply down on the west and south. In the 18th century the town was largely confined to the narrow western shore, behind the harbour. From the Rock both Algeciras across the bay and the Moroccan hills above Tangier can easily be seen with the naked eye.

On 24 July 1704, during the War of the Spanish Succession, the Spanish garrison surrendered to an Anglo-Dutch landing expedition led by Admiral Sir George Rooke. A six-month Spanish siege – the twelfth recorded – failed in 1704–05; and in 1713, as Article Ten of the Treaty of Utrecht, Spain ceded Gibraltar to Britain 'in perpetuity' (Britain also acquired the important Balearic island of Minorca, with its sheltered harbour at Mahon). A combined Franco-Spanish siege of Gibraltar failed after four months in 1727. During the following decades the defences were strengthened with new and improved artillery bastions, and by flooding part of the narrow neck of the promontory. In 1761, Major William Green began a major engineering programme lasting several years.

An anonymous contemporary print, showing the Rock from the north, where Spanish trenches and batteries cut the promontory. This was the site of the 'Great Sortie'.

TIMELINE

1713 Treaty of Utrecht cedes sovereignty over Gibraltar to Britain in perpetuity

1777 General William Eliott appointed governor of Gibraltar

1779 Spanish join anti-British European coalition in the American War of Independence; siege of Gibraltar commences

1781 'Great Sortie' wreaks havoc among Spanish artillery emplacements and siegeworks

1782 (February) British-held island of Minorca falls to a Franco-Spanish siege

1782 (September) Floating batteries deployed against Gibraltar but destroyed by British shore batteries

1783 Siege of Gibraltar is lifted after 43 months; Treaty of Paris ends American War of Independence

In May 1777 a new governor was appointed. Lieutenant-General George Augustus Eliott (1717–90), a younger son of a Scottish baronet, had unusually broad experience in the infantry, cavalry, artillery and engineers during more than 40 years' soldiering; his past service included the deputy command at the successful British siege of Havana, Cuba, in 1762. A stern and austere disciplinarian, he would never be held in affection by his men, but always in respect, for his professionalism and dedication to his duty.

In June 1778, France allied herself with the rebellious American colonists fighting Britain for their independence, and on 16 June 1779 Spain joined this anti-British alliance. Both sent fleets and armies that operated successfully against British forces in America, and there was a serious threat of an invasion of southern England; this time of maximum pressure on Britain also offered Spain an opportunity to achieve her main war aims by recapturing both Gibraltar and Minorca. On 21 June, Governor Eliott was informed that a state of war existed; landward communications with Gibraltar were cut, and Eliott began preparing his garrison of some 5000 British and Hanoverian soldiers for what promised to be a long ordeal (at that time King George III was simultaneously the Elector of Hanover). With a Franco-Spanish fleet manoeuvring in the English Channel, the chances of relief seemed slim.

A LEISURELY BEGINNING

Madrid may have decided upon a strategy, but no plan for these operations was yet in place, and it would be months before Spanish troops arrived before Gibraltar in any strength. In the meantime, Eliott tried to persuade as many of the mixed civilian population – about 3200 locals, Portuguese, Genoese, Jews and Moroccans, and some 500 British – to leave while they still could; rations could not be provided for them, and so they would have to depend upon their private means to feed themselves. (General Eliott set an example by having one of his horses shot to save its fodder; throughout the coming siege this dour 62-year-old Scottish vegetarian and teetotaller would deny himself anything but basic rations, and experimented to discover how little food he could get by on.)

The landward approach was well fortified, and the five British and three Hanoverian infantry battalions were sufficient to man it. However, Eliott was desperately short of artillerymen; in June

1779 he had only 485 of all ranks, to serve more than 550 cannon and mortars in his batteries and bastions, and on 3 July he transferred 180 infantrymen to be trained as gunners. In the harbour he also had a Royal Navy ship-of-the-line, HMS *Panther* (60 guns), the frigate HMS *Enterprise* (28 guns) and three powerful gunboats.

It was 18 July before the Spanish finally established a land blockade across the neck of the peninsula; the parched south of the country had few resources, and organizing food and other supplies for their garrison took a great deal of time. By early October 1779, they had 12,000–14,000 men in place – 16 infantry battalions and 12 cavalry squadrons, plus artillery and service troops. They were obviously too few for any assault along the narrow, flat peninsula under the mouths of the British batteries, and for political reasons Madrid dared not risk an attempt that might well end in bloody failure.

THE NAVAL BLOCKADE

The Spanish command had to hope that hunger and sickness would do their work for them; but this depended upon the ability of Admiral de Cordova to maintain a sea blockade – a task that would prove beyond his energy and competence, even though he had dozens of ships nearby in Cádiz. The squadron sent to lie off Gibraltar was commanded by Admiral Antonio de Barcelo, a rough and popular old fighting seaman; but Cordova only gave him one 74-gun and one 50-gun warship, with a variable number of lighter craft and gunboats. To watch all the approaches to Gibraltar he needed at least three times that many, and in fact his squadron was in some danger of destruction if the Royal Navy came out to engage him.

THE GIBRALTAR GARRISON, JUNE 1779

British battalions:
12th Foot (599 all ranks) – in post since 1769
39th Foot (586) – since 1766
56th Foot (587) – since 1770
58th Foot (605) – since 1770
72nd Foot (1046) – since July 1778

Hanoverian battalions:
Hardenberg's (452)
Reden's (444)
De la Motte's (456)

plus:
Artificer Company (122)
c.760 all ranks Royal Navy
Total: c.5,660 (with c.1,500 family members)

Reinforcements:
2/73rd Highlanders (1052) – on 25 January 1780
97th Foot – on 25 March 1782
Corsican Corps (83) – on 25 July 1782
25th & 59th Foot – on 18 October 1782
Royal Navy – c.300 during siege
Total in service March 1783: c.7000

Some of the blockade-runners were British, but many came from 'neutral' Portugal; they carried high-value, lightweight cargoes (such as the citrus fruit that would be increasingly vital to keep the garrison healthy), and also provided Eliott with reliable communications links and valuable intelligence. Nevertheless, Barcelo's inshore gunboats showed great energy and skill, and while fast, light vessels often managed to slip past the cordon and into the shelter of the shore batteries, the larger, slower supply ships that were needed to carry reinforcements and bulk stores seldom risked it, and paid a price when they did.

The first months passed with only intermittent exchanges of small-arms fire, but the rations were steadily consumed. On 10 December 1779 the governor reported that the last stores of food staples would be exhausted in about five months, that there was serious hunger among the remaining civilians, and that drinking water was also scarce. The Spanish had finished mounting about 90 heavy cannon and mortars in their lines, but as yet these had not fired a shot.

RODNEY'S CONVOY

By mid-September disunity and incompetence had lifted the Franco-Spanish invasion threat from England; and on 29 December a large stores convoy sailed for Gibraltar, escorted by Admiral Sir George Rodney with 21 warships. First reports to Admiral de Cordova underestimated the size of the escort, and the news seemed to present an opportunity for decisive action. Admiral de Langara sailed west through the Strait with 11 warships to intercept the convoy, while Cordova would lead 15 more out from Cádiz. When Cordova learned the true strength of the opposition he turned tail back to port; Langara was not informed, and sailed confidently out into the Atlantic. On 14 January 1780 he came up against Rodney, and in the ensuing 'Moonlight Battle' Langara and six of his ships were captured, while a seventh blew up.

On the 15th a fast brig from Rodney raced into Gibraltar with news of the convoy's arrival; and between 19 and 25 January it sailed in, complete with Rodney's prizes, amid cheers and gunfire salutes. Along with the food and ammunition, the transports carried the 2nd Battalion, 73rd Highlanders – at more than 1000 all ranks, an unusually strong force. They had been intended for the garrison on Minorca, but General Eliott persuaded Rodney to let him keep them instead.

GARRISON CASUALTIES DURING THE SIEGE

Killed and died of wounds – 333

Wounded – 1010
   (of which 138 disabled, 872 recovered)

Died of sickness – c.650

Discharged due to sickness – 181

Deserted – 43

Total killed, died, disabled,
   discharged & missing – c.1345

1780: HUNGER, SICKNESS AND BOREDOM

The land and attempted sea blockade continued, with varying success, throughout the next year, but the Spanish still declined to take any active steps on land. The morale of the garrison suffered from this inactivity; there were quarrels between senior officers, and indiscipline in the ranks. Some rare excitement occurred on the night of 6–7 June 1780, when Admiral Barcelo sent six fireships across the bay from Algeciras. Spotted in good time, they were slowed by cannon fire from HMS *Panther* and a battery on the New Mole, until longboat crews could grapple them and turn them into a current that took them clear.

The start of 1781 brought a serious setback. Light craft had been bringing in fresh food from Morocco, but in January 1781 Spain's prolonged attempts to bribe the sultan finally persuaded him to close his harbours and expel British diplomats. In Gibraltar, scurvy broke out among the garrison and civilians; basic foodstuffs would run out again by August, and without fresh vegetables and fruit the garrison could not last that long. By the end of March 1781 the weekly ration per man was down to 24 kilograms (52 lbs) of bread, 370 grams (13 oz) of salt beef, 510 grams (18 oz) of salt pork, 635 grams (22 oz) of butter, 340 grams (12 oz) of dried raisins, a half-pint of dried peas and a pint of

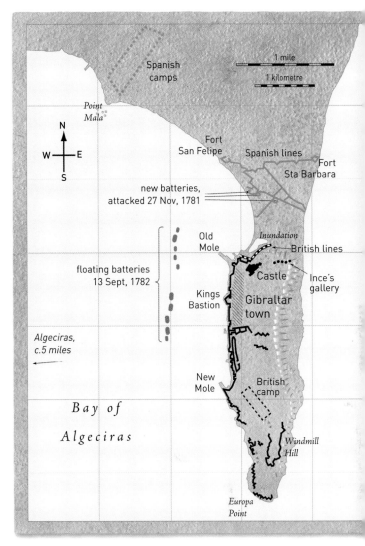

Map showing the narrow promontory of Gibraltar and the major actions that took place during the Great Siege of 1779–83.

beans. For those not on the ration strength prices were predictably high: up to 4 shillings a pound for beef – 1½ times what it cost in England. The poor in the town and the camp women had been reduced to scouring the slopes for dandelions by the time the Royal Navy again sailed in to the rescue.

APRIL 1781: DARBY'S FLEET

Following a plea by Eliott in mid-January, on 12 April 1781 Admiral George Darby arrived with 34 warships escorting nearly 100 transports from England. The utter inability of the Spanish fleet to prevent this clearly enraged their army command and the ships were greeted by the full strength of the Spanish land batteries – now some 150 pieces, which had never before mounted a massed bombardment. Once it started, however, it would persist, and Gibraltar would come under heavy fire every day for about 18 months. Darby left Eliott all the gunpowder he could spare from his ships' magazines, and when he sailed on 21 April he took with him about 1000 of the civilians and soldiers' dependants.

The bombardment soon reduced much of the town to smouldering ruins, and this had an unexpected result: some falling walls revealed large caches of food and alcohol laid aside by merchants waiting for prices to rise again, and when the word spread the redcoats naturally looted these, leading to drunken brawls and outbreaks of indiscipline. Governor Eliott restored order with the lash and the gallows (nevertheless, although he himself never drank anything but water, he usually allowed the town's taverns to stay open, realizing that his hard-pressed men had to have some outlet). Despite the wrecking of the town, the bombardment seldom affected the batteries and fortifications; any damage was soon repaired, and casualties were light. Eliott ordered the gunners to return fire whenever expedient, especially when working-parties were seen in the Spanish trenches and batteries.

NOVEMBER 1781: THE 'GREAT SORTIE'

Such work became very evident from mid-September, when the Spanish began digging by night a triple zig-zag of trenches forward from their main lines. By 15 November they had established a new parallel about 640 metres (700 yds) closer to the British lines, and soon afterwards had three new batteries in action. With intelligence gathered from deserters and observers, Eliott planned an attack: he wanted to damage these new works before General Alvarez received his reported reinforcements, and also to lift the morale of his much-tried garrison. The plan was for some 2500 men to go out by night, cross the northern no-man's-land as fast and as silently as possible, and capture the Spanish trenches and batteries from the estimated 650-strong guard force; they would then push forward a security line to hold off counter-attacks, while the rest destroyed as much material as they could, before falling back under the cover of the northern batteries. Eliott knew that the enemy batteries lacked firing-steps or flank positions for infantry; but he expected hard fighting and significant casualties, and had a strong reserve standing by. The preparations were made in great secrecy, under cover of bad weather.

As the moon set at about 2.45 a.m. on 27 November, Brigadier Ross led out his three columns of British and Hanoverians on either side of the Inundation. Each column was between 700 and 900 strong: two full battalions (12th Foot and Hardenberg's) and the assembled grenadier and light companies from seven others were divided between them, with additional gunners, engineers, pioneers and sailors to do the wrecking work.

Although enemy sentries gave the alarm before it reached the ramparts, the attack was still a remarkably quick and complete success. The Spanish guard force turned out to be only some 80 men of the Walloon Guards, who were overrun without difficulty. The 12th and Hardenberg's pushed out their security line, but no counter-attacks were made. Meanwhile battery positions were destroyed, guns and mortars spiked, and many fires soon lit up the night; old General Eliott

GIBRALTAR'S ARTILLERY

Between September 1779 and February 1783 the garrison's gunners fired a total of 57,163 roundshot, 129,151 explosive mortar and howitzer shells, 12,681 rounds of grapeshot, 926 of incendiary 'carcass' and 679 'light-balls'. These 200,000-odd rounds used up 8000 barrels of gunpowder. Additionally, the Royal Navy's gunboats fired some 4700 rounds. While rates of firing varied very widely from time to time, the daily average throughout the siege was thus c.160 rounds fired. In comparison, the Spanish fired a total of c.244,104 roundshot and shells from land and 14,283 from sea – this total of around 258,387 giving a daily average of some 195 rounds.

surprised everyone by turning up in the front lines himself, and was delighted with the cheerful work of destruction going on all around him. At 3.45 a.m. a textbook stage-by-stage withdrawal began, and – to the accompaniment of thunderous explosions from the blown enemy magazines – all passed safely back into the British lines by 5 a.m. The total cost had been just 4 men killed, 25 wounded and one missing. The Spanish forward lines continued to burn and explode throughout the morning.

THE LOSS OF MINORCA PUTS PRESSURE ON GIBRALTAR

Meanwhile, since 20 August 1781 the 2700-strong British garrison at Fort San Felipe guarding Mahon harbour on Minorca had been under siege themselves. The French Admiral Guichen had joined his 22 warships to Admiral de Cordova's 36 in the Mediterranean, and this fleet transported a final total of some 10,500 Spanish and 3800 French troops to the island. General Murray was under no illusions as to the outcome, but held out as long as possible to help distract enemy resources from Gibraltar. After six months' heroic resistance, Murray's last 660 fit men staggered out, with the full honours of war, on 5 February 1782. This left the Franco-Spanish force free to reinforce the siege of Gibraltar.

By late March, Eliott had received more supplies and another battalion, the 97th Foot; and in April the resourceful naval squadron under Captain Sir Richard Curtis began building 12 new gunboats. These were intended to counter Barcelo's coastal craft, but the crews interpreted their patrol mission liberally, and made night-time trips to spy out enemy activity in Algeciras. On 14 June they reported the arrival of a very large fleet of French warships and transports: fresh from his success on Minorca, Marshal the duc de Crillon was about to take overall command of the siege – the twenty-third of his career. He brought with him a numerous staff and the Régiments Lyonnais, Bretagne, Royal-Suèdois and Bouillon.

It was during June that Sergeant-Major Henry Ince of Colonel Green's Company of Artificers suggested that a tunnel driven through the Rock's northeast summit would allow the mounting of a gun in a useful position at 'the Notch'. So well did this work progress that a whole gallery with several gun embrasures would soon be built inside the northern cliff; this was the first of the 30 miles (48 km) of tunnels that are reputed to run within the Rock.

Crillon would soon have some 30,000 troops and 50 warships in the area, and was determined to enliven things after two and a half years of Spanish inactivity. His engineer, Colonel the Chevalier D'Arçon, had designed for the Spanish dockyards 'floating batteries'– battering-ships, massively armoured with timber on the landward side and decks – to bombard Gibraltar's strong western defences, thus allowing troops to land at the harbour.

September 1782: The Floating Batteries

A bombardment and landing from the west, with a simultaneous major Spanish effort from the north, would put the garrison in genuine danger. There was no secret about the enemy plans, and by the end of August thousands of Spanish and French sightseers were gathering to watch the coming spectacle. Eliott could only busy himself in deploying his garrison of 7500 men, strengthened by some 900 disembarked sailors. On 8 September he tried firing red-hot roundshot (so-called 'hot potatoes') against some venturesome Spanish batteries to the north, with excellent results, and ordered the preparation of grates and ovens near his batteries. On the night of 11–12 September there was an ominous probing attack on the northern lines.

In fact, Colonel D'Arçon was unhappy with the work done on his untested floating-battery designs; the caulking and pumps were unsatisfactory, and he argued for a postponement. Admiral Moreno, who was to command them, agreed; but Crillon – whose staff was riven by jealous quarrels – furiously insisted on immediate action. On the morning of 13 September the ten floating batteries approached the western shore of Gibraltar, with their pumps hosing water down their flanks to counter red-hot shot. Eliott ordered his furnaces lit to heat cannonballs, but this would take several hours. By 9.45 a.m. the largest vessels, *Pastora* and *Talla Piedra*, anchored about 915 metres (1000 yards) off the King's Bastion (where Eliott commanded in person), had opened fire. Meanwhile, eight more floating batteries began firing from further offshore to the north and south of them. The Spanish land batteries were also hammering the northern defences; but on the bay there was no sign of any other naval activity, nor of landing-craft – most of the allied commanders were sulking like Achilles in their tents.

'One of those astonishing instances of British valour, discipline, military skill and humanity that no age or country could produce an example of.'

Lord North (Prime minister 1770–82 and Home secretary 1783)
on the siege of Gibraltar

During the day-long duel the floating batteries were sitting targets, soon losing their rigging and thus the power to manoeuvre; but at first the thousands of strikes from the 150-odd British cannon firing cold shot made little apparent impression (though neither did the landward fire of the ships' 212 guns). By noon Eliott's ovens were at last able to supply red-hot shot, and infantry parties with iron stretchers gingerly carried it to the batteries. More hours of exhausting work by the guncrews passed without visible reward; but at last, at about 5 p.m., bucket-gangs were seen fighting a fire on the *Talla Piedra*, and an hour later the *Pastora* was also smoking. From then on the floating batteries steadily began to fall silent and to catch fire. Admiral de Cordova made no move to support, resupply, aid or evacuate the 5000-odd seamen aboard them, several hundred of whom were rescued after dark by Royal Navy longboats.

By noon on the 14th all but one of the ten floating batteries had blown up or burned down to the waterline, and the last, abandoned on a sandbank, was set ablaze by a British boat crew. The whole battle had cost 15 British soldiers and sailors killed and 68 wounded; the Spanish, meanwhile, lost more than 1800 killed, drowned, wounded or captured. In a private letter to General Eliott after peace was concluded, Crillon was withering in his criticism of the batteries, condemning them as 'second-rate machines' that had served him ill.

REINFORCEMENT AND PEACE

This victory was followed on 18 October 1782 by the abject failure of Admiral de Cordova's fleet to intercept a major relief convoy under Admiral Lord Howe, which carried not only supplies but two more British battalions. Gibraltar was clearly not going to fall, and by mid-November 1782 the daily Spanish bombardment began to tail off. On 2 February 1783 a Spanish vessel flying the flag of truce announced that a peace treaty had been signed; the siege had lasted three years, seven months and 12 days. On 10 March the frigate HMS *Thetis* sailed in with confirmation of the Treaty of Versailles.

The bloody price of assault
and resistance BADAJOZ
16 March–9 April 1812

'The capture of Badajoz affords as strong an instance of the gallantry of our troops as has ever been displayed. But I greatly hope that I shall never again be the instrument of putting them to such a test.'

General Lord Wellington, in letter to Lord Liverpool, War Minister (7 April 1812)

The third siege of the French-held town of Badajoz during the Peninsular War is popularly remembered for the savage treatment of the townspeople by British troops when they finally broke in. In military terms, however, it is more important as an example of the high cost to a besieger of storming a fortified place in haste, under real or perceived pressure from an approaching relief force.

THE NAPOLEONIC WARS

The 20-year world war that began (as the French Revolutionary Wars) in 1792 displayed a very different character to the somewhat formalized exercises through which generals had led the European professional armies of the mid-18th century. Generals now sought to manoeuvre quickly over long distances so as to position themselves for decisive victories, in costly confrontations between massed armies of conscripted peasants. Bold and talented commanders (notably, Napoleon Bonaparte himself) might destroy in a single day their opponent's ability to wage war, winning the prize of occupying his whole nation and even usurping his throne.

The traditional 18th-century science of warfare – involving protracted tactical manoeuvrings aimed at putting off a pitched battle for as long as possible – has been compared to complex financial dealings carried out entirely on paper credit prior to a final cash settlement. By that analogy, it may be said that once Napoleon had abandoned any particular passage of political intrigue in favour of a military solution, he dealt only in cash. In that spirit, he declared that a fortress could never defeat an army, but only delay it. Generals eager to get to grips with enemy field armies sought to minimize that delay, but the technical tools of gunpowder-and-steel warfare remained largely unchanged. A general might yearn to slash past a fortress into the open plains; but if he could not, then he still needed time, heavy cannon and specialist expertise. It has been calculated that between 1790 and 1815 some 65 fortified places surrendered on terms as soon as the besieger had achieved an undeniable advantage, but that about 16 held out until they were finally stormed.

The Storming of Badajoz (steel engraving by D.J. Pound, c.1850). The battle-hardened Wellington was deeply shocked at the terrible toll this assault took of his men.

Britain's greatest general for a century before and after, Wellington was a master of open-field tactics; but his Peninsular Field Army in Portugal and French-occupied Spain was for years denied both the equipment and the trained engineers to prosecute sieges. Before his campaigns the British army had not taken a European town by storm for 160 years, and it was woefully ill-equipped for the task; sieges were the occasions of Wellington's few outright failures, and even when successful they cost him dearly.

THE GATES BETWEEN PORTUGAL AND SPAIN

Britain, alone among the combatant nations in the French Revolutionary and Napoleonic Wars, never conscripted soldiers, so her volunteer field armies were always small. Wellington's expeditionary army in Portugal was always potentially outnumbered by any combination of two among the several separate French armies led by Napoleon's rival marshals in Spain. Consequently he had to play cat-and-mouse along the border, waiting for an opportunity to strike when one or other of them was distracted by campaigns elsewhere against the dispersed Spanish forces.

There were only two practical routes for armies through the frontier mountains: in the north, between the towns of Almeida on the Portuguese side and Ciudad Rodrigo in Spain; and in the south, between Elvas and Badajoz. Elvas remained constantly in Allied hands, but Wellington knew that he had to hold all four towns simultaneously before he could safely advance to engage in operations within Spain. Their French garrisons were sometimes vulnerable, but any threat would bring one or other of the French field armies marching west again to support them.

In the spring of 1811 Wellington followed Masséna's withdrawal into Spain via the northern corridor, but he sent a detached corps under William Beresford to watch the southern gates. While Wellington beat Masséna at Fuentes d'Onoro, Beresford tried to besiege Badajoz; but his resources were wholly inadequate, and he soon had to turn away to confront the advancing Soult at Albuera.

THE DULL NECESSITIES

The limitations of Wellington's army extended to a shortage of the simplest tools, which either had to be purchased locally in Portugal (a country already stripped by two French invasions), or shipped out from England. The following were among the necessities that were ordered for the third siege of Badajoz:

1000 shovels, 1200 pickaxes, 300 axes, 300 hatchets, 500 billhooks, 300 spades, 200 mattocks, 27,000 spikes and nails, plus dozens of saws, hammers and other tools for smiths and carpenters; 80,000 sandbags, 100 ballast baskets and 12 'chokers' to compress brushwood fascine bundles for lashing.

General Phillipon learned of the British shortage of tools, and offered a bounty to any of his men who managed to capture them during sorties; anything that won more delay for a relief force to arrive was worth trying.

Following that almost Pyrrhic victory, Wellington's army reunited to attempt a second siege; but again, Badajoz defied them. The arrival of either Marmont from the northeast, Soult from the southeast, or both, was inevitable within two weeks of Wellington's men 'breaking ground' on 30 May. When they tried to dig in on the chosen hill north of the River Guadiana they struck solid rock just 3 inches down. Wellington's long-awaited 'siege train' of heavy guns was still stuck in Oporto, so his senior artilleryman, Major Alexander Dickson, was forced to press into service 150-year-old bronze cannon from the walls of Elvas; the roundshot rattled loosely in their worn barrels, and their muzzles would droop and vent-holes blow out after only a few days' steady firing. Two failed assaults on the outlying Fort San Cristobal cost Wellington nearly 500 casualties, and on 16 June the news of Marmont and Soult advancing with 55,000 men forced him to raise the siege.

THE 1812 FRONTIER CAMPAIGN

Wellington's best opportunity came when Napoleon stripped his armies in Spain in preparation for his invasion of Russia. When Wellington learned that Marmont, opposite the northern corridor, was greatly weakened, and that Soult had moved away from the southern passes, he determined on a surprise winter advance to take both Ciudad Rodrigo and Badajoz. His army of some 45,000 troops arrived before Ciudad Rodrigo on 8 January; by now his iron heavy guns had arrived, after a four-month struggle over terrible roads, but he still feared that a probable month-long siege would allow Marmont to intervene.

In the event, the fortress – held by about 1800 men under the unimpressive General Barrié – fell to Wellington in just 12 days. On the very first night his crack light infantry captured a vital outlying fort on the Great Teson hill, 550 metres (600 yds) north of the town; at a cost of just 26 killed and wounded, the British had secured a position from which batteries could play on the most

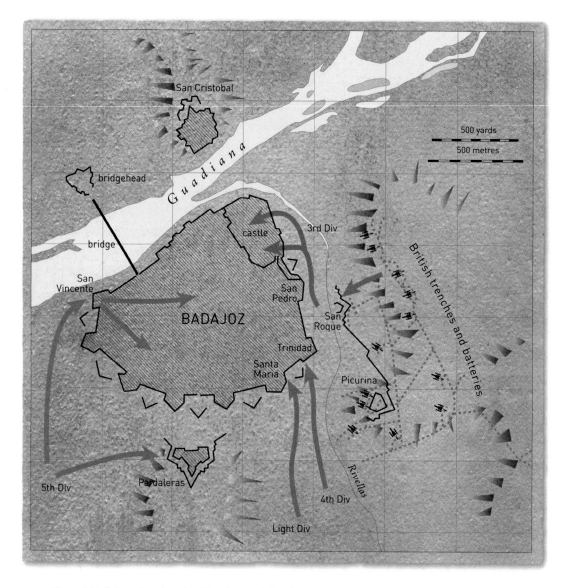

Map of Badajoz, showing the Picurina and San Roque outworks, the British batteries and the deployments for the final assault.

vulnerable part of the walls. In bitterly cold weather the infantry dug the first parallel and batteries on the Great Teson; the troops always detested this sort of work, but since the British army did not yet have a corps of trained sappers and miners the infantry were the only labour available. They worked in shifts of about 1000 men, rotating every day, and when they drove saps forward to open a second parallel about 274 metres (300 yds) from the defences they came under galling fire. Although the work was done by night the noise of pickaxes brought French flares, by whose light the diggings were raked with cannon-fire. The French made at least one successful sortie, and the diggers had to be guarded by equal numbers of troops under arms.

The siege guns opened fire on 14 January. Their initial siting was unsatisfactory, and they were hampered by the winter mists; but by nightfall on 18 January they had battered two breaches in the northwest wall. On the night of the 19th, assault units of the 3rd and Light Divisions crossed some 457 metres (500 yds) of open, moonlit ground before they could get down into the outer ditch and begin clambering up the debris in the breaches. A murderous fire from the defenders cost them some 200 dead and nearly 1000 wounded, but by daybreak Ciudad Rodrigo was in British hands. Marmont, still 20 miles (32 km) away, was incredulous; Wellington held three of the four gatetowers to Spain, and his redcoats would soon march south to seize the fourth.

BLOCKADE AND BOMBARDMENT

Badajoz was encircled on 16 March, when Wellington arrived with 31 infantry battalions (averaging perhaps 400 men each), 52 heavy guns under Major Dickson and about 20 trained engineer officers under Colonel Sir Richard Fletcher. Soult was far off to the south, with a detached British force across his path, but Wellington feared that Marmont could arrive within four weeks. In the event, Napoleon's long-range meddling delayed the marshal's start until 27 March; but Wellington, ignorant of this, felt that he was under the usual pressure of time. For their part the Badajoz garrison – some 4500 men, under General Armand Phillipon – were still confident of relief. Philippon had beaten off the second siege with energy and determination; he was well provisioned, and he and his chief engineer Colonel Lamare had used their time in strengthening the defences. The stage was set for a confrontation that would have an extra edge of bitterness, since the redcoats felt that they had a score to settle: the population of Badajoz was believed to be pro-French, and was known to have ill-treated British wounded in 1809.

The town stood in the angle of the River Guadiana to the north, and the smaller Rivellas to the east. As at Ciudad Rodrigo, its high walls were of medieval Moorish origin; but they had been strengthened according to the principles of Vauban, with projecting bastions, covered ways and

MOVING AND SUPPLYING SIEGE ARTILLERY

Breaching-guns were extremely heavy, and very slow to move along primitive dirt roads. A British 24-pounder was 2.7 metres (9 ft) long; complete with its carriage it weighed well over 3 tons, and required a team of 24 oxen, moving across country at perhaps no more than one mile (1.6 km) per hour. Huge numbers of draft animals – difficult to find in the Peninsula – were needed for a siege train; Wellington's for Almeida in 1811 numbered 1110 oxen for the guns alone, and very many more for the ammunition, tools and other stores. At Badajoz the 52 heavy guns needed 22,367 roundshot, and the lighter artillery another 24,983 rounds – say, 300 tons in all, plus 90 tons of gunpowder. These figures are a reminder that a siege was a daunting logistic undertaking.

deepened ditches. Strong modern outworks protected the immediate approaches – Picurina on the east, and Pardeleras on the south. This time Wellington would not risk the blind alley of San Cristobal on the north bank; he chose to dig his batteries and parallels on the eastern slopes, to pound the Trinidad and Santa Maria bastions from across the Rivellas. This would require the capture of Fort Picurina.

Ground was broken on the rainy night of 17 March, only about 137 metres (150 yards) from Picurina and within range of the guns of Colonel Thierry's 200-strong garrison. On 19 March, 1500 French troops made a sortie and rampaged through the siege lines, destroying much work. The rain continued for several days, and mud slithered back into the trenches as soon as it was shovelled out; but by nightfall on the 24th the guns could be brought up into the batteries, and the next day they opened fire on Picurina. The crumbling fort was assaulted by 500 infantry on the night of 25–26 March. Thierry's men shot many of them down before they reached the ditch, and then showered them with grenades and powder-charges; the scaling ladders proved too short for the walls, and the palisades too sturdy for the British pioneers' axes. Eventually, Irish soldiers from the 88th (Connaught Rangers) broke in through a damaged gun embrasure, and the fort was taken with the bayonet; the British lost just over 300 killed and wounded, but only a handful of Thierry's men escaped. The next day Phillipon bombarded Picurina, but by the night of 26 March the second parallel was incorporating its battered walls.

Three forward batteries were then installed, mounting 12 of Dickson's heavy 24-pounders, eight 18-pounders, and three 24-pounder heavy howitzers. The latter would act as mortars, lobbing explosive shells over the outer defences, and discouraging French night-time working-parties from clearing away the debris of bombardment from the ditch at the foot of the potential breaches – these ramps of rubble would be essential for the eventual assault. On 30 March the first batteries opened fire. On 6 April, Wellington finally accepted that the breaches in the Trinidad and Santa Maria bastions were 'practicable', but Phillipon and Lamare had not been idle. Each night parties had braved the blind-firing to clear away the rubble in the ditch, while others built retrenchments inside the breaches to seal them off, and dragged up cannon to guard them. When word came that Soult's 25,000 men were only three or four days' march to the south, Wellington ordered the assault for the night of the 6th.

THE ASSAULTS OF 6–7 APRIL

Units from General Leith's 5th Division were to make diversionary attacks on the San Vincente bastion at the northwest corner of the town, and on the Pardaleras fort south of it, while Colonel Power's Portuguese attacked positions over on the north bank of the Guadiana. On the eastern side of the town, a small detachment from General Colville's 4th Division would take the San Roque lunette; then General Picton's 3rd Division would advance across the Rivellas by a broken bridge and try to take the old castle in the northeastern corner of Badajoz by 'escalade' – that is, by climbing scaling-ladders against its walls (which stood up to 14 metres [46 ft] high in some places). All these attempts were secondary, however, since Wellington placed his real hopes on the two

FIRING SIEGE ARTILLERY

Breaching-guns had to be emplaced within a few hundred yards of the walls, as the velocity of the heavy iron shot dropped rapidly over quite short ranges. They and their crews – nine men for a 24-pounder – were therefore vulnerable to enemy fire, and had to be protected. Battery positions, floored with heavy timbers to prevent the massive guns bogging down, were usually dug 0.6–0.9 metres (2–3 ft) below the surface, and guns and crews were protected by raised earth banks consolidated with gabions and fascines. The army's lighter 8-pounder field pieces concentrated on trying to silence the defenders' guns, while the 24- and 18-pounders played on the walls themselves. Howitzers and, if available, mortars would meanwhile lob explosive shells from above, to hamper the defenders' attempts to repair damage or clear rubble from the breach.

Breaching masonry was a slow task for the relatively inaccurate smooth-bore cannon of the time. Under perfect conditions an experienced crew could fire a 24- pounder once every 3 to 5 minutes. First, they tried to cut a horizontal groove along the base of a wall, about 1.8–2.7 metres (6–9 ft) above the ground, to undercut the masonry above. Then they worked upwards from this to make vertical lines at several points; then, aiming between the vertical marks, they continued to pound the wall until it collapsed. This might take four or five days for a battery of four guns to achieve. Prolonged firing put a great strain on guns and their carriages, and constant maintenance and repairs were required.

breaches; that in the Trinidad bastion was assigned to Colville's 4th Division, and that in the Santa Maria to General Barnard's Light Division.

Wellington's orders were meticulously detailed. Each divisional assault column would be preceded by a 'forlorn hope', a small party of volunteers who would enter the ditch first with a couple of ladders, and sacks stuffed with grass for the following men to jump down on. The old name came from the Dutch *verloren hoop* ('lost party'), but there was never any shortage of volunteers for these virtual suicide missions – they knew that survival would bring rewards, promotion and universal respect. Behind them would follow the two divisional storming parties, each of 500 men carrying 12 scaling-ladders. These would be followed closely by 100-man firing parties, ordered to spread along the near edge of the ditch and keep the defenders' heads down. Strong reserves would stand ready in the rear.

The assault had been planned for 7.30 p.m., giving the French the minimum respite after sunset; in the event the clearly visible preparations took much longer, and the garrison had 2½ hours of darkness in which to make ready. Again, debris was cleared from the foot of the breaches, where mines linked by powder-hoses were buried, and another part of the ditch was flooded.

THE SACK OF BADAJOZ, 7–9 APRIL 1812

The crazed survivors of the storming-parties were described by one officer as resembling *'hell hounds vomited up from the infernal regions'*. They do not seem to have ill-treated the French prisoners; but they did what they liked to the Spanish population for three days and nights, before staggering back to their camps sated with drink, rape, theft and murder. Officers in those days led from the front, so most of their own had already fallen, and any unfamiliar officer who tried to restrain the men risked being shot on the spot. Even the Iron Duke – among the sternest disciplinarians of his age – recognized that he would simply have to let the madness burn itself out; although he had a gallows erected in the main square on the third day, it seems that none of his men were actually hanged. It is perhaps relevant that when Wellington saw his contorted, blackened dead piled in the breaches on the morning of the 7th he wept openly – an unprecedented moment of vulnerability for this hardened soldier.

Phillipon's French and German infantry were practised and prepared, and encouraged by their success in repelling Wellington the previous June. Cannon loaded with grapeshot stood ready to sweep the ditches and the heads of the breaches; on the battlements firepots, grenades, short-fused shells and powder-kegs lay ready, and each man had three loaded muskets to hand. Medieval-looking obstacles were now chained down in the breaches: *chevaux-de-frise* – wooden beams and planks bristling with old sword and bayonet blades and foot-long nails.

British officers' diaries and letters bear witness to a tigerish eagerness among the assault parties. Ensign Grattan of the 88th wrote:

> *'The spirits of the soldiers, which no fatigues could dampen, rose to a frightful height ... there was a certain something in their bearing ... every fine feeling vanished, and plunder and revenge took their place ... Badajoz was, therefore, denounced as a place to be made example of; and most unquestionably no city, Jerusalem exempted, was ever more strictly visited ...'*

The stormers had dumped their knapsacks, unbuttoned their red jackets and their shirts, and rolled their trousers; some countrymen even preferred to go barefoot, for a surer grip on the steep slopes. They pulled their slung cartridge-pouches round to the front for instant access, securing them by knotting musket-slings around their waists, and every man fixed his long bayonet. The order finally came at about 9.40 p.m., and the San Roque outwork was quickly taken; then, at 10 p.m., the main assaults went in opposite the breaches.

Some men drowned in the flooded part of the ditch, and at the foot of the breaches many hundreds of redcoats quickly became packed together, as the 'forlorn hope' struggled to climb into the Trinidad bastion above them. There was a sudden flare of light from a French incendiary; then the parapets flickered and thundered with musket- and cannon-fire. Grenades and powder-charges rained down on the helpless crowd lit up by the flames – and then the buried mines were detonated, hurling dismembered and burning bodies through the air. Those who did claw their way up the steep rubble were checked by the murderous *chevaux-de-frise*, and shot, bayoneted or brained where they stood. Officers' shouted orders were drowned out by gunfire, explosions, shrieks of pain and bellows of rage. Units became hopelessly mixed up, with confused groups clambering over the growing piles of dead and dying into whichever breach they saw, only to fall in their turn.

A TERRIBLE COST

This hellish chaos lasted for a full two hours; it was claimed that no fewer than 40 separate attempts were made on the breaches, but it is certain that no British soldier got into Badajoz alive by that path, and about 2000 were killed or wounded in an area perhaps 365 metres wide by 183 metres deep (400 yards x 200 yards). Wellington, appalled, had finally called the battalions back to rest when he received word that Picton's secondary attack on the castle, from which little had been expected, had actually succeeded.

The castle had been Phillipon's chosen final redoubt, but was not yet strongly garrisoned. At first the 300 Hesse-Darmstadt troops defending its battlements found it easy to shoot, bayonet or club the men frantically climbing the tall scaling-ladders, sending them tumbling to their deaths among the others clustered in the ditch over 15 metres (50 ft) below. However, the deadlock was broken when Colonel Henry Ridge of the 5th Foot (Northumberland Fusiliers) led a handful of men up a ladder slightly to one side where the wall was lower, and got inside an embrasure. He did not survive long, but more redcoats crowded up behind; they charged along the ramparts, clearing defenders from around the heads of the other ladders. Before long enough soldiers had got inside to drive the Germans first off the walls, and then right out of the castle.

Meanwhile, the attackers of the San Vincente bastion had also succeeded in getting a lodgement. Both these parties began clearing the streets from north to south; and when the defenders of the breaches heard bugles behind them, and saw the tricolour hauled down from the castle flagstaff, they first faltered, and then gave way. The wild-eyed survivors of the 4th and Light Divisions were at last able to climb up over the tangle of their burned and hacked comrades, and through the breaches into the streets. General Philippon escaped, crossing to San Christobal fort. From there he surrendered Badajoz, at about 7 a.m. the next morning.

The redcoats subjected the citizens of the town to a sacking of medieval ferocity, which continued for a full 72 hours; how many civilians were murdered is unknown. The total military casualties are estimated at 4000 British and 1000 Portuguese, but only some 1500 French – a reminder of the terrible arithmetic of storming a heavily defended place. For this price Wellington had secured all four of the frontier fortresses, and he would hold them for the rest of the war.

THE ALAMO

The sacrifice at the birth of American Texas

23 February – 6 March 1836

'*What are the lives of soldiers but so many chickens? ... If our soldiers are driven back, the next line in their rear must force those in front of them forward and compel them to climb the walls, cost what it may.*'

GENERALISSIMO ANTONIO LÓPEZ DE SANTA ANNA, REPORTED BY
CAPTAIN FERNANDO URISSA (5 MARCH 1836)

The 13-day defence of the mission at San Antonio de Béxar in the Mexican state of Texas, and the subsequent massacre of the garrison, was the defining moment in the birth of the independent Republic of Texas. This led inexorably to annexation by the United States nine years later, sparking the Mexican-American War of 1846–8, which led in turn to the USA acquiring California, with incalculable effects on her future power and prosperity. Apart from these undoubted strategic consequences, the battle claims our attention simply as an inspiring example of courage in the face of great odds. Any historical incident that passes into legend attracts myth-making and pointless argument over trivial details, but the essentials of the Alamo story are beyond dispute.

TEXIANS AND *FEDERALISTAS*

In 1823 the congress of the newly independent Republic of Mexico honoured a previous Spanish offer of generous grants to attract American pioneers to the sparsely inhabited state of Texas. The following year a new federalist Mexican constitution, based upon that of the United States, gave extensive freedoms to the constituent states. This was supported by the *Federalista* party, who also believed that American settlement would spur economic development; but it was opposed by conservative *Centralistas*, who were hostile to both the liberal constitution and the new 'Texians' from the north.

In 1834 General Antonio López de Santa Anna (1794–1876) led a coup that overturned the 1824 constitution, and in October 1835 a conservative congress stripped the individual states of their rights and installed a military government. When the *federalistas* resisted, the Texians flocked to join their Tejano fellow citizens in the name of their stolen constitution. In October 1835 a small force under James Bowie drove off a government battalion at La Concepción, and in December the 'Army of the People' captured some 1400 troops at San Antonio de Béxar. These were allowed to retreat south across the Rio Grande in return for General de Cos's parole, and – ignoring the appeals of their purely nominal commander-in-chief, Sam Houston – most of the militia then disbanded. They underestimated the vengeful ambition of Santa Anna, the self-styled 'Napoleon of the West'.

Dawn at the Alamo (1905; detail), an impression of the final assault painted by Henry McArdle, which hangs in the Texas State Capitol in Austin.

TIMELINE

1810 Miguel Hidalgo y Costilla declares Mexican independence from Spain, beginning a struggle that lasts for over a decade

1821 Short-lived First Mexican Empire proclaimed, with Agustín de Iturbide as emperor

1824 New republican constitution promulgated in Mexico, granting extensive rights to the constituent states

1834 Antonio López de Santa Anna seizes power in a coup in Mexico

1835 Texian force under James Bowie repels an assault by Mexican government troops on La Concepción

1836 (February–March) Siege of the Alamo mission ends in the slaughter of the entire garrison after a defence lasting 13 days

1836 (April) Sam Houston's force defeats Santa Anna's army at the Battle of San Jacinto and captures Santa Anna

1845 Republic of Texas joins the United States

A SECOND-CLASS ARMY VERSUS NO ARMY AT ALL

On 16 February 1836, Santa Anna crossed the Rio Grande with an 'Army of Operations' and made for San Antonio, while General Urrea's smaller force crossed futher south at Matamoros and moved on Goliad and the coastal settlements. The paper strength of the whole army had been 6000 when it set off from San Luis Potosí in January, but it had suffered badly from inadequate rations and water, and it lost many stragglers during the hardest winter in living memory. In all essentials the dictator's force resembled a division of one of the poorer Napoleonic armies. The Mexican treasury had been looted after independence, and the logistic services were rotten with corruption. The *soldados* were ill-clad, badly fed, thinned out by sickness, and driven into battle by a harsh and arbitrary discipline. Some of their disdainful officers were experienced professionals, but too many owed their ranks and decorations to political favouritism, and their practical care for their men was minimal.

However, the forces available to the Texas provisional government were almost non-existent – as, indeed, it was itself. It was not even in session, and authority was disputed; its rival factions had not had time to resolve their political differences, nor to do more than sketch a plan for an army, and General Houston suffered from a chaotic chain of command both above and below him. Texian militiamen were deeply egalitarian, and resented any attempt at regimentation by the few officers given regular commissions (there were hardly any regular enlisted men). Independent militiamen scattered in penny packets across the state totalled fewer than 800 in all, carrying their own miscellany of weapons, and led by officers whom they had elected. Most companies lacked organization or discipline, and any man could simply go home whenever he felt like it; no commander knew how many men he would have tomorrow, nor whether they would choose to obey him. Yet two months later this unpromising material would achieve a triumph of individual motivation and leadership over apparently hopeless unpreparedness.

'*The salvation of Texas depends in great measure on keeping Béxar out of the hands of the enemy ... Colonel Neill and myself have come to the solemn resolution that we will rather die in these ditches than give it up.*'

LETTER BY JAMES BOWIE TO GOVERNOR HENRY SMITH (2 FEBRUARY 1836)

SAN ANTONIO DE BÉXAR

This town on the old Spanish northern road was a necessary regional base which Santa Anna would have to take. It had, in the half-ruined mission station of the Alamo south of the town, a theoretically defensible post. In January 1836 this was commanded by a thorough-going professional, Colonel James C. Neill – but with fewer than 100 men. Others came in by handfuls: on 19 January, 30 volunteers arrived led by James Bowie, who went on to raise others among the local Tejanos (to whom he was well known). On 3 February a 26-year-old Texian regular, Lieutenant-Colonel William B. Travis, rode in with a couple of dozen troopers; others followed, from the volunteer New Orleans Greys; and on 8 February a dozen arrived from Tennessee, led by a former congressman and frontier legend – 'Davy' Crockett. However, by 10 February the garrison, though energized and encouraged by Neill's leadership, still stood at just 142 men. Their only realistic hope of reinforcement rested on a self-confessed incompetent, Colonel James W. Fannin, who was holding the presidio of La Bahia at Goliad, some 95 miles (152 km) to the southeast, with perhaps 500 men.

THE GENERALISSIMO

Antonio López de Santa Anna Pérez de Lebrón (1794–1876) dominated Mexican political life for 35 years, and was ruler of the Republic on 11 different occasions between 1833 and 1855. He had physical courage, charisma and cunning; but he was an indifferent military commander, an incompetent administrator and a cynical opportunist, motivated solely by vanity and hunger for power. He first showed his cruelty when serving as a Spanish officer against his rebellious countrymen in 1813 (before switching to the revolutionary side in 1821), and displayed it on many occasions thereafter. He made the mistake of declaring war on the USA in April 1846, and General Winfield Scott's victorious army marched into Mexico City in September 1847. Santa Anna's plotting for power, interspersed with periods in exile, lasted until 1865; he finally died in obscure poverty at the age of 82.

On 14 February Col. Neill left the Alamo, called away by desperate sickness in his family. As a regular officer Travis was named his successor, but the volunteers voted for Bowie; the gentlemanly lawyer and the drunken knife-fighter sensibly agreed to share the command (Crockett refused all authority). While the garrison worked on the defences and stockpiled supplies, Travis sent appeals for help to Fannin, and to the town of Gonzales about 70 miles (112 km) east.

On 23 February, although delayed by flooded rivers, Santa Anna reached San Antonio three weeks earlier than he had been expected, and after a brief skirmish the rebels fell back into the Alamo. Hoisting the red flag signifying 'no quarter' on the church tower, Santa Anna sent a demand that the garrison surrender unconditionally; Travis replied with a cannonball.

THE ALAMO AND ITS GARRISON

The main part of the 550-metre (600-yd)-long defended perimeter was a rectangular plaza with 3.7-metre (12-ft) stone walls, about 165 metres (180 yds) from north to south and 64 metres (70 yds) across. An unbroken line of buildings ran down the eastern side – the so-called Long Barracks – and there were a number of others inside the north, west and south walls. At the southeast the roofless chapel extended about 60 metres (65 yds) out to the east, adjoining to the north some buildings and two open yards (one with a well) lying in the angle of the L-shaped perimeter. The southeast corner was linked to the chapel by a diagonal run of timber palisade about 23 metres (25 yds) long.

On the north and west walls, in the northwest and southwest corners and in the apse of the chapel, Neill's engineer Major Jameson had built access ramps and reinforced platforms so that about half the 20-odd guns abandoned there by the Mexicans could be raised to fire over the parapets. Other cannon were emplaced in an open battery inside the main south gate; in an earth-and-palisade lunette outside that gate; along the southeast palisade; and in corners of the cattle pen and corral, to command the eastern wall. The guns were mostly 6- and 8-pounders; but there was a kind of 12-pounder carronade on the west wall, another 12-pounder among three guns in the chapel and a powerful 18-pounder in the southwestern corner.

How many men Travis finally had to defend the perimeter is still the subject of research. The accepted number used to be 189; but there is uncertainty over how many Tejanos were present, and some believe the garrison may have reached about 250 rifles. They were mainly Texian and Tejano volunteers, the latter led by Captain Juan Seguin. Texian regulars included Captains Dickinson and Carey and their artillerymen, and Travis's cavalrymen. The rest were volunteers from the United States – the New Orleans Greys, Crockett and his Tennesseeans, and various other individuals. Whatever the true total, they were far too few to defend 550 metres (600 yds) of walls against simultaneous assaults from different directions, while lacking any flanking fire from supporting outworks. About 25 women, children and other non-combatants were also relying on their protection.

THE SIEGE

Santa Anna had perhaps 2000 men at the Alamo: 300–400 cavalry, about 200 sappers, perhaps the same number of gunners and some 1800 infantry. The latter were three regular battalions (the

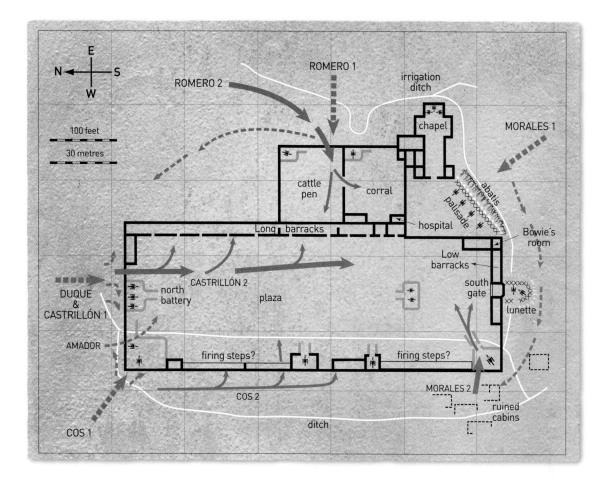

Plan of the mission station at the Alamo, showing the main defensive points and the sequence of assaults on 6 March by Santa Anna's separate columns.

Aldama, Jimenez and Matamoros), and two of the partly trained *Milicia Activa* (the Toluca and San Luis). A battalion was officially 640 strong, with one light, one grenadier and six fusilier companies, but these units actually mustered only 300–400 men each; most of them carried flintlock muskets, though a few in the *cazador* light companies had rifles. The most professional unit was probably the Sapper battalion (*Zapadores*); both the equipment and the training of the artillery had been neglected.

On 23 February batteries were constructed north, northeast, south and southwest of the Alamo, and the following morning one of their 17-inch howitzers reportedly opened the bombardment by lobbing an explosive shell into the plaza. The Mexicans had about the same number of cannon as the garrison; of perhaps 17 field pieces only two 12-pounders could be considered wall-smashers, but the walls of the old mission had never been built to withstand artillery fire. The Mexicans believed that with breached defences, provisions running low and no sign of a relief force, the rebels would soon surrender without any necessity for them to storm the walls in the face of grapeshot and rifle-fire.

It was also on 24 February that Bowie collapsed, seriously ill, and was taken to a room in the southeastern corner; with his endorsement, Travis assumed sole command. He sent off another call for help, though declaring his determination to hold out whether it came or not. On the 25th a fight took place outside the southern walls when Crockett's men –assigned the defence of the southeastern palisade – sortied to clear snipers from the cover of some neighbouring shacks, which they then destroyed. That day Travis sent out Captain Seguin with another appeal for support. On the 26th, Fannin finally left La Bahia and began to march 320 men towards San Antonio; but a chapter of foolish accidents halted him immediately, and the next day his men easily persuaded him to give up the plan.

The cannonade was relentless; the long-range accuracy of the defenders' rifles kept Mexican heads down, but the walls and buildings were showing damage. Travis's appeals were getting through, but there was no recipient who could act upon them. The Texian leaders were not due to reassemble until 2 March, and Houston – with neither troops, nor authority to lead any – was away on a mission to his Cherokee contacts. The Alamo's call did not fall on wholly deaf ears, however; on the night of 29 February help arrived – just 32 heroic volunteers from Gonzales slipped into the mission, and even such a small reinforcement stiffened morale.

On 3 March, however, Santa Anna also received reinforcements. By that night, when Travis sent another courier out, he had given up all hope of Fannin coming to his aid: *'If my countrymen do not rally to my relief I am determined to perish in defence of this place, and my bones shall reproach my country for her neglect.'* The rider also took out some mail from the defenders, and a letter from a Gonzales volunteer, Isaac Millsaps, mentioned that while the walls were crumbling the garrison had so far suffered no deaths. He said that Travis was to address them all that evening; this was the occasion of his (possibly apocryphal) *'drawing of a line in the dust'*, and inviting any man not willing to die to step over it and leave – only one did.

On 4 March the Mexicans moved guns to a new battery only about 230 metres (250 yds) to the northeast. Although Texian riflemen made life perilous for the crews, these now did serious damage to the north wall, and that night had to be spent in trying to shore it up. Meanwhile Santa Anna had announced his intention to assault the walls on 6 March; this surprised his officers – particularly General Castrillón, who considered such a potentially costly tactic unnecessary. But the Generalissimo clearly felt he needed a dramatic victory for political reasons, and when he issued his orders on 5 March he was callously unconcerned about probable casualties.

THE ASSAULT

The cannonade was halted late on 5 March: the defenders, constantly under fire for 12 days, would be unable to resist sleeping in the unaccustomed lull, and Santa Anna ordered that his men should advance in silence early the next morning. The most recent and untrained recruits were excused, but some 1700 infantrymen would be committed.

'*Fellow Citizens, I am besieged by a thousand or more Mexicans, under Santa Anna ... The enemy have demanded a surrender at discretion, otherwise the garrison is to be put to the sword, if the fort is taken. I have answered the demand with a cannon shot, and our flag still waves proudly from the walls. I shall never surrender or retreat ...*
VICTORY OR DEATH.'

ALAMO CO-COMMANDER LIEUTENANT-COLONEL WILLIAM B. TRAVIS, OPEN LETTER 'TO THE PEOPLE OF TEXAS AND ALL AMERICANS IN THE WORLD' (24 FEBRUARY 1836)

The north wall was allocated to Colonel Duque, with 400 militiamen of the Toluca and San Luis battalions; on their right, General de Cos led 200 regulars from the Aldama and 100 San Luis militiamen against the northwest corner. Simultaneously, Colonel Romero with 300 regulars from the Matamoros and Jimenez battalions would attack the east wall; and Colonel Morales would lead 100 *cazadores* detached from the Matamoros, Jimenez and San Luis against the southeast palisade. Santa Anna's 400-strong reserve of regulars, under Lt.-Col. Amat, comprised the *Zapadores* battalion and the *granadero* companies detached from the Aldama, Jimenez and Matamoros. Meanwhile, some 370 cavalry – many armed with lances – were to patrol the outer edges of the battlefield.

The assault columns moved forwards, carrying scaling ladders, axes and crowbars, at 5.30 a.m. on 6 March. At first they kept silent, as ordered, but before long some broke into battle-cries, and the garrison ran to their posts. Under Travis's orders the three guns in the northern battery, loaded with scrap-iron, tore great gaps in the attacking ranks, while riflemen – some with as many as four weapons ready to hand – began picking off individuals. Colonel Duque was wounded, and his militiamen lost all order; on their right, General de Cos's regulars fared little better against the northwest guns. But still they pressed forward, firing at the Texians exposed on the parapets, until they reached the north wall and put up their ladders. As the first men climbed in a storm of bullets, Travis fell with a ball in his head; but his riflemen killed the scaling parties at point-blank range, and cleared the ladders.

The soldiers of de Cos's and Duque's units (the latter now commanded by General Castrillón) became mixed together, huddling against the foot of the north wall where the defenders' cannon could not reach them. Meanwhile Colonel Romero's troops had taken heavy casualties from the chapel guns, sweeping the east wall; his men, too, lost cohesion, and ran around the northeast corner to join the crowd under the north wall. At the southeast palisade, the cannon and Crockett's

THE AFTERMATH

On 2 March the reconvened Texian convention at Washington-on-the-Brazos had already declared Texas an independent republic, and on the 4th they confirmed Houston as commander-in-chief. Santa Anna's insistence on killing the entire Alamo garrison rebounded on him: it caused outrage in the USA, and stirred the Texian leaders into action. But by 11 March, Houston still had only 374 men and, despite many protests, he sensibly withdrew deeper into Texas. The highly capable General Urrea was meanwhile snapping up several small Texian detachments, including troops unwisely dispersed by Fannin. On 19 March that officer abandoned Goliad and withdrew northeastwards pursued by Urrea. Trapped in the open at Coleto Creek, the volunteers formed square and put up a stout fight, until the arrival of Mexican cannon forced their surrender. On 27 March the wounded Fannin and about 340 other prisoners were murdered at La Bahia on the orders of Santa Anna, thus ensuring his lasting reputation as a butcher.

Meanwhile Houston continued to withdraw, gathering troops as he went, and Generals Santa Anna, Urrea and Filisola followed him. On 21 April, Houston had about 900 men (including Juan Seguin's Tejanos) when he caught Santa Anna and some 1250 travel-weary Mexicans (including the Aldama and Matamoros battalions that had fought at the Alamo) carelessly camped beside the San Jacinto river. In just 18 minutes a wild charge – to the battle-cries 'Remember the Alamo! Remember La Bahia!' – overran the Mexicans. About 650 were slaughtered without mercy, and the rest taken prisoner; Houston's casualties were nine killed and 30 wounded. Remarkably, next day the painfully wounded Houston spared the life of the captured Santa Anna, who sent orders for Urrea and Filisola to retreat. Their army disintegrating in terrible weather, they fell back across the Rio Grande. The US, British and French governments subsequently recognized the independent Republic of Texas.

riflemen had repulsed Morales' light companies; the survivors ran westwards and around the south-west corner, to take cover in ruined cabins. The assault was losing momentum and direction; although they had inflicted losses, the Mexicans still did not have a lodgement on the walls. At this point Santa Anna committed his reserve.

The *Zapadores* advanced on the north wall; when they opened fire at the few Texians still visible, many of them shot low, into their own troops crowded at the foot of the wall. Under the lash of this new danger, some of these were ready to climb again, but their ladders were mostly smashed. However, the gun damage and hasty repairs had left plenty of hand- and footholds; General Juan Amador set an example of courage and others followed. They reached the parapet at the northwest corner and – somehow overlooked in the noise and smoke – they dropped down and managed to open a small postern gate. This was the turning point of the battle.

No Quarter

The Texians abandoned the north wall, some retreating into the Long Barracks, as a scrambling firefight raged across the open ground. At roughly the same time, General de Cos's men had spread down the outside of the west wall, and began smashing their way though blocked-up doors and windows with axes and crowbars, penetrating and clearing some of the western buildings and emerging into the plaza. Down in the southwest corner, Morales' *cazadores* managed to get up the wall and capture the 18-pounder gun; and over on the eastern perimeter, Romero's soldiers broke into the cattle pen and corral and captured the two guns there – the crews of all three of these pieces were killed or driven back before they could spike their guns, which the Mexicans now turned against the defenders.

The Texians fighting in the open plaza were quickly overwhelmed by superior numbers and firepower from two directions, but the dwindling survivors fought on from the cover of the Long Barracks and the chapel. Romero's men blew their way into the Long Barracks from the east with the captured cannon, while those coming from the north wall smashed their way in from the other side. In savage fighting inside the barracks all its defenders were killed; the stormers gave no quarter, and any Texians who fell were bayoneted – as were the casualties in the hospital. Meanwhile, Morales' light infantrymen had charged down the ramp from the southwest gun battery and were clearing the southern part of the compound. James Bowie was killed in his sickbed, and the last men fighting – including Captain Dickinson – fell back inside the chapel, defending a sandbag barricade. A considerable number (some believe as many as 75) broke out at the southeast and tried to escape across country, but after a stubborn fight they were all killed by Colonel Ramirez y Sema's lancers. The captured 18-pounder was used to blast a way into the chapel, where the last defenders were silenced at about 6.30 a.m. Perhaps six were taken alive, but Santa Anna ordered them hacked down on the spot.

The Generalissimo, who had lost perhaps 600 of his men in an hour, was unmoved by the corpses of both sides strewn in heaps around the compound; but he allowed a few surviving non-combatants to leave, including Mrs Susanna Dickinson and her daughter Angelina and Travis's slave Joe, and it was they who carried the story of the Alamo to the world.

A Victorian epic in an ugly war LUCKNOW

30 June–17 November 1857

'*In the sky of India, serene as it is, a cloud may arise, at first no bigger than a man's hand, but which growing bigger and bigger, may at last threaten to overwhelm us with ruin.*'

LORD CANNING, GOVERNOR-GENERAL OF INDIA (AUGUST 1855)

The five-month siege of Lucknow was probably the most famous of the many endured during what the British in India called the Great Mutiny (and which Indians refer to as the First War of Independence), which lasted from 1857 to 1859. During this conflict both sides committed widespread atrocities, but in Victorian Britain the defenders of Lucknow became an archetype for heroism. The first force sent to rescue the garrison arrived too weakened to do anything but join them under siege. When the second relief column broke in six weeks later, it was obliged to extract the survivors and shepherd them to safety on a retreat through enemy territory.

THE TINDERBOX

By the 1850s the 250-year-old British East India Company (EIC) had expanded from a simple trading enterprise into a vast civil and military administration, governing and protecting much of India as a supervised but independent agency of the British crown. Its large private army was divided between the three regional 'presidencies' of Bengal (with two-thirds of the troops), Bombay and Madras; the great majority were native soldiers – sepoys – led by British officers, in units modelled on those of the British army. In 1857 the EIC had 311,000 Indian and 16,000 European troops, in contrast with just 24,000 British regulars – 'Queen's troops' – then in India.

The 18th-century British had mixed freely with a culture that they admired, and avoided meddling in religious matters; EIC officers often married Indian women, and forged strong bonds with their troops. By the 1850s this easy-going atmosphere had fallen victim to Britain's new mood of assertive bourgeois Christianity, which had unleashed on India energetic missionaries and administrators convinced of their duty to spread enlightened Western values among the 'benighted heathen'. Reforms to customary law were deeply resented, while a growth in racial prejudice harmed both the careers of Indian employees and relationships within the EIC army. High-caste Hindus – heavily represented among the sepoys – suspected all reforms as attempts to subvert their culture. Experienced officers and officials warned that there was a real danger of uprisings, but their superiors remained complaisant.

Attack of the Mutineers on the Redan Battery at Lucknow. An unattributed illustration from an 1860 history of the Indian Mutiny shows the desperate defence of the battery on 30 July.

TIMELINE

1608 The East India Company is granted its first trading concessions in India

1813 First Christian missionaries are licensed to preach in India

1853 The first railway in India is opened in Bombay

1856 East India Company annexes the province of Oudh

1857 (May) Siege of Lucknow begins as Lawrence fortifies the town against attack

1857 (September) A relief column under Sir Henry Havelock fights its way from Cawnpore to Lucknow

1857 (November) Lucknow evacuated by the British; death of Sir Henry Havelock

1858 Lucknow retaken by British forces; East India Company wound up, as the Crown assumes sovereignty over India

1876 Queen Victoria is proclaimed empress of India

THE SPARK

In February and March 1857 a rumour that cardboard-wrapped powder-and-shot cartridges for the newly issued Enfield rifles were greased with animal fats that offended religious taboos led to cases of insubordination in several Bengal Native Infantry and Cavalry (BNI/BNC) regiments stationed north of Calcutta. These were harshly punished, and at Barrackpore the 19th BNI was disbanded; yet this warning was not heeded even when there was another outbreak in the 3rd BNC at Meerut north of Delhi – nearly 700 miles (1120 km) northwest of Barrackpore. The mutineers had no co-ordination nor any central plan, but were simply giving vent to common feelings of rebellious hatred.

On 10 May, sepoys based at Meerut massacred their British officers and their families and marched on Delhi. Local EIC commanders were paralysed with shock, and most Queen's troops were deployed far away in the Northwest Frontier and Punjab regions. By 13 May growing numbers of mutineers had gathered in Delhi, slaughtered Europeans and Christian Indians, and proclaimed the revival of the Mughul empire. While a British force was hastily scraped together to retake Delhi, mutinies burst out all over northern India, with isolated outbreaks further to the south; many British men, women and children perished in horrific bloodbaths.

British commanders – dispersed over great distances, with unreliable communications – were forced to improvise relief forces and logistics at short notice, from their few British troops and Indians of as-yet uncertain loyalty. The EIC administration collapsed, and mobs of mutineers numbering tens of thousands roamed the countryside seeking violent confrontation. Some Indian civilians joined them, turning on their neighbours in a tide of bloodshed and looting.

Two of the EIC centres cut off by this wave of murderous anarchy became particularly notorious: Cawnpore (Kanpur) and Lucknow, towns about 40 miles (64 km) apart and both some 220 miles (350 km) southeast of Delhi.

THE APPROACHING STORM

At Lucknow in mid-May the EIC commissioner in Oudh province, Sir Henry Lawrence, heard rumours of impending trouble. He began to gather his small force of British troops and local European volunteers, and to fortify and provision a perimeter for future defence. On 30 May killings and destruction signalled mutinies among the four local units, but when Lawrence sent British troops against them the mutineers drifted away without attacking the town.

On 6 June, at Cawnpore on the Ganges to the south of Lucknow, Sir Hugh Wheeler was besieged with about 300 British soldiers and 500 civilians. The mutineers chose as leader a disaffected native prince, the Nana Sahib, maharajah of Bithur. Wheeler had chosen an indefensible position; with rations and ammunition running low, on 27 June he surrendered to the Nana Sahib on the promise of safe conduct to sail away down the Ganges. When the British reached the river they were ambushed and massacred, apart from some 200 women and children dragged back to the town and imprisoned in a small building.

On 29 June, when Lawrence heard a report of some 500 mutineers at Chinhat, some 10 miles (16 km) from Lucknow, he foolishly took about 600 of his troops out to face them. On 30 June they were attacked by at least 5000 rebels, and suffered more than 300 casualties and several cannon lost

THE CARTRIDGE AFFAIR

Two-thirds of the EIC's Bengal sepoys, recruited in the conservative north, were high-caste Brahmin or Ksatriya Hindus who were extremely sensitive about their religious status. In 1857 BNI and BNC regiments, previously armed with smooth-bore muskets and carbines, received the first issues of the new rifled Enfield weapons. Still muzzle-loaders (whose paper cartridges had to be torn or bitten open to pour the powder and bullet down the barrel), these rifles took a new type of greased cartridge. In January 1857, during an argument at the Dum-Dum arsenal, an 'untouchable' low-caste workman taunted a haughty Brahmin soldier that the cartridges were greased with a mixture of beef- and pork-fat, and thus ritually defiling to both Hindu and Muslim soldiers who handled them. The rumour spread like wildfire through the restless Bengal army; Hindu ringleaders, already suspicious and resentful at British enlistment of 'untouchable' Sikhs and Gurkhas, claimed that this was a secret plot to destroy the army's religious purity.

There probably was animal tallow on the cartridges – the question of religious sensitivities had simply not been considered. When the troops' resentment was reported most officers dismissed it too lightly, and when insubordination did occur the sepoys were punished harshly. In fact ammunition was soon issued ungreased, so that soldiers could grease it themselves with mutton-fat and wax; but this concession came too late – the cartridge affair was the tipping-point in an already dangerously unstable situation.

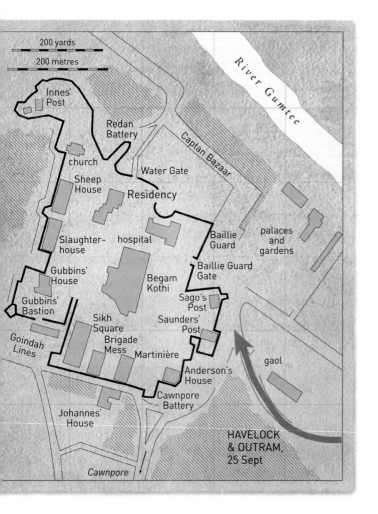

Map of Lucknow, showing the perimeter around the Residency and other defended buildings, and the route of the first relief force.

before escaping back into Lucknow. The mutineers pursued them, the city mob rose to kill and plunder, and the siege began.

THE RESIDENCY

Lawrence and his engineer, Major Anderson, had traced an irregular perimeter about 1.2 miles (1.9 km) long enclosing the Residency and nearby buildings on a rise in the north of the town, overlooking the bank of the Gumtee river. Individual houses and public buildings had been strengthened and loopholed, and tied into a perimeter using existing walls extended by entrenched earthworks, timber palisades and rubble and sandbag barricades. The garrison had more cannon than they could properly man; but these could not sweep the faces of the perimeter with flanking fire except from the Redan Battery in the north, and in the northeast around the Baillie Guard.

The only places where the enemy could mass for frontal attacks were on the sloping ground above the riverbank to the northeast, commanded by guns in the Redan; and in an area partly covered with ruins outside the west face, dominated by several strongpoints. Yet Lawrence's refusal to destroy many buildings close outside the perimeter angered his senior combat officer, Colonel John Inglis of the 32nd Foot; these misplaced scruples meant that more stealthy attackers could approach under cover through narrow streets outside Anderson's House and the Cawnpore Battery in the southeast corner, and Gubbins' House and Bastion in the southeast. The buildings outside – for instance, the native houses of the Captan Bazaar in the north, and Johannes' House close to the southern wall – also ensured that the garrison would come under constant sniper fire.

British soldiers of the 32nd Foot held the Redan and Cawnpore batteries, and were distributed between some other strongpoints to stiffen volunteers and Indian defenders; 50 men from the 84th Foot formed a reserve in the Residency building. Nearly half the garrison were loyal Indian sepoys:

men of the 48th and 71st BNI held the Hospital Post – the former banqueting hall – and others from the 13th defended the Baillie Guard Gate, while Sikh irregulars were posted south of this, and across in Sikh Square. At any one time about 30 men held each post.

The monsoon rains had just begun, but the weather was still swelteringly hot. There was plentiful drinking water from several wells, and for the first weeks Lawrence's stockpiles of food, firewood and ammunition seemed sufficient for his 1720 troops and the 1280 non-combatants (including some 600 women and children) who depended upon their protection. However, medical supplies were always short, and the lethal shock of amputations without anaesthetic awaited many of the wounded. Neither was there adequate drainage out of the perimeter, and sanitation and hygiene would become a serious problem.

JOHN INGLIS AND HENRY HAVELOCK

In the first 24 hours of the siege Lawrence sent a letter out by a Sikh courier to General Sir Henry Havelock (1795–1857) at Allahabad, some 130 miles (209 km) to the southeast, doubting the garrison's ability to hold out for more than 20 days.

Initially about 6000 mutineers were actively engaged in the town, but this number soon rose to at least 10,000. At first their professional training and solidarity made them formidable enemies, but these qualities faded as men from different units drifted apart and became muddled together with civilians. Above all they lacked command and control: fighting with 19th-century weapons depended upon simultaneous obedience to the orders of officers, and without officers the rebels' attacks lacked all co-ordination. While their smooth-bore muskets were outranged by the garrison's rifles, the besiegers had enough ammunition, and were close enough, to keep up constant and dangerous sniping, and they could lay down withering fire on the defences to cover assaults. At first (though not for long) they also seemed to have plenty of artillery ammunition; on 2 July, Sir Henry Lawrence was killed by a shell exploding in his quarters – fired from an 8-inch howitzer lost during his mishandled sortie to Chinhat.

Command was then taken by Colonel Inglis of the 32nd, who would prove the soul of the defence. He sent out sorties to spike enemy guns and clear snipers from advanced posts, which lifted morale during the weeks of weary endurance of constant enemy fire, punctuated by occasional mass attacks which forced the garrison to stay vigilant at all times. It took them a while to learn the habits of caution when moving around, and during the first week they lost 15 to 20 casualties each day to sniping.

At Allahabad, where he was frantically trying to gather a relief force for Cawnpore and Lucknow, General Havelock was told on 3 July of the massacre of the Cawnpore garrison and the imprisonment of the women and children. He redoubled his efforts; and on 7 July he marched north with about 2000 troops, half of them British – including many young soldiers, who collapsed from heatstroke under the 38°C (100°F) sun during the forced marches of the next ten days. Havelock's men fought their way through 3500 rebels at Fatehpur on 12 July, and others at Aong and Pandu Nadi on the 15th. On 16 July the Nana Sahib led 10,000 men to face Havelock outside

Cawnpore. His cannon raked the British infantry, whose own guns could not yet get up; but the 64th Foot led a wild bayonet charge into the grapeshot, and when their cannon were captured the mutineers retreated. Havelock entered the town on 17 July – to discover something ghastly.

When news of his approach had reached the Nana Sahib on the 15th, he had ordered the murder of the 206 British women and children. Local butchers were sent into the stifling, cramped bungalow with their knives, and spent all night hacking their victims to death; next morning their remains were thrown down a 50-foot dry well, which the bodies filled to within 1.8 metres (6 ft) of the top. Havelock was a devout man, but he could not face recovering the pitiful, violated corpses for Christian burial; he had the well filled, and the service spoken over its sealed cap. His soldiers' incredulous shock soon travelled around India and the world. To the Victorian British the atrocity at Cawnpore damned all mutineers as devils incarnate, and for the next two years many thousands of summary executions would add a new horror to British operations. As early as 31 July the wise British governor-general, Lord Canning, gave public orders forbidding indiscriminate revenge; but he was sneeringly dubbed 'Clemency Canning', and soldiers continued to festoon the trees with hanged corpses.

In Lucknow, a major attack on 20 July was beaten back with some difficulty from the Redan Battery and Innes' Post, the entrenched salient at the north; such massed assaults were spotted by look-outs during their careless assembly, giving time to reinforce the threatened sectors. On the 22nd, a raid out of the southwest corner cleared buildings at Goindrah Lines.

On 25 July, Havelock led his 1500 surviving men – exhausted and cholera-ridden – towards Lucknow; but the Nana Sahib's far stronger forces manoeuvred against him, and after fighting his way through 4000 of them at Bithur on 16 August he had no choice but to fall back to Cawnpore to await reinforcements.

At Lucknow, the mutineers now tried driving mines under the defences; but Anderson's deputy Captain Fulton counter-mined, with former tin miners from the Cornish 32nd Foot as his leading hands, and they dominated the consequent fierce underground skirmishes. On 10 August two mines were blown short of the Martinière and Sago's Post, and the assault parties were shot down; attacks that developed at many other points were also driven off – the besiegers may have been weakened by sending so many troops out to face Havelock. On 16 August infantry fire from the Johannes' House silenced the gun crews in the Cawnpore Battery, so the next day Lieutenant Innes and men of the 32nd began digging an offensive mine of their own near the Martinière. On the 21st it was blown, a sortie cleared the ruins of Johannes' House, and the Cawnpore Battery got back into action.

SEPTEMBER: ENDURANCE
By mid-September many buildings – the Residency, Anderson's and Gubbins' Houses, the Brigade Mess – were crumbling under repeated artillery strikes, and anyone not needed at the barricades had to shelter in basements and fortified ground floors. The mutineers shifted their guns around from place to place, but counter-battery fire was sometimes successful.

THE BENGAL PRESIDENCY ARMY

In 1857 the army of the EIC's Bengal presidency was particularly restless. A new regulation made all troops liable for service overseas, which for Hindus automatically involved religious pollution requiring expensive purification rituals. Many of the sepoys had been recruited in the princely state of Oudh, and were outraged when it was annexed to EIC adminstration in 1856; this damaged both their pride and their pay terms. Sir Henry Lawrence, commander of the Lucknow garrison in Oudh, was one of the old India hands who prophesied disaster: '*We act contrary to common sense, and in neglect of the lessons of history, in considering that the present system can lead to anything but a convulsion. We are lucky in its having lasted so long.*'

In 1857, of 123 regular and irregular Indian units of the Bengal army, 59 mutinied and 37 others were disarmed or disbanded for unreliability – i.e. 78 percent. At that time there were only three EIC European battalions in Bengal. In May 1857 there were single Queen's units at Calcutta, Dinapore and Lucknow, and two at Meerut - just five battalion-size units of British regulars, stretched over some 750 miles (1200 km).

When the Great Mutiny broke out, all Gurkha and most Muslim and Sikh units of the Bengal army remained loyal. So did the whole of the Madras and most of the Bombay army, which played an important part in the 1858 campaigns in central India.

The now dwindling rations went mainly to the fighting men, though they found the lack of tobacco hard to bear. A shortage of fresh food was causing cases of scurvy, to add to the many victims of cholera (the greatest killer), smallpox, dysentery, gangrenous wounds and skin diseases. The lack of sanitation and the unburied bodies of animals attracted tormenting swarms of flies. In the packed hospital, several wounded were killed where they lay by snipers' bullets penetrating to the middle of the building; windows had to be barricaded shut, temperatures reached 38°C (100°F) even at night, and some of the besieged simply went insane. The British women had at first felt helpless in the absence of their accustomed servants, but most had now rallied tirelessly to help in any way they could – not only nursing, but even loading rifles at the ramparts. Babies were born, but many did not survive the desperate shortage of milk; of 270 children in Lucknow, 54 would die, as would 14 women.

On 5 September the garrison repulsed a third massed attack: mines under Gubbins' House and the Brigade Mess again exploded short, but the storming parties seemed even more determined than previously, and minor local attacks were now almost continuous.

THE FIRST RELIEF

By 19 September, Havelock had at last been reinforced by General Sir James Outram to a strength of some 3200, including 2000 English and Scottish infantry, and could march north from Cawnpore.

THE LUCKNOW GARRISON

On 1 July, Lawrence had *c.*1720 troops comprising:

Europeans (c.1000)
700 of the 32nd Foot (Cornwall)
50 from the 84th Foot (York & Lancaster)
*c.*100 East India Company artillerymen
153 civilian volunteers

Indians (c.720)
200 from the 13th Bengal Native Infantry
120 from the 71st Bengal Native Infantry
57 from the 48th Bengal Native Infantry
60 from the 7th Bengal Native Cavalry

*c.*160 Sikhs from disbanded Oudh Irregulars plus recalled pensioners

From 25 September, Havelock and Outram joined the garrison with several Indian and six European infantry units:
5th (Northumberland) Fusiliers
64th Foot (2nd Staffordshire)
78th Highlanders (Ross-shire Buffs)
84th Foot (York & Lancaster)
90th (Perthshire) Light Infantry
EIC Madras Fusiliers

On the 23rd they defeated 11,500 mutineers about 4 miles (6.4 km) south of Lucknow, and their morale was further lifted by news of the recapture of Delhi on 20 September. They now had to plan a route to the Residency in the north of the town that would not trap them in costly street-fighting. This meant taking a canal bridge – in clockface terms, at 7 o'clock to the town; then swinging right to follow the canal through the southeast and eastern outskirts, until they almost reached the Gumtee river (at about 2 o'clock); then wheeling left, to drive westwards through an area of palaces, mosques, and parkland until they reached the Residency (at about 12 o'clock).

The drive into Lucknow on 25 September faced hard fighting from the start, and when they reached the northeast quarter the Kaisarbagh and Manzil palaces had to be taken by bombardment and storming. A final struggle by the 78th Highlanders and 14th Sikhs through the gauntlet of an entrenched and loopholed street past the gaol took many lives, including that of Brigadier James Neill, but at last the relief column and the defenders joined hands at the Baillie Guard Gate; the break-in had cost Havelock and Outram 535 casualties. Meanwhile, at a cost of 244 men (but not a yard of their defences) the garrison had held out not for Lawrence's predicted 20 days, but for 88; now they would have to endure for another 53.

Outram, who now assumed command, did not have enough carts for the sick, wounded and families, nor enough men to escort them. Reinforced by some 2500 bayonets, the garrison could extend the perimeter greatly, and fortify a separate strong complex – the Alambagh, 3 miles (5 km) down the Cawnpore road. The discovery of a secret cache of grain (in puzzling circumstances) provided enough food for them all while they awaited a stronger relief force. The mutineers reimposed the siege, in even greater strength; but although mining and bombardment were frequent, there were no more massed attacks, and communications with the outside were more reliable.

CAMPBELL AND THE FINAL RELIEF

A new commander-in-chief had arrived in India – the great Scottish soldier General Sir Colin Campbell (1792–1863); and on 12 November two columns from Cawnpore and Delhi, totalling about 4500 men, united under his command at the Alambagh. An Irish civilian slipped out in disguise to warn him of the mutineers' deployments, and consequently he chose to loop right around to the east outside the town before driving in through the northeast quarter in the footsteps of Havelock and Outram.

The attack began on 14 November, but it was the 16th before it reached the heavily fortified Secundrabagh palace in the northeast, held by more than 2000 mutineers. This was bombarded, and then stormed by the 4th Punjabis, 53rd Foot and 93rd Highlanders. Pounding on to the west, they took the Shah Najaf mosque, and that evening the garrison saw the 93rd's colours flying from the minaret, just 365 metres (400 yards) away. At 3pm on 17 November the old 32nd Foot Mess building was taken by the 2nd Punjabis, and Captain Garnet Wolseley (1833–1913) then pressed straight on to attack the Moti Mahal palace with soldiers of the 53rd (Shropshires); as they fired into the loopholes an explosion breached its west wall, and a sortie by the garrison's 90th Light Infantry broke through and met them in the smoke and dust. The second relief had cost Campbell 541 casualties.

With Tantia Topi's Gwalior army manoeuvring nearby, Campbell could not tarry. Between 19 and 23 November, 1500 non-combatants and wounded, and all the troops, were smoothly evacuated through leap-frogging rearguards. At the rendezvous in the Dilkusha park, on 24 November, the sick and worn-out General Sir Henry Havelock died, in the knowledge that the defenders of Lucknow were safe at last.

'The rise and fall of empires are not affairs of greased cartridges.'

CONSERVATIVE POLITICIAN BENJAMIN DISRAELI, BLAMING THE MUTINY ON IGNORANT DISREGARD OF INDIAN TRADITIONS (27 JULY 1857)

The campaign that cut the Confederacy in two

VICKSBURG

19 MAY – 4 JULY 1863

*'I cannot, in words, tell you my joy over this result. It is great,
Mr Welles, it is great!'*

PRESIDENT ABRAHAM LINCOLN, ON BEING TOLD BY SECRETARY OF THE NAVY
GIDEON WELLES THE NEWS OF VICTORY AT VICKSBURG ON 4 JULY 1863.

Vicksburg is an example of a siege with a classic purpose – the freeing of a strategically important waterway from interdiction by an enemy fortress. While the Union victory was obviously of immediate value, in retrospect it also became clear that the first week of July 1863 – when the Confederacy suffered two great defeats almost 1000 miles (1600 km) apart – could be seen as the turning-point of the American Civil War. On the same evening that white flags were raised over Vicksburg on the Mississippi, in Pennsylvania far to the northeast General Robert E. Lee's Army of Northern Virginia began their retreat from the bloody field of Gettysburg.

The fall of both Vicksburg and, by rapid consequence, the smaller fortress of Port Hudson above Baton Rouge, gave the North control of the Mississippi from its source to its mouth and cut Texas, Arkansas and western Louisiana off from the rest of the Confederacy. His success there also confirmed the claim of General Ulysses S. Grant to his subsequent supreme command of the Union's armies, which brought the final victory. Famously, when a political spokesman for his jealous rivals tried to persuade President Lincoln to dismiss Grant during the winter of 1862–3, the president replied *'I can't spare this man – he fights'*. Lincoln had great need of a general who might win him a victory: after a year of Union setbacks his political position was weakening, and it was feared that Britain and France might soon recognize the Confederate government of Jefferson Davis.

'THE GIBRALTAR OF THE CONFEDERACY'

Vicksburg, a town of some 5000 people, stood on steep bluffs about 60 metres (200 ft) above the east bank of the Mississippi, roughly 300 miles (480 km) as the river turns north of its mouth on the Gulf of Mexico. It was an important trading centre with rail links to the north, east and south, and a hub of the covert supply route via Mexico – increasingly vital to the Confederacy, given the tightening US Navy blockade of the Atlantic and Gulf coasts. The wide river itself made attack from the west impossible, and the surrounding countryside in all other directions was an overgrown wilderness cut by many waterways. When Grant was given command of the Union Army of the Tennessee in October 1862 his operations were constrained by great difficulties in moving his troops across country.

A maze of gulleys and high ridges around Vicksburg provided ideal vantage points for its defenders to repulse attacking Union troops. This unsigned contemporary print depicts an assault in which both sides are using grenades.

TIMELINE

1859 Convention at Vicksburg demands the resumption of slave imports to the USA, banned since 1807

1860 Abraham Lincoln wins the US presidential election

1861 American Civil War begins with Confederate bombardment of Fort Sumter, South Carolina

1862 Battle of Antietam in Maryland checks Confederate advance on the northern states

1863 Fall of Vicksburg in Mississippi and victory at the Battle of Gettysburg in Pennsylvania turn the tide of war irrevocably in favour of the Union

1864 General Sherman's 'March to the Sea' drives deep into Confederate territory, destroying Atlanta and capturing Savannah

1865 (April) Confederate forces surrender at Appomattox, bringing the American Civil War to an end

The fortification of Vicksburg was supervised from June 1862 by a 25-year-old engineer, Major Samuel H. Lockett, who had been a star of his class at West Point. Troops and plantation slaves built a 9-mile (15-km) circuit of defences, mostly along a high, curving ridge 1–2 miles (1.6–3.2 km) outside the city, and anchored on the Mississippi at each end. Lockett tied his redoubts, entrenchments and gun batteries into many natural obstacles. The yellow clay soil dug and packed well; the complexes of earth ramparts – up to 7.6 metres (25 ft) thick, and fronted with ditches up to 3 metres (10 ft) deep by 5.5 metres (18 ft) wide – were enhanced with log palisades, gabions, fascines and sandbags, and the plentiful cotton bales from Vicksburg's wharfs; internal trenches and 'bombproof' shelters protected the troops manning them. Spaced along the landward front were 77 positions mounting 102 cannon, with ten major forts commanding the six roads and one rail track leading into the city; strongpoints every few hundred yards were linked by trenches and belts of rifle-pits. The perimeter was almost continuous, and the fields of fire overlapped to cover every approach. The 3-mile (5-km) riverside had another 13 batteries mounting 50 guns, to prevent Union shipping passing below.

GRANT'S MANOEUVRES

In late 1862 Grant began a march southwards from Memphis, Tennessee, coupled with an amphibious thrust by General William T. Sherman's corps to the confluence of the Mississippi and Yazoo rivers about 7 miles (11 km) north of Vicksburg. This attempt to force the Confederate General John C. Pemberton to withdraw or divide his forces north of the city was frustrated by Rebel cavalry raids on Union supply lines. In late March 1863 Grant's army was stuck on the west bank of the Mississippi about 20 miles (32 km) north of Vicksburg, while he needed it on the east. A small force managed to march down the west bank to New Carthage, below Vicksburg; and Admiral David Porter offered to take his flotilla south past the city's guns to meet the troops and carry them across to the east bank.

At the cost of much hard labour Grant's army reached New Carthage by the end of April. Meanwhile, under heavy fire, Admiral Porter had stormed south past Vicksburg on the night of

16–17 April, and on the night of 22–23 April repeated the feat with a supply convoy. On 30 April the first 20,000 of Grant's troops were landed unopposed on the east bank at Bruinsburg.

THE BIG BLACK RIVER CAMPAIGN

Grant now outmanoeuvred both Pemberton and his theatre commander General Joseph E. Johnston further off to the northeast, by a stroke of Napoleonic audacity. Sherman made feints south from the Yazoo to hold Pemberton's attention, while Colonel Benjamin Grierson's cavalry were sent rampaging for 600 miles (965 km) through the Confederate rear. Grant knew he had to defeat Pemberton's 25,000 men around Vicksburg, and Johnston's unknown strength at Jackson, separately; so he deliberately force-marched his army to the northeast of Vicksburg and got between them, risking an advance without a secure supply line (he never even told his nervous superiors in Washington of his plan). His men marched very light, living off the country, while a single road was maintained to bring up ammunition and minimal provisions. The plan worked brilliantly: Johnston's communications with Pemberton had been cut before he reached Jackson on 13 May with only 6000 men, and the next day Grant routed him and drove him north.

Then Grant turned west for Vicksburg; confronted by Pemberton holding a strong position at Champion Hill on 16 May, he still bundled the Confederates back with heavy casualties. By 19 May, when Pemberton fell back within the Vicksburg defences, Grant's troops had already inflicted some 12,000 casualties for a loss of about 4400 of their own. Johnston at once sent word that Pemberton should abandon Vicksburg, but President Davis ordered that it be held.

THE ENTRENCHMENTS

Now Grant was back in safe contact with his supply lines, with naval flotillas on the Mississippi and Yazoo, while Pemberton was almost encircled. In all, the Union army was spread over some 15 miles (24 km) from the Yazoo down to the Mississippi south of the city, but the actual entrenchments were about 9 miles (15 km) long. Like Lockett's, they were earthworks revetted and sheltered with

'THE ANACONDA PLAN'

Winfield Scott (1786–1866), the former US Army general-in-chief, was 75 years old in January 1861 when he was recalled from retirement to advise President Lincoln; he had battlefield experience stretching back to the days of Napoleon, and had led the successful advance from Veracruz to Mexico City in 1847. Scott advocated ignoring the clamour for an advance on the Confederate capital of Richmond, Virginia, in favour of an 'Anaconda Plan' that would divide and squeeze the Rebel states by gaining control of the Mississippi Valley. His plan was rejected; but although he retired on grounds of ill-health that October, he lived long enough to see the soundness of his strategy recognized and followed to success by Ulysses S. Grant.

logs, gabions, fascines, cotton bales and planking from dismantled houses. Sherman's XV Corps held the short right-hand sector, north of the Graveyard Road, where they would also be responsible for guarding against interference by Johnston; on their left the line south to near the Baldwin's Ferry Road was held by General James Birdseye McPherson's XVII Corps. These were two of the most capable and admired generals in the Union armies. However, the longest sector in the south was held by XIII Corps under General John A. McClernand, an incompetent braggart who owed his rank solely to political influence. Although he had four divisions, there would remain a four-mile (6.4-km) gap in the Union investment along the southern riverbank, through which Rebel parties could slip in and out until mid-June, when the arrival of Herron's and Lauman's divisions finally closed it.

These reinforcements raised Grant's strength from about 50,000 to 71,000 men, of whom 30,000 could then be faced to the northeast to guard against any move by Johnston, who was trying to scrape an army together 30 miles (48 km) away. By the end of June, Grant had 248 guns in some 90 batteries; though most were lighter field pieces, Admiral Porter did land some heavy naval guns and crews.

Within Vicksburg, only some 18,500 of Pemberton's roughly 31,000 men were 'effectives' available to hold the perimeter; still, Major Lockett's defences inspired confidence. One Union officer reported his first sight of them: '*A long line of high, rugged irregular bluffs ... crowned with cannon ... to the right and left as far as the eye could see. Lines of heavy rifle pits, surmounted with head logs, ran along*

LIEUTENANT-GENERAL ULYSSES S. GRANT (1822–85)

Grant had entered West Point unwillingly; he did well in the Mexican War, but in 1854 was persuaded – by boredom, separation from his family and a reprimand for heavy drinking – to resign his commission. As a brigadier-general of volunteers he earned praise for capturing Forts Henry and Donelson on the Tennessee and Cumberland rivers in February 1862 – the latter campaign involved overcoming difficult terrain and co-operating with Navy river craft. Although badly mauled at Shiloh in April 1862, that October he was given command of the Union Army of the Tennessee.

Initially an unambitious officer, disdained as dull and 'ordinary' by more glittering products of West Point, Ulysses Grant was practical, energetic, determined, tenacious, brave and humane; his common-sense plans and clear orders earned him the trust of his subordinates, and his modesty and decency their loyal affection. His Big Black River campaign in April–May 1863 laid the sure foundation for his success in the siege of Vicksburg.

Grant went on to lift the siege of Chattanooga in October 1863, and to destroy Braxton Bragg's army at Lookout Mountain and Missionary Ridge the following month; promoted to lieutenant-general, he was then transferred east and appointed the Union general-in-chief. Robert E. Lee and his Army of Northern Virginia were still formidable; but in April 1865 the man who had taken Vicksburg for President Lincoln brought the war to an end at Appomattox.

Major Confederate positions

River batteries with heavy guns:

(A) Upper Water Battery

(B) Wyman's Hill Battery

(C) Marine Hospital Battery

Landward forts, each usually with a few field guns, and infantry garrison from listed units:

(1) Fort Hill (Vaughn's Tennessee brigade)

(2) 26th Louisiana Redoubt

(3) Stockade Redan (large complex; units from Cockrell's & Green's brigades of Gen. Bowen's Missouri & Arkansas division, and Hebert's mainly Mississippi & Louisiana brigade of Forney's division)

(4) 3rd Louisiana Redan

(5) 21st Louisiana Redan, or 'Great Redoubt'

(6) 2nd Texas Lunette

(7) Railroad Redoubt, or 'Fort Pettus' (Alabama units & Texas Legion from Stevenson's division)

(8) Square Fort, or 'Fort Garrott' (20th Alabama)

(9) Salient Work, or Horn Work (57th Georgia)

(10) South Fort (Georgia & Tennessee units from Reynolds' & Barton's brigades)

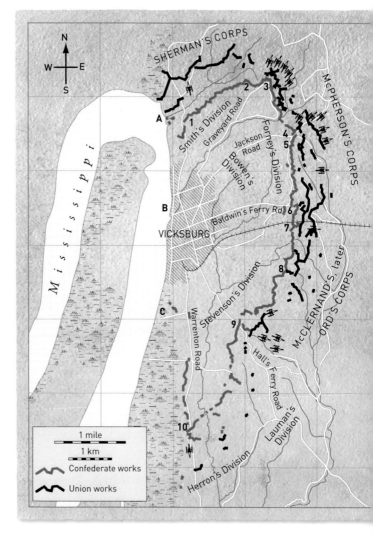

the bluffs connecting fort with fort ... The approaches to this position were frightful – enough to appal the stoutest heart.' The defenders' northern sector, from the riverbank to the Graveyard Road, was entrusted to General Martin Luther Smith's division, with three brigades from Mississippi, Louisiana and Tennessee; the centre, from Graveyard Road to the Alabama & Vicksburg Railroad, was held by General John H. Forney's division, with two brigades of Mississippi, Louisiana and Alabama regiments, plus the 2nd Texas. Both these divisions were relatively fresh; General John S. Bowen's tired Missouri and Arkansas division was placed in reserve behind Forney, to send forward reinforcements as needed. In the south, from the railroad down to South Fort, General Carter L. Stevenson had four brigades from Georgia, Alabama and Tennessee.

THE ASSAULTS

Initially Grant tried to take Vicksburg by assault, but on 19 May a first attempt around the Stockade Redan failed at the cost of 1000 casualties. A second, launched on 22 May after a heavy bombardment, was much more ambitious: 35,000 men of all three corps attacked nearly 3 miles (5 km) of the defences between the Stockade Redan and South Fort. The broken terrain forced them to attack on narrow ridges between the gullies, exposing them to murderous fire; although some got into the ditches at the foot of the enemy ramparts, the attempt finally failed with 500 killed and 2700 wounded. Many casualties could have been avoided had General McClernand not sent a misleading and premature report of success; the heroic Iowa soldiers of Lawler's brigade had indeed broken into the Railroad Redoubt, but could not hold it against a Texan counterattack. (Grant finally dismissed McClernand on 18 June, replacing him with his deputy General E.O.C. Ord.)

Accepting that there was no quick solution, Grant patiently settled down for a siege; its progress to final success was entirely conventional, with few outstanding incidents. These included the detonation of a Union mine under part of the 3rd Louisiana Redoubt on 25 June; but the garrison, forewarned, had pulled back to interior defences before it was blown, so Leggett's brigade of General John A. Logan's division could not fight their way beyond the crater. (A second mine detonated on 1 July achieved no significant results.)

THE SIEGE

Grant's men broke ground some 550 metres (600 yds) from the defences, and at 14 points protected saps were steadily driven forward, to be linked by a web of parallels, 'bombproofs' and gun emplacements. By 3 June, Sherman's sharpshooters were already sniping gun crews in the Upper Water Battery; the next day some saps were within 137 metres (150 yds) of the defences, and by the 8th a couple of them were within 27 metres (30 yds). There were few Confederate sorties, but sniping was constant and deadly, and in close encounters both sides exchanged improvised hand grenades. Their scant numbers compared with the length of their perimeter meant that – unlike their attackers – Confederate units were never relieved from the trenches to rest.

The Union artillery bombardment only slackened three times daily at mealtimes, and at night the Rebels had to stay on the alert against attacks. They – and the town's civilians – took cover when they could in 'rat holes' dug in reverse slopes; few civilians were killed, but many houses were

SNIPERS

Sharpshooters caused many casualties on both sides. One famous Rebel sniper was the one-eyed Private Elliott of the 30th Alabama, at the Square Fort, who it was claimed could drop a Yankee at 915 metres (1000 yds) with his Belgian rifle. Opposite the 3rd Louisiana Redan a Union sniper, Lt. Henry C. Foster of the 23rd Indiana, was called 'Coonskin' from his distinctive cap; he eventually built a timber tower armoured with railroad iron and fitted with an angled mirror to peer behind the Rebel ramparts. In the Stockade Redan, Confederate Gen. Martin E. Green was killed by a Federal sniper shortly after declaring *a bullet has not yet been molded that can kill me*.

HUNGER

Although the garrison reportedly began the siege with stores for 60 days, these ran short 12 days' sooner. In early June the daily ration was about 142 grams (5 oz) of dried peas, 284 grams (10 oz) of cornmeal, 227 grams (8 oz) of meat (bones included), with a little lard, salt and sugar. Coffee soon ran out, and Confederate sentries would trade tobacco for it with Union pickets. On 15 June, Gen. Pemberton wrote to Gen. Johnston that on reduced rations he could hold out another 20 days – an accurate forecast. The engineer Maj. Lockett wrote that for several days before the surrender on 4 July the garrison had been on quarter-rations only. The town's civilians also went hungry, and in June butchers were selling horse, mule, dog and rat meat. Bread was made of equal parts cornmeal and dried peas, which according to one contemporary commentator, '... *had the properties of india-rubber and was worse than leather to digest'*.

burned down or damaged by shells and mortar bombs. For their part, the Union front-line infantry had to dig tunnels through the bluffs to reach their rifle-pits safely, and most movement was carried out in silence and under cover of darkness. By night the sentries of both sides were so close that they could chat and even make small trades; by common consent, they were not fired upon.

For the defenders – increasingly tired, hungry and thinned by disease – the ordeal was drearily repetitive, day after baking day, night after chilling night. To their officers they showed a stoic cheerfulness, but with little hope of any rescue they became increasingly despondent. Pemberton set little store by Johnston's promises of relief, including a message in late June that Johnston was approaching the Big Black river and hoped to reach him on 6 July; from early in the siege Pemberton had doubted that his men had the energy left for a break-out, and this was now doubly true. In the event Johnston's force was too small and too hesitant to present any real threat to Grant's strong reserves. It was 6 July that had been chosen for a final assault on Vicksburg, but this proved unnecessary: on the evening of 3 July two Confederate officers rode out under white flags to parley.

Grant and Pemberton – who had known each other in the Mexican War – met between the lines. Pemberton tried to bluff, but the only concession that Grant would agree was to allow the disarmed garrison to go home under parole; he believed that most of them would probably be happy to keep their written oath and drift off home. On the national holiday of 4 July 1863, after a brief ceremony, General Logan's division took possession of Vicksburg – with about 29,500 prisoners, 170 guns and 60,000 rifles. Confederate casualties during the siege had been nearly 2900 – many fewer than the 4900 Federal losses, nearly all suffered in the abortive assaults of 19 and 22 May.

PARIS

A besieged city's ordeal arouses international public opinion

20 September 1870–26 January 1871

'*The sufferings of Paris during the siege? A joke for two months; but in the third month the joke turned sour. Now nobody finds it amusing any longer, and we are moving rapidly towards starvation.*'

EDMOND GONCOURT, DIARY ENTRY (7 JANUARY 1871)

The siege of Paris was prosecuted with military efficiency by General Helmuth von Moltke's Prussian-led German forces, steered by Chancellor Otto von Bismarck; nevertheless, it had more significance as a political than as a military episode. The technical means and tactical methods employed by both sides had not changed since Vicksburg a few years beforehand; but the spectacle of the citizens of this glittering European capital reduced to eating dogs and rats, under indiscriminate shellfire – a spectacle broadcast by foreign journalists and private correspondents caught up in the siege – had a 'real-time' effect on overseas public opinion. Such civilian sufferings had been a commonplace of urban sieges throughout history, but now they seemed to many a barbaric anachronism. In a period when international attempts to limit the horrors of war were gaining support, they caused sufficiently widespread revulsion to reverse the sympathies of many who read about them.

Many foreign commentators had felt sympathy with Prussia when, on 19 July 1870, the French emperor Napoleon III declared war with irresponsible haste and little cause, and von Moltke's destruction or encirclement of France's vainglorious armies within just six weeks seemed a kind of poetic justice. However, during the subsequent siege sympathy turned instinctively towards the underdog: Prussian intransigence seemed cruelly excessive, and a worrying harbinger of what a unified Germany with a militarist government might mean for Europe as a whole. This sympathy would soon be complicated by horror at the French government's bloody crushing of the insurrection by the Commune of Paris in May 1871 – an insurrection that was a direct consequence of the Prussian siege.

THE FALL OF THE EMPIRE

Since Bismarck's long-term goal of unifying Germany under Prussian leadership made conflict inevitable at some point, he cleverly isolated France diplomatically while manipulating French public opinion into feverish demands for a premature war. In summer 1870 the French military proved themselves hopelessly outclassed in organization, staff work and operational leadership.

An unsigned contemporary illustration from the *Illustrated London News* shows German troops and French civilians watching a balloon escape from Paris.

TIMELINE

1851 Louis Napoleon stages a coup d'état to install himself as Emperor Napoleon III of France

1862 Bismarck appointed prime minister of Prussia

1866 Prussia crushes Austria in the Seven Weeks' War

1870 Bismarck engineers the outbreak of the Franco-Prussian War; von Moltke's forces swiftly overrun French army and lay siege to Paris

1871 (January) German Second Empire is established under Prussian leadership

1871 (February) Peace of Versailles ends the Franco-Prussian War

1871 (May) Thousands killed as French government forces under General MacMahon crush the Paris Commune

Their soldiers fought bravely when given opportunities to do so, and made the Prussians pay a high price in lives; but their leaders mostly allowed themselves to be herded blindly around the countryside by the German generals until their armies could be taken apart with surgical precision. By mid-August one of the two French field armies was trapped and inactive at Metz; and at Sedan, on 2 September, Napoleon himself was taken captive with more than 100,000 men of the second.

Three days later his empire fell, and a Third French Republic was proclaimed, with General Jules-Louis Trochu, the military governor of Paris, as president of a provisional Government of National Defence (based partly in Paris and partly at Tours). Foreign Minister Jules Favre attempted to secure a peace settlement without making territorial concessions, but in vain. Although many French citadels still held out, and 200,000 German troops were tied down around Metz, General von Moltke continued to drive a broad corridor across northern France; its eventual borders would be roughly a line through Sedan and Amiens in the north, and through Dijon and Orléans in the south.

By 17 September, German patrols were on the outskirts of Paris; the next day a thrust out of the city towards the approaching German southern pincer, by some 28,000 French troops, was driven back. On 20 September cavalry of the Army of the Meuse and the Third Army linked up at Versailles, encircling Paris from the north and south respectively. Over the following weeks some 206,000 infantry, 34,000 cavalry and 1100 guns established a discontinuous 50-mile (80-km) 'Iron Ring' of entrenched positions and batteries, commanding the city and its approaches from distances of between 2 and 6 miles (3.2–10 km) from the walls. Large numbers of these troops were set to gathering in the harvest from the autumn fields as the Prussians settled down to wait.

THE WALLS AND THEIR DEFENDERS

The city of Paris measured only about 7 miles by 6 miles (11 x 10 km), with a population of some 2 million enclosed within its ramparts. These had been built in the 1840s by King Louis-Philippe's prime minister Adolphe Thiers, and were of formidable strength. An outer ring of major artillery forts had been built between 1 and 3 miles (1.6–5 km) outside the ramparts, around all except the

BALLOONS AND PIGEONS

The air link between Paris and the outside world was the first example of the 'third dimension' that would play a central part in sieges from the 1940s onwards. Seven man-carrying balloons were found in the city, and soon many others were being manufactured under the high roofs of the disused railway stations. Since silk was unobtainable they were made of varnished cotton, and filled with highly inflammable coal-gas – the crews risked a terrible death if Prussian sharpshooters hit them, but only five of 65 balloons launched fell into enemy hands, and only two balloonists died. The balloons were at the mercy of the winds, but they successfully carried out of the city 164 passengers, 381 homing pigeons and nearly 11 tons of messages including some 2.5 million letters, providing the outside world with a commentary on events and conditions. The pigeons released to return to Paris were less successful – out of 302 attempts, only 59 reached their lofts – but these carried extraordinarily long miniaturized texts ingeniously printed on collodion membranes. This tenuous link allowed Trochu to receive tantalizing fragments of information about the operations of the provincial armies.

northwest quadrant, to keep enemy guns out of range of the city itself. The ramparts themselves were massive earthworks faced with masonry walls, inside a ditch 9 metres (30 ft) deep and 14 metres (45 ft) across; 94 bastions for artillery studded this belt, commanding the glacis and approaches. Both sides understood that Paris, if strongly garrisoned, was a fortress-city that could defy any realistically possible Prussian assault attempt – and on paper, at least, her garrison was about twice the strength of the besieging army.

The regular troops were provided by General Vinoy's XIII Corps and part of XIV Corps, plus some 3000 from I Corps led by General Ducrot, and a division of about 8000 naval troops. All but two of the 30-odd army infantry regiments were second-line, assembled from the depot battalions of many different units and filled out with reservists and volunteers; nevertheless, reinforced by a few battalions of gendarmes, this Second Army gave Trochu perhaps 75,000 trained and disciplined infantry. But the bulk of his manpower was far less impressive. About 20,000 of them were Gardes Mobiles raised in the Seine region – territorials who elected their own officers, and who boasted at most a few weeks of disjointed pre-war training. These Parisian 'Mobiles' had already shown themselves to be undisciplined and unreliable, but they were better than the third and largest part of the garrison.

AN UNCERTAIN MILITIA
In the weeks before the siege began the Garde Nationale de Paris had grown exponentially, from about 24,000 to more than 330,000 men. In early September, France and her new Republican government had imagined that the fall of the empire would persuade the Prussians simply to go

home, without exacting any further punishment. When this was revealed as a delusion, the country rallied behind the Republic and prepared to fight on: the conflict changed from being an Imperial adventure to a people's war. Parisians flocked to enlist in district National Guard units; but many from the hungry workers' quarters joined mainly for the pay and rations, and most guardsmen received no meaningful training whatever. They too elected their own officers; these were of very variable quality, ranging from courageous and knowledgeable former regular soldiers to political revolutionaries and shady opportunists.

Eventually, the Paris National Guard would form 236 small 'war battalions' of the younger men, with a total strength of about 104,000, backed by a 'sedentary' reserve of some 227,000 more. Many units were outspokenly hostile to the 'quitters' of the Imperial army, and resented any attempt to bring them under proper military control; most National Guard units were negligent and drunken, and some actually mutinous. They could be employed, at best, for manning static defences and checkpoints.

While labourers strengthened the ramparts, Trochu took stock of his resources. The capital did at least have large arsenals and many factories, and rifles and ammunition (though of varied and sometimes obsolete patterns) were available for most of the National Guard. The forts and bastions mounted nearly 2000 cannon of various models, mostly bronze muzzle-loaders with ranges of up to 3500 metres (3800 yds). Food stocks also seemed adequate; during September and October much had been brought into the city, including livestock – 40,000 cattle and 250,000 sheep grazed in the Bois de Boulogne. Trochu calculated that he had enough supplies to last 80 days, until early December. Nevertheless, by early October the bourgeoisie were already beginning to eat horsemeat – then only recently introduced by Parisian butchers as cheap food for poverty-stricken workers.

COMMUNICATIONS BY AIR

Many Parisians were confident of relief, despite the virtual destruction of the French regular army; the provisional government energetically began raising new armies of raw conscripts in both the north and the south, hoping to punch through to link up with a break-out by the Paris garrison. Trochu – an able analyst, if an uninspiring leader – was less optimistic; but at least rudimentary co-ordination would be possible. On 23 September a balloonist named Durouf launched from the city and landed at Evreux 3 hours later, carrying a 113-kilogram (250-lb) cargo of despatches, and others soon followed his example. The prevailing winds and lack of control prevented balloons from flying back into the city; but some took carrier pigeons out, and soon a fragile two-way communications link was established between Trochu and the Tours government.

On 7 October the interior minister, the charismatic young lawyer Léon Gambetta, was flown out to Tours, where his energy would do much to accelerate the raising of the provincial armies. Soon facing a threat of interference from the new Army of the Loire to his south, with guerrilla *francs-tireurs* harassing his lines of communication, and needing to maintain the two major sieges of Paris and Metz simultaneously, von Moltke could do little more than keep a tight grip on the captured territory, mop up bypassed garrisons and guard against any sorties from Paris.

THE SORTIES OF OCTOBER

From the start, Trochu faced political unrest by Parisian factions determined to influence his command decisions, who used their allies in the National Guard as leverage. Some of these radicals, innately hostile to all things military, still believed the old revolutionary myth of the irresistible power of the *levée en masse* – the illusion that free patriots did not need formal training or staff organization, but could throw back invaders by their sheer ardour and solidarity. They frequently demanded that Trochu show more aggressiveness, urging sorties in which he had little faith and which had no discernible military object beyond harassing the besiegers.

A first attempt on 30 September had been stopped dead by the quicker-firing, longer-ranged Prussian artillery; but on 13 October, Trochu ordered General Vinoy to plan another, towards Châtillon and Bagneux to the south. It was launched on the 19th; many Mobiles were too busy electing their officers to take part, and after some initial success this glorified raid was abandoned. Trochu ordered General Ducrot to mount a larger-scale attack on 21 October, to break through in the west at St Cloud and on towards Bougival some 4 miles (6.4 km) beyond the Seine. Again, this made some progress, up the slopes to Bouzenval; the village was captured and held against a counter-attack, but then had to be abandoned (though the retreat was carried out in good order).

Vinoy's troops were simply unequal to holding off concentrated German counter-attacks outside the range of the city's guns, and his Mobiles usually disintegrated under fire; the civilians

BOILED HOOVES AND ELEPHANT À LA CARTE

Food became seriously short for all classes from mid-November, and the poor were suffering outright famine by December. Although soup-kitchens were set up to feed them, and there was an official meat ration (on 1 October, 900 g/32 oz daily per person, but halved by 26 October), there was no overall control of food distribution, so wealth or poverty decided who ate and who went hungry. Butchers advertised themselves as 'canine and feline specialists'; a genuine rabbit cost 30 francs – about 8 days' wages, at the workman's average of around 4 francs per day – and people made increasingly thin soup from bones, hooves and offal. Fat rats sold for 1.5 francs each, and vegetables became so scarce that a cabbage cost 50 francs. Ruthless speculators hoarded all food stocks to send prices higher, releasing them at times of encouraging rumours of relief, only to withdraw them again when these were disappointed. But while those poor who were not supported by National Guard allowances faced starvation, the wealthy still ate – and often exotic fare, such as the slaughtered animals from the zoo. Elephant meat was sold, as was antelope, ostrich and giraffe; reportedly, nobody could face the monkeys (too much like human babies), and no butcher could afford the hippopotamus.

One thing that never ran short was alcohol, and many Parisians tried to dull their hunger and despair by getting dead drunk as often as possible.

were unable to grasp this, and the regulars in their turn bitterly resented the insults of militiamen who stayed safely inside the walls. Morale plunged when news of the surrender of Marshal Bazaine's army at Metz on 27 October reached the city – a disaster that freed 100,000 Germans of the Second Army to move against the Army of the Loire, while others reinforced the Iron Ring. It was also on 27 October that a raid northeastwards from Paris overwhelmed a small enemy force at Le Bourget; this was hailed in the streets as a great victory – but on 30 October a counter-attack retook the village and inflicted 1200 French casualties. On 31 October revolutionary guardsmen burst into Trochu's headquarters in the Hôtel de Ville, holding him a virtual captive and abusing him for some hours.

THE FALSE HOPES OF NOVEMBER

A hastily organized plebiscite endorsed Trochu's authority; and before long, despite the growing hunger in the city, morale was lifted by the news of an unaccustomed French victory. On 9 November the raw Army of the Loire had defeated a Bavarian corps (which they outnumbered three to one) at Coulmiers, and was able to re-occupy Orléans. Although Paris is 70 miles (112 km) from Orléans, political activists demanded a break-out to the southeast to link up. Trochu had been planning a sortie through what he believed to be a weak point in the ring, northwest towards Rouen, but he could not resist the pressure to alter his preparations.

The attack would be towards the strongest Prussian defences, across the River Marne (then in winter flood). An attempt to warn Gambetta to co-ordinate operations by the Army of the Loire was not made until 24 November, just four days before the planned attack. The balloon carrying the despatch was blown so far off course that it eventually landed in Norway (the despatch bag, jettisoned over the sea to save weight, was – miraculously – found and delivered to Tours, but far too late). The 'Great Sortie' went ahead on 28–30 November, with Trochu and Ducrot leading 80,000 men out past Fort Vincennes towards Champigny and Villiers. They crossed the Marne on the 30th, and held their bridgehead against the initial counter-attacks; but again the Prussian artillery proved too strong, forcing them back across the river on 3 December with 12,000 casualties. (At least a net gain of some 600 captured horses meant five days' meat supply for the city's butchers.)

THE DISAPPOINTMENTS OF DECEMBER

The supreme effort had been pointless, anyway: simultaneously, General d'Aurelle's Army of the Loire had been defeated at Loigny near Orléans, and the Prussians retook the city, forcing the provisional government to withdraw to Bordeaux. The Army of the Loire was driven back in two separate halves; eventually General Bourbaki took part of it east to try to relieve the besieged frontier fortress of Belfort, while General Chanzy's dangerously outnumbered force manoeuvred south of besieged Paris, mesmerized by its symbolic significance. An Army of the North had also entered the fray by now, but after some initial successes had been defeated at Amiens on 27 November. Von Moltke's troops, like the French, would soon be suffering heavy losses from sickness and exposure in this harshest winter in living memory; but he no longer faced any credible threat of interference in his siege from Gambetta's brave but incompetent armies of barely trained conscripts.

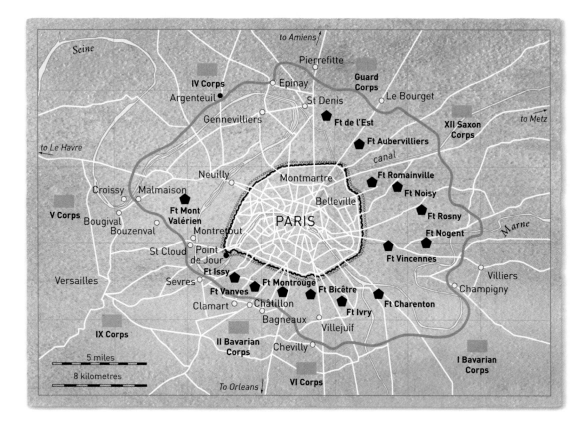

Map of the siege of Paris, showing the investiture of the French capital and its main outlying forts by von Moltke's infantry and artillery.

On 21–22 December the garrison mounted yet another attack, by 50,000 men against the whole northeast quadrant of the siege lines, with feints in other directions. Since some units emerged on the 20th and lit their overnight campfires around the forts, the Prussians were ready for them. French artillery in the forts and with the infantry duelled with Saxon field batteries, and the major fighting took place around the loopholed houses of Le Bourget. Both sides suffered from the hard-frozen ground and extreme cold, and in the end nothing significant was achieved: harassing the besiegers paid no real dividends without a strategic goal in view, and there was no chance now of linking with General Faidherbe's Army of the North.

As the sortie fell back on 22 December, Trochu informed the Bordeaux government that the city had only enough food until 20 January. During the week ending 17 December deaths rose to 2728 – more than twice the normal rate for that month, and including disproportionate numbers of children. A balloon letter reported a ration equivalent to 30 grams (1oz) of horsemeat per head per day, or salt fish in lieu, and that no supplements were now to be found at any price. The trees felled in the Bois de Boulogne before the siege had all been burnt, and in a month so cold that the Seine froze over the shortage of fuel was lethal for people weakened by hunger, pneumonia and typhoid.

THE COMMUNE: THE SECOND SIEGE AND 'BLOODY WEEK'

Incensed by the surrender terms agreed by the Thiers government, socialist, revolutionary and simply patriotic groups in Paris backed the National Guard when it refused to be disarmed. In mid-March 1871 the government and army withdrew from the city to Versailles, and Paris declared itself a self-governing Commune. On 3 April a National Guard march on Versailles was driven back in disorder, and regular officers shot some prisoners out of hand; the Commune arrested hostages, and a spiral of bitterness spun into mutual terrorism. With German agreement, Thiers built up an army of 100,000 (mostly unwilling) regulars led by Marshal MacMahon; the city was again shelled from mid-April, and on 21 May troops entered through an unguarded gate at the Point du Jour. Only a few thousand of the 200,000-odd National Guards actually fought at their barricades; their political and military leadership was hopelessly disorganized and disunited, and the army – advancing carefully behind artillery support, to minimize their casualties – captured the last eastern slums of Belleville on 28 May. Both sides committed atrocities during this 'Bloody Week' (*la semaine sanglante*): the Communards murdered hostages and burned down much of the city centre, and the army carried out widespread summary executions. The army lost about 1000 dead, the Communards at least 20,000, most of them after capture.

JANUARY: BOMBARDMENT AND DESPAIR

General von Moltke was coming under increasing pressure from Bismarck to take more active steps to bring the siege to a close, and from 5 January 1871 the previously intermittent and focused German bombardment was extended from the forts to the city itself. At a rate of some 500 shells every 24 hours, about 12,000 would fall inside Paris, night and day, during the next three weeks. Around 1400 buildings were damaged, mainly in the southwest; only 97 people were killed and 278 wounded, and the experience seems to have toughened rather than sapped civilian morale. However, foreign newspaper readers were horrified by stories of children in the streets and sick in the hospitals being blown to pieces.

Between 7 and 12 January, Chanzy's Army of the Loire was driven back yet again, and for good, in the battle of Le Mans. On the 19th the Army of the North – which had achieved some limited success early in the month – was finally defeated at St Quentin. In the east, Bourbaki's Second Army of the Loire was broken at Héricourt outside Belfort on 15–17 January; when the Prussian pursuit closed in on the 26th, Bourbaki shot himself (incompetently), and the survivors of his army straggled over the frontier into Swiss internment. On 18 January, in an act of calculated humiliation, Bismarck proclaimed King Wilhelm I of Prussia the emperor of the new German

Reich, in the Gallery of Mirrors at the Palace of Versailles. The reaction of the Parisian politicians was a frenzied demand that Trochu make another sortie.

This pointless spasm of hatred took place on 19 January, when Generals Vinoy, Ducrot and Bellemarre led about 90,000 men westwards to attack the Bouzenval heights yet again, in freezing fog. For the first time large numbers of National Guards were included in the mixed columns with the regulars and Mobiles. Yet again the French made initial progress, and yet again they were driven back; General von Kirchbach's V Corps did not even need the help of the alerted Bavarian reserves. Trochu estimated that about 400 of the 3000 casualties were caused by National Guards firing into the backs of men ahead of them.

The will of the provisional government to continue the war now collapsed – as did all discipline in Paris, where news of Chanzy's defeat at Le Mans was published on the 20th (and where the death toll rose to 4500 in this final week). Trochu, his authority destroyed, resigned as governor in favour of General Vinoy. On 22 January revolutionary National Guards traded volleys with Mobiles guarding the Hôtel de Ville; the next day Foreign Minister Favre sought talks with Bismarck. An armistice was signed on 26 January, and French capitulation came into force at midnight on the 27th. Prussia's peace terms were signed at Versailles on 26 February by the new government of Adolphe Thiers; they included the ceding to Germany of Alsace and part of Lorraine, and payment of a huge indemnity. They also insisted on a gesture which cut Parisians to the heart: on 1 March 1871, some 30,000 German troops paraded in triumph down the Champs-Élysées.

'But the ghastliest sight in Père-Lachaise [cemetery] was in the south-eastern corner, where, close to the boundary wall, there had been a natural hollow. The hollow was now filled up by dead ... There they lay, tier above tier, each successive tier powdered over with a coating of chloride of lime – two hundred of them patent to the eye, besides those underneath hidden by the earth covering layer after layer. Among the dead were many women.'

SCOTTISH WAR CORRESPONDENT ARCHIBALD FORBES ON THE EXECUTION OF PARISIAN
COMMUNARDS, IN *THE DAILY NEWS* (26 MAY 1871)

The 'Rats' who clung on behind Rommel's shoulder TOBRUK

10 April–7 December 1941

'*The Australians fought with remarkable tenacity. Even their wounded went on defending themselves with small-arms fire, and stayed in the fight until their last breath. They were immensely big and powerful men, who without question represented an élite formation of the British empire.*'

LIEUTENANT-GENERAL ERWIN ROMMEL (WRITING OF HIS ATTACKS ON TOBRUK OF 30 APRIL–3 MAY 1941)

Tobruk – a purely military siege, with no significant civilian involvement – was a prime example of the defence of a strategic harbour, which offered a base for operations against the enemy's lines of supply passing its landward defences. Holding it in 1941 also helped prevent an Axis invasion of nearby Malta, from which British aircraft and submarines were ravaging Rommel's seaborne supply lines from Italy to North Africa. Its retention, behind his 'left shoulder' during his lunges eastwards towards Egypt and the Suez Canal, divided his forces at a time when the main British and Dominion army there was relatively weak and badly led. Its story is somewhat akin to that of Gibraltar, with repeated relief by the Royal Navy, and sorties out of the perimeter.

'SIEGE WARFARE' SINCE 1870

Conflicts after 1870 offer many dramatic but conventional stories of small colonial garrisons cut off by non-European enemies (or by rival colonists, in the case of Ladysmith and Mafeking during the Second Anglo-Boer War). One siege on a huge scale – that of Port Arthur during the Russo-Japanese War (1904–05) – seems in retrospect to prefigure the static horrors of the Great War. When that unique catastrophe arrived it produced, at Kut el-Amara in Iraq (1916), one textbook case: a garrison whose fate was sealed by the inability of a relieving British/Indian force to fight its way through a skilfully deployed Turkish 'circumvallation'.

On the Western Front the fighting from 1915 to 1917 in many ways resembled one vast, linear siege. It was specifically in order to avoid repeating that unparalleled carnage that armies – most notably, the German *Wehrmacht* – developed during the 1930s a doctrine of fast, mobile warfare (*Blitzkrieg*) spearheaded by the new generation of tanks and ground-attack aircraft. This involved seizing vital choke-points by sudden coups-de-main, but bypassing most defended places to strike

A German tank crosses a defensive tank ditch filled in by *Afrika Korps* sappers during the siege of Tobruk.

deep into the enemy's rear areas, creating conditions in which demoralized garrisons would either surrender or could be captured at leisure by the slower-moving mass of infantry and artillery. The German Panzer (armoured) divisions and *Luftwaffe* (air force) proved the success of the formula in 1939–40; and in 1941 a Panzer division and a light motorized division were diverted to help Italian forces recapture their lost territory on the North African coast. This 1000-mile (1600-km) strip of desert was key to the domination of the Mediterranean Sea, and potentially offered the hope of strangling British global communications through the Suez Canal. The *Deutsches Afrikakorps* was commanded by a leading exponent of the new lightning tactics, General Erwin Rommel (1891–1944).

THE ARENA

Only a narrow coastal corridor of Italian Libya to the west and British Egypt to the east, lying between the coastal escarpment and the virtually impenetrable sand-seas of the greater Sahara to

THE TOBRUK GARRISON, APRIL–SEPTEMBER 1941

9th Australian Division (plus):

20 Infantry Brigade: 2/13th, 2/15th & 2/17th Infantry Battalions

24 Inf Bde: 2/28th, 2/32nd & 2/43rd Inf Bns

26 Inf Bde: 2/23rd, 2/24th & 2/48th Inf Bns

18 Inf Bde (ex-7th Division): 2/9th, 2/10th & 2/12th Inf Bns

2/12th Regiment Royal Australian Artillery

2/3rd AT Regt RAA (part), 2/4th Light AA Regt RAA (part)

2/3rd Pioneer Bn, 4x field companies RA Engineers

British

1st, 104th & 107th Regts Royal Horse Artillery, 51st Field Regt Royal Artillery, 3rd AT Regt RHA

51st Heavy & 14th Light Anti-Aircraft Regts RA

1st Bn Royal Northumberland Fusiliers (MG bn)

3rd Armed Bde: 1st Royal Tank Regt, D Sqn 7th RTR

3rd King's Own Hussars/ King's Dragoon Guards (composite)

Indian 18th Cavalry Regt (as inf bn)

The total strength on 18 April was c.35,300; many of these served no purpose, and the removal of non-combatants reduced the ration strength to c.24,000 by the end of June.

Garrison infantry, 25 October 1941

Australian 2/13th Inf Bn, 2/15th Inf Bn (part)

Polish Carpathian Rifle Bde (3 bns)

British 70th Division:

14 Inf Bde: 2nd Bn Black Watch, 2nd Bn York & Lancs Regt, 1st Bn Beds & Herts Regt

16 Inf Bde: 2nd Bn Leicester Regt, 1st Bn Essex Regt,2nd Bn King's Own Royal Regt

23 Inf Bde: 4th Bn Border Regt, 1st Bn Buffs, 1st Bn Durham Lt Inf

the south, was suitable for large-scale operations. An arid wilderness apart from a few small towns along the single east–west highway, this environment required that an army's every need – ammunition, fuel, food and stores of every kind – be imported by ship, and then trucked up to the front lines. The distance from the Italian rear port at Tripoli to the British equivalent at Alexandria was about 1100 miles (1770 km). Planning and executing any campaign between these was above all a logistic exercise, and possession of the very few harbours between these base areas was crucial. Tobruk, a little coastal town about 200 miles (320 km) west of the Libyan/Egyptian frontier, offered much the best sheltered harbour. It was an essential supply entry point for any army – either British heading west, or Axis driving east – and an aggressive garrison could threaten all traffic past Tobruk.

ITALIAN ROUT, GERMAN RESPONSE

In September 1940, Italy sent five divisions of her large but outdated 10th Army across the frontier from Libya and established several large fortified positions inside Egypt. On 9 December, General O'Connor's 30,000 British, Indian and Australian troops began Operation 'Compass' to expel them and carry the war into Libya. By the time O'Connor halted in mid-February 1941 at El Agheila, about 500 miles (800 km) into Libya, he had taken 133,000 prisoners for the loss of 2000 of his own men killed and wounded. Tobruk, with its 25,000-strong garrison, was taken in just 36 hours (21–22 January 1941), at a cost of about 50 Australian dead and 300 wounded.

Hitler could not allow his inept ally to fail; in mid- February, General Rommel and his first troops landed in Tripoli and moved forward to confront the British. General Wavell (1883–1950), British C-in-C Middle East, had now been obliged to send much of his desert army to fight the Axis invasion of Greece. Rommel attacked on 24 March, and over the next fortnight – thrusting, feinting and hooking round the desert flank – he bundled the British advanced forces back to the Egyptian frontier in confusion. Determined to hold Tobruk, Wavell entrusted it to General Leslie Morshead's 9th Australian Division, supported by British artillery and machine-gunners and about 45 tanks. On 9 April 1941, in a sandstorm, some 35,000 weary, confused troops withdrew inside the town's battered perimeter.

THE DEFENCES

A rectangle of bare, rocky territory on the escarpment behind the harbour had been laboriously fortified by the Italians. This enclave measured about 16 miles long by 11 miles deep (25 x 18 km), with a perimeter of some 32 miles (52 km). The outer ring was formed by concreted dug-outs for 30–40 men each, connected by concealed trenches with weapons positions every few hundred yards and partly protected by belts of barbed wire. Nearly half the perimeter, on the east and southeast, was also protected by an anti-tank ditch, though in places this 2.1-metre (7-ft) deep cut had been partly filled in. About 22 miles (35 km) inside this 'Red Line' – which the defenders set about improving with minefields – was an inner ring of concreted bunkers and trenches, which the Australians would also improve; this would be termed the 'Blue Line'. In all, there were about 140 outposts.

This double perimeter would have to be held by 12 battalions of Australian infantry, giving each an apparently impossible frontage of nearly 3 miles (5 km). Each brigade in the Red Line kept one of its three battalions behind it in the Blue Line; and each battalion in the Red Line kept one of its companies dug in half-a-mile behind it. In both cases these inner lines were covered by machine guns and anti-tank guns, and over some weeks the Blue Line would be strengthened with continuous wire and minefields. The tanks, armoured cars and light armoured infantry carriers formed a small mobile reserve; there were too few infantry to guard the coastline, and the town and harbour were entrusted to the anti-aircraft gunners. Up to 25 April a squadron of Hawker Hurricane fighters was based at the airfield, before heavy shelling forced them to withdraw.

FIRST ASSAULTS

By 11 April German and Italian troops had completely invested Tobruk. The headstrong Rommel planned both to thrust on 100 miles (160 km) eastwards towards the defensive line being cobbled together by the British around Sollum, and also to take the port. Given the ease with which the Italians had been ousted in January, and the garrison's lack of time to organize the defences, he did not anticipate great difficulty; but on the night of 13–14 April a probing battalion from his 5th Light Division was destroyed west of the El Adem road. They broke through the 2/17th Battalion, but when tanks of the Italian 'Ariete' Armoured Division went through the gap and moved north they were stopped dead at the future Blue Line by 25-pounder artillery and anti-tank guns, and withdrew. A third attack further to the west on 15–17 April, by the 'Ariete' and 'Trento' Divisions, was so thoroughly defeated by 2/48th Battalion that they took some 800 Italian prisoners.

The thwarted Rommel was distracted by operations around Sollum, and gave the garrison two weeks' respite to work on the defences; nevertheless, during this time, there were repeated heavy air raids by both Junkers Ju87 'Stuka' dive-bombers and level bombers from Derna and Tmimi, which flew a total of 1550 missions during April. A number of ships were sunk in the harbour, and the

THE 'SPUD RUN'

The Royal Navy lifeline to Tobruk along 'Bomb Alley' from Alexandria and Mersa Matruh was costly in ships and lives. During April 1941, six ships were lost, plus another eight during May. Isolated losses continued, but from June the RAF was sometimes able to provide daylight cover, rendezvousing with the returning ships east of Tobruk at dawn. During June a total of 1900 troops were delivered to Tobruk, with a daily average of 97 tons of stores landed, and 5148 were shipped out. The replacement of 9th Australian by 70th British Division between 19 August and 25 October involved the transfer in one direction or the other of some 81,400 men. By the time the 242-day siege ended on 10 December, the Royal Navy had delivered to Tobruk 34,000 men, 72 tanks, 92 artillery pieces and 34,000 tons of stores.

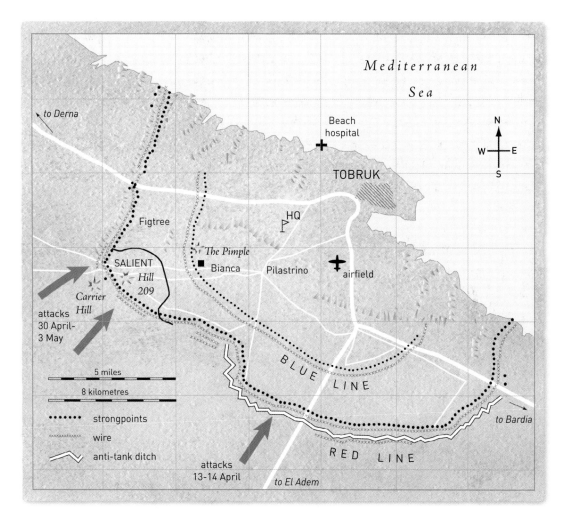

Map of the siege of Tobruk, showing the Italian defences taken over by the Australian and British garrison, and the main points of the German and Italian assaults.

town was almost levelled; few RAF patrols could be flown over Tobruk in April, and the anti-aircraft gunners took a while to learn how to counter the dive-bombers. Meanwhile, General Morshead pursued an extremely aggressive defence. Night reconnaissance and fighting patrols were constantly sent out; in ten days 26 Brigade took 1700 prisoners, and a single night sortie by its 2/48th Battalion, beyond Carrier Hill, brought in no fewer than 370. It was not unusual for a single brigade to send 300 men out on any one night, and this sort of stealthy hunting expedition suited the Australian temperament well.

THE EASTER BATTLE

By the end of April both sides had been reinforced, and Rommel determined to remove this drag on his operations. He planned a break-in at the southwest corner of the enclave, on both sides of

TIMELINE

1940 (Sept) Italian forces advance from Libya into Egypt

1941 (January) British, Indian and Australian forces rout the Italians and capture Tobruk

1941 (April) The German Afrikakorps under Erwin Rommel pushes back the Allies and lays siege to Tobruk

1941 (December) Tobruk relieved by the British Eighth Army in Operation 'Crusader'

1942 (June) Surprise attack by Rommel after his victory at the nearby Battle of Gazala succeeds in capturing Tobruk and its 33,000 South African defenders

1942 (October) At the Second Battle of El Alamein, General Bernard Montgomery defeats Rommel, forcing a retreat that ends with the capture of Tunis and German withdrawal from North Africa; Tobruk falls to the Allied advance in November

Hill 209 (Ras el Medauar); units from 15th Panzer Division on the left, and 5th Light on the right, would punch gaps that the Italians of the 'Ariete' and 'Brescia' Divisions would then exploit. From the afternoon of 30 April air raids and artillery softened up the Red Line – held in this sector by 2/24th Battalion, in 22 concrete outposts; sappers gapped the minefield and wire, and at 8 p.m. the assault went in. Despite savage resistance the outnumbered 'Diggers' were pushed back, and by first light on 1 May a deep, wide salient had been created. However, when the Panzers advanced through it to exploit to north and east they were stopped by the new minefield and anti-tank guns of the Blue Line, and hit by some of the reserve tanks. Rommel threw in reinforcements, and by that night the Germans had taken a salient 2 miles (3.2 km) deep along a 3-mile (5-km) front, including the valuable observation point of Hill 209. Australian counter-attacks failed, and by nightfall on 3 May both sides were exhausted. They settled down in and around 'The Salient' for months of deadly positional warfare – attritional fighting that was almost as punishing as that at Gallipoli in 1915.

THE LONG SLOG

During May the garrison settled down to endure the harsh conditions. Water was short, and tasted brackish; two wells and an Italian desalination plant produced about 40,000 gallons a day, and more was shipped in from Egypt, but the garrison (averaging 30,000 men) had to get used to a daily ration of 3 pints maximum for all purposes. Food was in fairly good supply, but very monotonous – mainly bully-beef, biscuits and tinned fruit. For the 'Rats of Tobruk' – a term coined by Joseph Goebbels' sneering English-language propaganda broadcaster, the Irish fascist William Joyce ('Lord Haw-Haw') – there were no sports or entertainments, since any concentration of men presented a vulnerable target. Air raids and shelling were frequent, falling on the harbour gangs as often as upon the perimeter defenders.

Life in the Red Line meant crouching in baking, cramped dugouts all day, and in the Salient it was even more dangerous. Since the Easter fighting had punctured the hardened defences, both sides faced one another from shallow foxholes and slit trenches hammered with difficulty into the rocky ground. Movement in daylight brought down instant fire, and the Australian snipers earned a lethal reputation in the Axis front line. So intolerable were conditions that an unspoken truce was observed for two hours after dusk, allowing men to bring up supplies and ease their cramp; the Afrikakorps would signal the end of this lull by firing a burst of tracer straight up into the air. Even in daylight both sides evolved a marginally humane routine for evacuating casualties from the front line: when a Red Cross flag was lifted, the enemy would switch fire to another target until the stretcher-bearers had come and gone.

In the Blue Line outposts men were usually spared direct fire, but suffered endless choking dust and maddening swarms of flies and fleas. Men were rotated between the two lines and the reserve positions, where they spent much of their time not resting but labouring. The lucky rear-echelon troops in the ruined town (and the AA gunners, for one day each week) got a coveted chance to swim off the sheltered beaches. Health was generally good, but most men suffered from distressing desert sores – slow to heal, for lack of fresh vegetables and fruit in their diet.

'BOMB ALLEY'

The life of Tobruk depended entirely on the Royal Navy, whose Inshore Squadron ran the gauntlet from Alexandria on moonless nights to bring in men and supplies and to take out casualties and prisoners. This 'Spud Run' was performed by British and Australian destroyers, minesweepers, gunboats, sloops, some heavy beach-landing craft and a miscellany of small commandeered merchant craft. (At this time the Mediterranean Fleet was extremely hard pressed by the fighting off Crete.) These vessels ran the risk of mines, shells from the shore, bombs from the Stukas and torpedoes from aircraft, E-boats and U-boats. During the siege the clearly marked hospital ship *Vita* was sunk by dive-bombers, and thereafter the wounded were taken out by destroyer. Even moonlit nights were perilous, yet some daylight voyages were unavoidable, and losses among the light craft were severe. The trawlers and schooners would attempt to sneak in just before dawn, tying up to unload in the cover of one of the wrecks in the harbour before slipping out again after dark.

Troops, munitions, tanks and guns were shipped in by destroyers. Typically, perhaps three destroyers and a minesweeper would leave Alexandria at 8.30 a.m., so as to enter the mineswept channel at Tobruk just before midnight. They were quickly unloaded by Indian stevedores; wounded and prisoners were embarked, and if the schedule was not too disrupted by air raids they could be away again before dawn.

THE SALIENT

Throughout the summer Rommel was constantly worried by the running sore of Tobruk behind his left flank, forcing him to bring every last shell and litre of petrol from hundreds of miles to his rear. Even their arrival in Tripoli was always uncertain thanks to British operations from Malta, and from June 1941 the invasion of the USSR took priority over Africa. For his part, General Morshead was equally preoccupied with the ground lost in the Salient, whose unfortified perimeter now needed five times more defenders than the original bunkers; Rommel was forced to use high-quality German motorized infantry (needed at the Egyptian frontier) to hold Hill 209, and while clashes

'THE DESERT RATS'

Like most military legends carelessly repeated by journalists, the origins of this famous nickname – nowadays perpetuated in references to the British army's 7th Armoured Brigade – are complicated.

Firstly: the vehicle sign of a red jerboa – a jumping desert rodent – was adopted early in 1940 by the British Army's Mobile Division/Egypt. This was redesignated 7th Armoured Division in November 1940, with its tank units forming 4th and 7th Armoured Brigades; the overall divisional sign remained the red jerboa, but 4th Armoured Brigade adopted it in black, and 7th originally in green. In April 1941 a unit of 7th Armoured Brigade, 1st Royal Tank Regiment, was among the scattered elements that withdrew inside the Tobruk perimeter.

Secondly: during the siege Nazi propaganda broadcasts sneeringly referred to the defenders of Tobruk as being 'trapped like rats' and the whole garrison delightedly adopted the nickname 'Rats of Tobruk'.

Thirdly: Modified as 'Desert Rats', this was later loosely applied to the whole of British 8th Army in North Africa, and to its post-war veterans.

Fourthly: Since the disbandment of 7th Armoured Division after the end of the Second World War the jerboa sign has been preserved – in black and red respectively – by 4th and 7th Armd Brigades; but the press insist on applying the name 'Desert Rats' specifically to the 7th.

took place all around the perimeter it was that southwest sector that saw the bitterest fighting.

In mid-May, Wavell ordered an attack from the Sollum line and a simultaneous operation by the Tobruk garrison. Wavell's Operation 'Brevity' failed, and on 15–16 May the besiegers made a push north out of the Salient to try to reach the Figtree position; they only took a third of their objectives, but Morshead's counterattacks on the 17th suffered heavy losses for no gain. In mid-June Wavell launched the much more substantial Operation 'Battleaxe', which was stopped on the line Hafid Ridge–Fort Capuzzo–Halfaya Pass – partly by the deadly 88 mm dual-purpose gun, here revealed for the first time in its anti-tank role – and was forced back on 17 June by a Panzer counter-attack. (Soon after, General Wavell was replaced as theatre commander by General Auchinleck.) Again, Morshead had co-ordinated attacks on the Salient, and during the rest of that month 20 Brigade continually nibbled away at it, shoving the Germans slowly back for 915 metres (1000 yds). On this new line, about 4 miles (6.4 km) long, they established hardened defences with minefields.

Morshead – whose nickname was 'Ming the Merciless', after the villain in the Flash Gordon comic strip – always hungered to recapture the whole Salient, and he ordered several costly and fairly pointless attempts that smacked of the Great War. The last were in the first week of August, when 24 Brigade took heavy casualties in failed assaults; thereafter the Salient settled into 'active defence', punctuated by the usual patrols and raids.

REPLACING THE AUSTRALIANS

During August, after a four-month ordeal, the Australian government began pressing for their 9th Division to be relieved by other troops. The first brigade was shipped out between 19 and 29 August, being replaced by the Free Poles of General Kopanski's Carpathian Brigade. The rest of the division were pulled out progressively during September and October, and by 25 October the Australians were gone (except for 2/13th and half of 2/15th Battalion, whose evacuation ship was sunk on the inbound voyage). Their replacements were the British 70th Division, whose GOC, General Scobie, took over the Tobruk command on 23 October. When the Poles moved into part of the Salient they were at first unwilling to maintain the evening truces, but Kopanski warned that breaking them suddenly would warn the Germans opposite that new troops were in the line – knowledge that they would exploit. The Carpathian Brigade worked tirelessly to improve the shallow positions, and by December they had chipped some trenches deep enough for a man to stand safely.

NOVEMBER: OPERATION 'CRUSADER'

In early November, British intelligence received – through 'Ultra' decoded radio intercepts – many details of a German assault being planned for the 23rd. General Auchinleck brought forward his own planned Operation 'Crusader', a major offensive to destroy Rommel's armoured units and drive him back beyond Tobruk. General Scobie prepared a simultaneous break-out towards the southeast by a whole brigade group with tanks, to link with the advancing 8th Army.

In the event 'Crusader' involved weeks of fighting and many confused movements by both sides, with the key Sidi Rezegh ridge some 15 miles (24 km) southeast of Tobruk changing hands several times between 20 November and 5 December. Breaking through German strongpoints south of the Bardia road on 20–22 November cost Scobie many of his tanks, and after his men had created a broad corridor the planned link-up had to be postponed for days, leaving this protruding 'tail' from the perimeter terribly vulnerable to attacks. The 1st Essex reached El Duda on the 26th, linking next day with 19th New Zealand Battalion and some tanks from Sidi Rezegh. However, holding El Duda until the Afrikakorps finally retreated westwards on 5 December took hard fighting, in which 4th Border and the 2/13th Australians distinguished themselves; the latter battalion could thus claim to have been 'first in, last out'. On 7 December, South African troops and British tanks reached Tobruk's eastern perimeter; and on the night of the 9th/10th the Polish brigade finally recaptured the whole Salient. The siege was over, after 242 days. Ultimately, Tobruk would fall to Rommel six months later, but his triumph would result from a surprise attack rather than by siege warfare.

Heroic defences of key Soviet cities during the 'Great Patriotic War'

LENINGRAD AND STALINGRAD

15 SEPTEMBER 1941–27 JANUARY 1944
22 NOVEMBER 1942–2 FEBRUARY 1943

'*The ring around Leningrad has not yet been drawn as tightly as might be desired, and further progress ... is doubtful. Considering the drain on our forces on the Leningrad front ... the situation will remain critical until such time as hunger takes effect as our ally.*'

COLONEL-GENERAL FRANZ HALDER,
GERMAN ARMY CHIEF-OF-STAFF (12 SEPTEMBER 1941)

The siege of Leningrad was remarkable mainly for causing a greater localized loss of civilian lives than at any other place during the Second World War except the Nazi extermination camps. The total number of deaths can never be known; the official Soviet figure was 632,000, but many historians suggest that 1 million is a more realistic estimate. While the siege continued for two and a half years, the greatest number died during the winter of 1941–2; the city was never entirely cut off from outside supplies, but before spring 1942 these were inadequate to sustain life during a north Russian winter. Thereafter the lifelines became rather more efficient; the population was halved by evacuations, and the city was no longer under any serious threat of assault.

JUNE–JULY: OPERATION 'BARBAROSSA'

Peter the Great's 18th-century watergate to the West, St Petersburg – which was renamed Leningrad in honour of the leader of the Bolshevik Revolution in 1924 (and reverted to its original name in 1991) – is a port city at the eastern end of the Gulf of Finland, a finger of the Baltic Sea. It stands at the mouth of the Neva river at the southwest foot of the Karelian Isthmus; the Neva crosses the isthmus from the vast Lake Ladoga on its eastern shore, only some 30 miles (48 km) from the city. The Finnish frontier across Karelia – forced back by the USSR in the Winter War of 1939–40 – still lay only about 100 miles (160 km) north of Leningrad.

The German plan for the invasion of the USSR, Operation 'Barbarossa', envisaged the effective destruction of the huge but outdated Red Army, and the occupation of Russia up to a line stretching roughly from Archangel in the Arctic to the Caucasus in the southeast, thus securing for near-bankrupt Germany much of the country's vast agricultural, oil and mineral resources. The invasion was launched on 22 June 1941, with inadequate forces and logistics, but gambling upon the superior equipment and skill of the *Wehrmacht* to achieve a series of shock victories and deep penetrations by three great Army Groups – North, Centre and South. In Russia's huge spaces,

During the siege of Leningrad conditions were desperately harsh for civilians and soldiers alike. Here, women collect water from ruptured pipes in the frozen ground on Nevsky Prospect.

TIMELINE

1939 The Soviet Union and Nazi Germany conclude a non-aggression pact

1941 (June) Germans launch Operation 'Barbarosssa', the invasion of the Soviet Union

1941 (August) Siege of Leningrad begins

1942 (September) Battle to take Stalingrad begins

1942 (November) Zhukov orders massive counter-offensive against German forces at Stalingrad

1942 (December) German attempt to relieve Stalingrad pocket fails

1943 Field Marshal von Paulus surrenders; the survivors of the German 6th army are taken into Soviet captivity

1944 (January) The siege of Leningrad is lifted after 880 days

destroying Stalin's armies was more important than capturing territory; since most of the German armies relied on horse-drawn transport and marching infantry, the key would be the achievement of great encirclements of Soviet armies by fast Panzer and motorized divisions.

Army Group North, commanded by Field-Marshal Wilhelm Ritter von Leeb (1876–1956), at first raced eastwards from East Prussia through Soviet-occupied Lithuania, Latvia and Estonia; it comprised the 16th and 18th Armies, plus General Hoeppner's 4th Panzer Group of tank and motorized infantry divisions. Their ambitious mission was to reach and take Leningrad by 21 July. Hitler harboured an obsessive hatred for the cradle of the Bolshevik Revolution, and spoke of killing or driving out all the inhabitants, razing their city to the ground and giving the ruins to Finland: '*The venomous nest Petersburg, out of which Asiatic poison has for so long gushed into the Baltic Sea, will disappear from the face of the Earth.*'

The Red Army was no match for the *Wehrmacht* in the frontier battles, and Leeb was advancing south of Lake Peipus by 10 July; but then the Soviets scraped together a defensive line on the Luga river, which held until late August. The marshy, forested terrain was far more difficult country than the steppes to the south, lending itself to stubborn defence; German fuel consumption was three times the anticipated figure, and in August the advance slowed to *c*.3 miles (5 km) a day.

AUGUST–SEPTEMBER: INDECISION, THEN ASSAULT

Hitler had planned to capture Leningrad before he switched the 4th Panzer Group south to support Army Group Centre's push on Moscow, but for about six weeks from late July he and his generals argued over how best to exploit their unexpectedly rapid victories – they could not be strong enough on all sectors simultaneously. Hitler still wanted to take Leningrad first; a strong group argued for immediate concentration on Moscow; and on 21 July the Führer avoided a choice by switching the weight of the punch southwards into the Ukraine, to encircle and destroy Soviet forces around Kiev. This brilliant success deceived him into believing that the Red Army was effectively finished, and in early September he agreed to a push on Moscow. However, he left 4th

Panzer Group with Leeb for the time being, ordering a swing around the south of Leningrad to link up with Finnish armies advancing from the north on both sides of Lake Ladoga. But the Finns were not interested in an aggressive war of conquest; by 7 September they had regained their lost Karelian territory, and stopped about 6 miles (10 km) north of Leningrad.

Leeb outflanked the Luga line in late August, and on 1 September the first German shell fell on Leningrad. On the 8th the city suffered its first major air raid, and the Germans took the important transport hub of Shisselburg on the shore of Lake Ladoga, 10 miles (16 km) to the southeast. On 10 September their capture of the Duderhof heights gave them artillery observation of the city from just 7 miles (11 km) south; outlying towns fell on the 11th and 12th; soon the *Wehrmacht* reached the coast west of the city, and 1st Panzer Division was in the suburb of Aleksandrovka, the southwest terminus of the Leningrad tram lines. On 15 September the envelopment was complete; but Leeb's worn-out troops could advance no further. On 17 September the tanks of 4th Panzer Group and the Stuka dive-bombers of 8th Air Corps were withdrawn to take part in the assault on Moscow. Army Group North had advanced nearly 600 miles (965 km); now its 300,000 men settled down to besiege Leningrad. On 21 September, Stalin issued his own merciless orders: the city would be resupplied, and was to resist to the last.

THE DEFENCES

The city itself was about 8 miles wide by 10 miles deep (13 x 16 km), but the whole encirclement took in an area of about 2850 square kilometres (1100 sq mi), and contained some 250,000 defenders – about 40 army divisions, plus the Baltic Fleet, and some 400 aircraft; west of the city a separate coastal enclave around Oranienbaum also held out. The defenders were short of artillery and many other necessities that could not be produced locally, but the city had about 50 factories building KV-1 heavy tanks, guns, mortars, small arms and munitions. On 9 September the Red Army chief-of-staff – Stalin's finest general, Georgi K. Zhukov (1896–1974) – was sent in for a few weeks to organize the defences, before rushing back to save Moscow (air communications would be maintained throughout the siege – the *Luftwaffe* was not strong in this sector).

The city's inner and outer defence rings were tied into natural obstacles such as the many canals. In the centre, units of volunteers, *Komsomol* young Communists, police and NKVD handled civil defence tasks and internal security. The inner defence line, following the city's peripheral railway circuit, was manned by militia and Interior Ministry troops, and the thick outer line through the suburbs by regular troops. More than a million men and women had been put to work by the Party to dig and build these defences; the city would eventually be ringed with about 620 miles (1000 km) of earthworks, 400 miles (640 km) of anti-tank ditches, 185 miles (300 km) of timber obstacles, 5000 pillboxes and 370 miles (595 km) of barbed wire entanglements and minefields. The Baltic Fleet and Ladoga Flotilla provided naval gunfire support from west and east. The garrison was strong enough to hold this perimeter against assaults, although with the whole western USSR torn apart by the still-advancing *Wehrmacht* there was no realistic chance of a military relief. However, by far the greatest challenge was simply keeping the city alive.

PREPARATIONS FOR THE SIEGE

The effective ruler of Leningrad was the Communist Party chief, Andrei A. Zhdanov (1896–1948); he would prove ruthless at mobilizing his hard-pressed citizens into labour corps, but skilful at inspiring their will and endurance.

When the siege began the civil population was at least 2½ million; on 12 September it was reckoned that the city had cereals for 30 days, flour for 35, meat for 33 and fats for 45 days. In all, the city needed to import about 1000 tons of food each day, in addition to fuel and munitions; and since the Germans had taken the southern shore of Lake Ladoga, the only lifeline was across the lake from Novaya Ladoga to Osinovets – a 16-hour voyage, under German air attack, with inadequate shipping and no proper unloading facilities. Supplies reached the far shore of the lake by rail via Tikhvin and Volkhov, then by road and water up the Volkhov river; with the USSR's production of grain and meat reduced by wartime chaos to between a third and a half of normal, merely getting Leningrad's needs to the railheads was difficult enough.

All food stocks in the city were centralized, and ration rates were graduated. Soldiers and manual workers got the most, then office workers, then the rest; initially the first category got 1.6 kilograms (3½ lbs) of meat a month, the second 0.9 kilograms (2 lbs), and the rest just 0.45 kilograms (1 lb), with cereals and fats pro rata. At first many people walked out into the countryside to grub up potatoes, but the first hard frosts in October put a stop to this. That month the garrison made a counterattack south across the Neva, in the hope of linking with a push westwards by General Meretskov's Volkhov Front. This failed, and on 8 November came news of catastrophe: 150 miles (240 km) to the east, the Germans had pushed out a salient and captured the railhead at Tikhvin.

THE CRISIS OF NOVEMBER AND DECEMBER

In November ice began to close the water lifeline across Lake Ladoga, but it would be weeks before this froze hard enough to support convoys; the ice between Kabona and Osninovets had to be

'*The mortuary itself is full. Not only are there too few trucks to go to the cemetery, but, more important, not enough gasoline to put in the trucks, and the main thing is – there is not enough strength left in the living to bury the dead.*'

LENINGRAD RESIDENT VERA INBER,
DIARY ENTRY (26 DECEMBER 1941)

THE EXTREMES OF DESPERATION

Starvation in Leningrad soon surpassed anything seen in Paris in 1870–1. By September 1941 the rationed bread was already only 50 percent rye flour, mixed with oats, barley, soya beans and malt, and when these ran out they were replaced with sawdust. Scientists were ordered to come up with some kind of substitute for bread made from the few materials available in bulk – cellulose from paper-pulp factories, and cottonseed. By the end of November an edible cellulose concoction was being produced (edible, in the sense that it was not actually poisonous), but the daily ration provided only about one-tenth of a worker's calorific requirements. Any half-starved draft horses killed on the streets by shelling were rapidly butchered where they lay, and their flesh mixed with saltpetre, pepper, garlic and leather dust, to be issued as 'sausage'; another batch was produced from sheep gut, mixed with fish scraps from a glue factory and flax seeds. Working parties were set to scouring every corner of the city for anything that could be eaten: dust was swept from the floors of mills and bakeries; a sunken bargeload of grain was recovered and mixed into a sort of cake with rice husks and cocoa dust. Yeast and seaweed were turned into 'soups', and soap into 'jelly'; wallpaper was even stripped so that the flour-and-water paste used to hang it could be recycled.

In later years a man who had survived that first winter as a child recalled his worst and most indelible memory: that as he had watched both his father and his mother die of starvation, 'I wanted their bread more than I wanted them to stay alive'.

consistently 18 centimetres (7 ins) thick for horse-drawn sleighs, and 23 centimetres (9 ins) for lorries with a one-ton load. In the meantime, the city faced starvation; an airlift of 200 tons per day was planned from 16 November, but this was never achieved, and anyway would have fallen 80 percent short of the city's needs. On 22 November a first convoy was attempted, but this was followed by a partial thaw; in the last week of the month less than two days' supplies got through. On 26 November eight lorries left Leningrad, returning the next day with just 33 tons of food. Daily convoys continued, but their loads varied between 100 tons and less than 20 – a tiny fraction of the city's requirements.

A new road had to be built to bypass Tikhvin to the north, looping 220 miles (350 km) through swamps and forest from the railhead at Zaborye. With immense labour and at great cost in lives, it was completed on 6 December, but it was so primitive that it was almost useless for wheeled traffic. Then, on 9 December, there occurred probably the most decisive event of the whole siege: Tikhvin was recaptured by General Fedyuninsky's 54th Army. The Finns from the north had reached the Svir river, linking the south of Lakes Ladoga and Onega, but now they settled down to purely defensive operations. The *Wehrmacht* had been suffering appallingly from its lack of preparation for the Russian winter, and in temperatures of –52°C (–61°F) frostbite casualties soon rivalled combat losses. The Germans were soon driven right back to the west bank of the Volkhov river; rail links from Zaborye to Volkhov were restored, and with them regular convoys over the 'ice road'.

LIFE IN THE CITY

However, the ice was not wholly reliable until January 1942; in December the average daily supply load was only 800 tons of all necessities, and the of the inhabitants would remain almost unimaginable right through the winter. During November, 11,000 people had starved to death (the official euphemism was 'death from alimentary dystrophy'); in December this increased to nearly 53,000 – even the first-category rations for soldiers and workers now provided less than 1000 calories daily. By January all the cats and dogs had been eaten; those few citizens who still had jewellery or furs traded them for a crust of bread; people were murdered for their ration cards, and there is no doubt that cannibalism took place.

There was no fuel for heating, and many power stations closed down. What electricity there was went to factories; homes were connected to the supply for only one hour per day, kerosene for oil lamps ran out and the city fell into icy darkness. There were no private telephones or newspapers, no electricity for radios, so the suffering was increased by a sense of hopeless isolation. People chopped up their furniture and floorboards to feed crude stoves, which caused more deaths from poisonous fumes and accidental fires – these sometimes spread and burned for days, for lack of power to pump water. In temperatures of around –30°C (–22°F) outdoors, and –14°C (6.8°F) indoors, the starving died in their sleep, in the street, at their workbenches; children of 12 were particularly vulnerable, since at that age they lost their special rations. While air raids were few, artillery fire on the southern quarters continued. This was a constant danger to exhausted, famished workers trudging miles to and from those factories that still operated, or housewives queuing all day at ration stations; many corpses were simply covered by snowfalls until revealed by the spring thaw. There was no hot water, and the sanitary system failed, so people lived in freezing filth; conditions in the city's hospitals were unspeakable.

By the end of December some 35,000 people had left the city, some in ration lorries but most by walking out across the frozen lake, where many died in blizzards. During January 1942 supplies coming in at last caught up with daily consumption, and ration scales inched upwards. But this could not rebuild health after cumulative starvation, and the death toll continued to multiply: to 120,000 during January, and about 280,000 in February – 10,000 every day. However, in January some 11,300 women, children and sick were evacuated; by the end of March the total had reached about 514,000, and in April another 163,000 left, easing pressure on rations for those remaining. By the spring children, at least, were getting enough regular meals to keep them alive.

1942: THE THAW

Supply ships could not cross the lake until June 1942, but preparations began in February. A 21-mile (34-km) branch rail line was laid from Voibokalo up to Kabona on the eastern shore, speeding up bulk transport and saving petrol, and by June an underwater fuel pipeline was in operation.

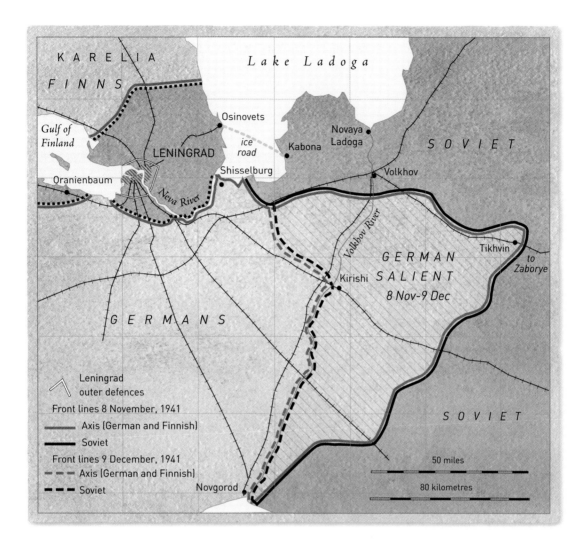

Map of the siege of Leningrad, showing the Soviet defensive lines around the city and the German positions from 1941 until the break-through in January 1943.

During the summer another half-million Leningraders were shipped out, reducing the population to about one million, and before the ice returned in November 100,000 tons of food had been stockpiled for the following winter. Meanwhile, fresh Soviet divisions had been shipped into the enclave, and in the winter of 1942–3 preparations were completed for outside forces to drive a land corridor through to Leningrad from the east.

1943–4: RELIEF AND BREAK-OUT

Operation 'Iskra' was launched by the Leningrad and Volkhov Fronts, with massive artillery preparation, on 12 January 1943, and on the 18th the two army groups linked hands. A 6-mile (10-km)-wide corridor was captured along the southern shore of Lake Ladoga; new railway lines and bridges were built; and on the 526th day of the siege the first train steamed into the Finland Station. The task of rebuilding Leningrad was daunting, and all those between the ages of 15 and 60 who were not already doing vital war work were mobilized. But though life was still terribly harsh, and the death toll continued (diseases returned with the warm weather, and some 6000 citizens were killed that summer and autumn by German shelling) at least starvation was no longer a serious danger.

On 14 January 1944, in heavy snow and fog, the three-pronged Operation 'Neva II' was launched southwards and westwards by the Leningrad and Volkhov Fronts, with a total of 1,241,000 troops, 23,100 guns and rocket-launchers, 1475 tanks and 1500 aircraft. Against them, General Küchler's worn-out Army Group North had not much more than half that number of men, less than half the artillery, and only a quarter of the tanks and aircraft. The outskirts of the city were rapidly cleared, and by 20 January the *Wehrmacht* was falling back in ruin all the way to the Luga river. At 8 p.m. on 27 January 1944 – after 880 days of siege – the Leningrad skyline was lit up by coloured rockets, searchlights and the celebratory thunder of 300 guns.

STALINGRAD, SEPTEMBER–NOVEMBER 1942: STREET-FIGHTING

The German defeat at Stalingrad is commonly referred to as a siege; in fact, the battle was probably more significant for the intensity of the street-fighting between mid-September and late November 1942, before a siege was imposed.

Stalingrad was an important industrial and river-port city straggling for some 18 miles (29 km) down the banks of the Volga. In summer 1942 it was a necessary German military objective, as a northern flank bastion behind the left shoulder of their deep thrust south towards the Caspian oilfields and the Caucasus. In July the 4th Panzer Army was detached from the 6th Army, commanded by General Friedrich von Paulus (1890–1957) and sent south to bolster this advance by Army Group A, leaving Stalingrad to 6th Army with some weakly equipped additional Axis divisions. Paulus's troops broke into the northern outskirts of Stalingrad on 23 August 1942, and Hitler ordered a general assault on 15 September; but the stubborn resistance by General Chuikov's 62nd Army increasingly goaded the Führer into an obsession with capturing the city as a symbol of Soviet defiance, and all sane military arguments against committing troops to what threatened to become a cul-de-sac were ignored. While Hitler remained mesmerized by Paulus's struggle for the devastated streets of the city, the flanking defensive fronts – on the Don bend to the northwest, and on the Volga to the southeast of the city – became increasingly precarious; they were thinly held, mainly by Romanian, Italian and Hungarian divisions, as Hitler fed German reinforcements into the meat-grinder of Stalingrad.

The east bank of the Volga remained in Soviet hands throughout; although costly street

'NOT ONE STEP BACK!'

JOSEPH STALIN, ORDER ISSUED TO ALL RUSSIAN FORCES (28 JULY 1942)

fighting took the Germans as far as the west bank at points in the south and centre of the city, the defenders were seldom cut off from reinforcement and supply; at a terrible price, riverboats and barges crossed the 2-mile (3.2-km)-wide Volga every night, and from the east bank Soviet artillery and rocket-launchers pounded the German positions. Street-fighting is always very costly in lives: like combat in thick jungle, it is characterized by short-range duels between infantrymen stalking each other in heavy cover – in this case, in rubble-choked streets or the sewers beneath them, between buildings gutted by bombing and shelling – and every hundred yards of progress have to be paid for with the lives of the first men to break cover. Off the open steppes and bogged down in this vast maze of blind-faced apartment blocks, collapsing warehouses and mountains of smouldering rubble, dominated by crazily teetering walls and chimney-stacks, the Germans were unable to utilize their skills in mechanized warfare. The infantry demanded that tanks come forward and provide close fire support for their rushes, but the Panzer regiments were steadily worn away; tanks are notoriously vulnerable to short-range infantry anti-tank weapons if committed to street-fighting, due to their crews' poor visibility.

The Red Army showed a new level of flexible tactical skill, with command and control devolved down to small units which prepared meticulously for sudden assaults on limited objectives – a single building, sometimes a single storey within a building. Desperate fighting raged from room to room, and from one blast-furnace or stamping-mill to another across the dim caverns of ruined factories. Hitler aided Chuikov in October by ordering a pause in the advance for a concentrated air and artillery bombardment, thus knocking down more concrete houses-of-cards and creating more cover for the *frontoviki* to exploit in this murderous 'rat warfare'.

NOVEMBER 1942 – FEBRUARY 1943: THE FAILURE OF THE 'AIR BRIDGE'

On 19 November, with Hitler distracted by the Allied offensives in North Africa, Marshal Zhukov launched his long-prepared Operation 'Uranus' – massive counter-offensives north and south of Stalingrad. The transfer of troops from the inactive front facing the Japanese on the Chinese and Manchurian frontiers had given Zhukov a total of nearly 1 million men in 12 armies. Hopelessly outnumbered and outgunned, the Romanian, Italian and Hungarian expeditionary corps were swept aside; the armies of Generals Yeremenko and Rokossovski met at Kalach west of Stalingrad on 22 November, and as these two pincers closed around it, the 6th Army was indeed besieged.

A break-out during the following week might have succeeded, but, on 24 November, Hitler ordered Paulus to hold fast in 'Fortress Stalingrad'. In this decision he was influenced by the wildly irresponsible boast of Field-Marshal Hermann Göring that his *Luftwaffe* could supply the 6th Army entirely by airlift into the airfields at Pitomnik and Gumrak, respectively in the south and north of the German enclave. Paulus's staff estimated their needs at 700 tons a day immediately and twice that figure later, once they had consumed their accumulated reserves; Göring was told by his own staff that the airlift might manage 350 tons daily for a brief period, with no allowance for extreme weather or for losses; but he told Hitler that his obsolete Junkers Ju52 trimotor transport planes could deliver 500 tons a day, without qualification.

Hitler refused to consider a withdrawal by Paulus, and the failure of Field-Marshal von Manstein's attempted break-in to reinforce him from the southwest on 23 December finally sealed the 6th Army's fate. Manstein was thereafter preoccupied by trying to hold a corridor open for the retreat of Army Group A from the Caucasus during January 1943, which was achieved only with difficulty. The *Luftwaffe* hardly ever delivered more than 250 tons of supplies per day; their best result was on 19 December, when 154 aircraft flew in 289 tons. On 4–6 January 1943 they averaged less than 150 tons daily, and from the 7th to the 21st less than 100 tons. The Red Army launched its final thrust into the city on 10 January; on the 16th they took Pitomnik, and Gumrak fell on the 23rd. The *Luftwaffe*'s valiant attempts to keep the air bridge open had saved about 34,000 of Paulus's wounded, but had cost Germany 488 largely irreplaceable transport aircraft and 1000 aircrew.

The Russians continued their assaults while the 6th Army starved and froze; on 26 January they split the enclave in two; Paulus and the southern pocket surrendered on 31 January, while the last resistance in the north was snuffed out on 2 February. Since the November counter-offensive alone some 60,000 Axis troops had been killed inside the encirclement and perhaps 130,000 captured; of about 92,000 of those prisoners taken when the last pockets surrendered, nearly half would die of starvation and neglect by the spring, and only perhaps 5000 would ever return home, long after the end of the war. Total German casualties during the whole battle were just short of 300,000 men, a figure equalled among the other Axis nations. Stalingrad was, beyond all argument, the turning-point of the war against Germany.

Soviet military casualties for the whole campaign were nearly 486,000 dead and perhaps 600,000 wounded; to these must be added an unknown but certainly large number of the civilian population, whose evacuation had been forbidden (the Barykady ordnance factory had still been repairing tanks and guns as the *Wehrmacht* approached its walls). Remarkably, nearly 10,000 civilians had survived the whole battle under the ruins on the west bank of the Volga.

'Surrender is forbidden. Sixth Army will hold their positions to the last man and the last round, and by their heroic endurance will make an unforgettable contribution to the establishment of a defensive front and the salvation of the western world.'

MESSAGE FROM ADOLF HITLER TO FIELD-MARSHAL FRIEDRICH VON PAULUS
(3 JANUARY 1943)

Hard-pressed French paratroopers in Dien Bien Phu await another Vietminh assault on 24 March 1954. These shallow trenches were in the centre of the camp.

DIEN BIEN PHU

13 March–7 May 1954

*'I look forward to a Vietminh assault ... Their artillery will be
troublesome for a while, but we will silence it.'*

LIEUTENANT-GENERAL RENÉ COGNY, COMMANDING
FRENCH GROUND FORCES NORTH VIETNAM (JANUARY 1954)

The fall on 7 May 1954 of Dien Bien Phu, a jungle fortress in North Vietnam held by a full division of French troops, to a Vietminh army led by General Vo Nguyen Giap (born 1911), destroyed France's will to continue fighting to maintain her colonial rule over Indochina. The crucial miscalculation of the French high command was their misplaced faith in air power: they believed that Dien Bien Phu could not be besieged, because it would have a 'vertical' line of supply, reinforcement and casualty evacuation, invulnerable to an enemy without an air force of its own. They relied upon air transport for its creation, garrisoning, supply and resupply; and upon ground-attack aircraft – alongside artillery – to guarantee the ground defences of its perimeter.

'THE DIRTY WAR'

The left-wing press and intelligentsia in France gave this name (*la sale guerre*) to a conflict that had been dragging on since 1946, when France, after having suffered the humiliation of defeat and occupation in the Second World War, tried to regain control of its Indochinese colonies. The power vacuum left by the lackadaisical Japanese occupation, and later sudden surrender, had allowed the Vietminh Communist underground movement to gain a foothold beyond their remote bases in the forest hills and swamps, which they successfully defended until 1949. The Communist victory in China then provided Vietnamese Communist leader Ho Chi Minh (1890–1969) and his military chief Vo Nguyen Giap with a generous supplier of arms and training, in camps across the border from the Vietminh heartland. It was there, in northern Tonkin, that Giap inflicted a shocking defeat on the French in October 1950, and thereafter the drain on French blood and funds only increased. By 1953 the French public were sick of optimistic rhetoric from a series of short-lived governments lacking any coherent policy, punctuated by disappointing news of battlefield failures.

The French Far East Expeditionary Force (CEFEO) had to rely on volunteers; all its conscripts were committed to fulfilling France's NATO commitment in West Germany or to garrisoning its North African colonies. Although it included some first-class units – notably the paratroops and the Foreign Legion – the CEFEO relied heavily on North and West African colonial troops and local Vietnamese recruits, and the need to provide them with French cadres left all combat units chronically short of experienced officers and NCOs. (At Dien Bien Phu, less than 20 percent of the garrison would be from mainland France.)

From 1950 the USA had begun replacing the CEFEO's sparse and worn-out equipment; but the need to maintain security all over Indochina prevented French generals from assembling a strong mobile reserve of manoeuvre units to take the initiative. Meanwhile, Giap's new Chinese-style divisions grew steadily in their safe havens beyond the CEFEO's reach; and in late 1952 he opened a new front by marching them into the remote, roadless Thai Highlands above the Laotian border, where French motorized forces could not follow.

THE 'AIR–GROUND BASE'

This concept appeared to offer a solution to the CEFEO's inability to operate effectively in North Vietnam outside their Red River Delta base areas around Hanoi and Haiphong. In December 1952, at Na San in the Thai Highlands, the French prepared an airstrip in the path of Giap's advance, and used their growing air transport fleet to fly in thousands of troops with artillery and supplies to fortify a ring of hill positions surrounding it. Maintained by a constant airlift, this bastion held off Giap's attacks, costing his regiments the sort of loss rates they had suffered during his premature attempt to fight his way into the Delta itself early in 1951. In late 1953, when faced with another Vietminh advance in the border hills, the French commander-in-chief General Henri

THE MATHEMATICS OF AIR RESUPPLY

It is not surprising that the small French air force in Vietnam failed to meet the needs of the Dien Bien Phu garrison for parachuted ammunition and other supplies, totalling at least 180 tons per day. In March–April 1954, available men and machines fell well short of its 'paper' strength. Its maximum capacity, for all operations throughout Indochina, was 76 C-47 Dakotas (76 x 2.5 tons = 190 tons) and 18 C-119 Flying Boxcars (18 x 6 tons = 108 tons) – a grand total of 298 tons, for missions to support Dien Bien Phu and simultaneous major operations elsewhere. In practice, Dien Bien Phu might hope for nightly missions by about 40 C-47s and 12 C-119s, with a total capacity of 172 tons – of which a proportion always fell outside the shrinking perimeter.

Each C-119 carried 6 one-ton pallet loads, which rolled out of its tail doors in about 10 seconds; but each C-47 carried 25 packages each of 100 kilograms (220 lbs), and these had to be manhandled out of side doors by the despatchers, one pack at a time. Even while the drop zone (DZ) was at its maximum size it was only about 1200 metres (1300 yds) long. Flying at 105 mph (170 km/h), a C-47 would pass the DZ in about 25 seconds, so dropping a whole load meant turning and making several runs – sometimes 10 or more. This meant repeatedly flying straight and level through a storm of flak.

On the ground, the DZ gangs had to find and gather up (in the dark) 40 x 25 = 1000 separate 100-kilogram (220-lb) packages, and 72 one-ton pallets, before dawn brought heavy enemy fire down on the DZ. Vital supplies often lay unretrieved for days, visible but out of reach.

TIMELINE

1946 French troops reoccupy Indochina (Vietnam), sparking conflict (First Indochina War) with anticolonial Vietminh forces

1950 General Giap defeats the French at Lang Son and Cao Bang

1952–3 Vietminh take over much of Laos

1953 (November) French forces reinforce the airstrip at Dien Bien Phu with 9000 troops

1954 (May) Siege of Dien Bien Phu ends with the capture of over 11,000 French and allied troops

1954 (August) French agree to withdraw from Indochina; Geneva Accords divide Vietnam at the 17th parallel

1959 Second Indochina War breaks out as US-backed South Vietnam fights northern insurgents

1968 US forces successfully withstand a siege at Khe Sanh during the Tet Offensive

1975 US forces withdraw from South Vietnam and the country is unified under communist rule

Navarre (1898–1983) decided to repeat this formula at Dien Bien Phu, 185 miles (300 km) northwest of Hanoi. The garrison's mission was not primarily to lure Giap into costly attacks through their minefields and barbed wire: they were tasked with making deep sorties into the surrounding hills to dominate the region, and their defences were merely insurance against a possible (though hoped-for) assault.

By early 1954 the camp commander, Colonel de Castries (1902–91), had 12 battalions of Colonial and Legion paratroopers and Legion, North African and Vietnamese infantry, dug in on hills to the north and east of the central camp on the Nam Youm river, and on the valley floor to the west and south. The 10,000-strong garrison were supported by 28 howitzers, 10 tanks, 9 fighter-bombers on the airstrip, and every kind of service troops. However, Giap's reaction was both faster and stronger than anticipated. He mobilized hundreds of thousands of peasants as porters, and to build new roads through the jungle hills, by which he marched some 50,000 troops hundreds of miles across country. Largely evading the French air force, he used these roads to bring in not only supplies for a long battle, twenty-four 75 mm mountain guns and fifty 120 mm heavy mortars, but also his new and unsuspected trumpcards: thirty-six 105 mm howitzers and the same number of 37 mm anti-aircraft guns, provided by China.

The Vietminh noose soon tightened around the base, checking all French attempts at external operations, until the garrison (designated Operational Group Northwest, whose French acronym was GONO) was closely confined. Meanwhile, major French operations in the south reduced the availability of transport planes to supply the camp; and French confidence that their spotter planes and howitzers could locate and destroy Giap's gun positions proved mistaken, since these were patiently and cleverly dug in and camouflaged under cover of night. Even so, the crack paratroop and Foreign Legion battalions were still convinced that they could defeat any outright assault with heavy loss, though some North African and Vietnamese units were less robust.

Map of Dien Bien Phu, showing the French fortified positions on hilltops around the airstrip and the main camp area.

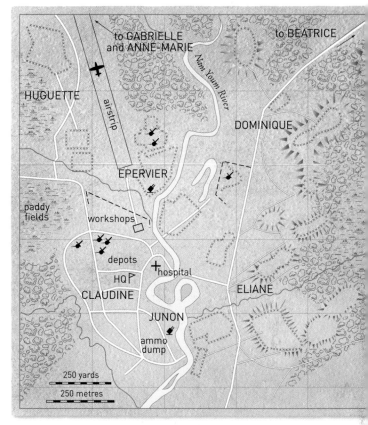

The Storm Breaks

On 13 March 1954 Giap unleashed his artillery in a devastating bombardment that smashed guns, aircraft, barbed wire, trenches and bunkers. The camp's own artillery proved unable to reply effectively (its colonel would commit suicide 48 hours later), and for a while GONO's command staff were paralyzed. That night the Legion battalion holding the northeast strongpoint codenamed 'Béatrice' was battered by shellfire and overrun by human-wave assaults; on the night of 14–15 March the same fate befell the Algerian unit on strongpoint 'Gabrielle' due north of the camp, and on 17 March most of the low-lying northern 'Anne-Marie' positions had to be abandoned. A whole corner had been knocked out of the defence plan.

The shortage of airlift capacity had denied GONO the engineer stores it needed; the roofs of bunkers and fighting positions were mostly far too lightly constructed, and the barbed wire too thin. The Vietminh artillery was far stronger and more destructive than it had been at Na San; the perimeter was far longer and the defenders more widely spaced, and the only counter-attack attempted by the central reserve (to Gabrielle) failed. The Vietminh attacks were sacrificial, accepting terrible losses – particularly from French artillery – in order to get close enough to swamp the defenders.

The airlift was the key to GONO's survival, but the Vietminh made it perilous with their new regiment of Russian AA guns in the hills around the camp. The airstrip, under shellfire, was closed to all but risky flights to evacuate the mounting numbers of seriously wounded, and on 28 March aircraft movements had to cease altogether; from then on any reinforcements and resupply had to be dropped by parachute. Dien Bien Phu had become a siege.

The Siege

The next main phase of mass infantry assaults by night lasted from 27 March to 5 April; some of the eastern hill positions at 'Dominique' and 'Eliane' were lost, but others were held or even recaptured. For the following three weeks the Vietminh concentrated on replacing their already massive expenditure of men and ammunition, and meanwhile they sapped and trenched ever closer to isolate the remaining strongpoints. In late April they strangled the important 'Huguette' positions guarding the open ground of the airfield; the rainy season had now started, and in the partly flooded valley the trench-fighting was as grim as anything seen at Verdun in 1916. French casualties mounted fast, and the scenes in the overcrowded dug-out hospital – as vulnerable to shellfire as the rest of the camp – became appalling. By 24 April the original perimeter had shrunk by 50 percent, and the garrison was down to 3250 combat-ready infantry.

Between 14 March and 6 May, three paratroop battalions and part of a fourth were dropped into Dien Bien Phu. So too were individual replacements for artillery and tank crews, and many untrained volunteers who made their first jumps into the cauldron by night. These reinforcements were never enough to allow GONO to regain the initiative in the grinding trench-fighting all round the perimeter – where defending units were always greatly outnumbered – but merely prolonged the garrison's agony.

As the siege dragged on and the possible drop-zones within the camp shrank, the shortfall in the tonnage dropped each night worsened, and an increasing proportion of the air-drops, including vital artillery ammunition, fell into Vietminh hands. The core premise of the operation – that a camp of divisional strength could be sustained by airlift and air-support alone while under attack – proved false: the French did not have enough transport or ground-attack aircrews, the camp was too distant from the Delta airbases and the enemy AA guns were too numerous and elusive. Little by little, every necessity began to run short.

The fact that the infantry held out as long as they did was remarkable; under the leadership of inspirational officers, such as the paratrooper Colonel Pierre Langlais, the fighting by individual battalions and companies for the eastern hill and northern valley positions was heroic, resourceful and often locally successful. However, although Vietminh morale had been badly shaken by their enormous casualties, by 1 May Giap was ready to launch a renewed assault.

By 4 May the Vietminh were closing in on the central camp from east and west; on 7 May the last vital hill strongpoints of 'Eliane' were overrun, and the Vietminh reached the east bank of the

'*I would like to emphasize that ... insofar as the free world is concerned, the French Union forces at Dien Bien Phu are fighting a modern Thermopylae.*'

US UNDER-SECRETARY OF STATE WALTER BEDELL SMITH (19 APRIL 1954)
COMPARES DIEN BIEN PHU TO THE HEROIC STAND OF THE SPARTANS
AGAINST PERSIAN INVASION IN 480 BC

SENIOR GENERAL VO NGUYEN GIAP

In civilian life a history teacher, Giap learned guerrilla warfare with Mao Tse-tung's Communists in China during the Second World War. As Ho Chi Minh's military leader he oversaw the Vietminh take-over of North Vietnam after the Japanese surrender, and prepared remote bases for eventual war against the French. In 1946-9 he directed and honed his forces in basically defensive guerrilla activity, but from late 1949 Communist Chinese aid enabled him to organize, arm and train regular regiments and divisions.

His surprise victory on Highway RC4 in October 1950 led to French withdrawal from the Tonkin/China border region and eased future cross-border co-operation. His costly defeat in a premature invasion of the Red River Delta early in 1951 nearly caused his dismissal in disgrace; but he learned from this error, patiently rebuilding and practising his regular force until the delivery of field and AA artillery by China in late 1953 allowed him to accept the challenge of Dien Bien Phu.

Giap's victory made his position in the North Vietnamese hierarchy unassailable for many years, and he remained at the head of the military throughout the US war in South Vietnam and the final invasion of 1975 – though how much operational authority he actually wielded in the 1970s is questionable. His death has not been reported at the time of writing; at the age of 95, the revered Father of the People's Army was seen in public during the Dien Bien Phu 50th anniversary celebrations in 2004.

river at almost all points. Colonel de Castries ceased fire that afternoon, after 54 days of resistance. The Vietminh allowed about 860 of the wounded to be repatriated, but marched some 9000 prisoners – including perhaps 3000 wounded – for hundreds of miles to distant prison camps; many died on the march.

The French government fell, and peace negotiations began; by the end of July a ceasefire was agreed, and France evacuated the whole of North Vietnam by early October. The Vietminh began freeing prisoners in mid-August; of those taken at Dien Bien Phu, some 4000–5000 never returned from their captivity of just four months. (The figures are uncertain because hundreds of légionnaires from countries then behind the Iron Curtain are thought to have been repatriated directly.)

The French army remained in South Vietnam until April 1956, but the US-backed government of President Ngo Dinh Diem had already been installed there in June 1954, and US involvement was constant thereafter.

AFTERMATH: A MISUNDERSTOOD LESSON?

The outright defeat of a Western professional army with air support, at the hands of an Asian independence movement, shocked the world. It proved that hit-and-run guerrillas could (with

200 DIEN BIEN PHU

CASUALTIES AT DIEN BIEN PHU

The initial garrison plus later reinforcements totalled c.15,100 men, of whom 18.6 percent were French, 26 percent Foreign Legion, 17.5 percent North African, 1.6 percent West African and 36.3 percent Indochinese. Total casualties are believed to have been:

    Killed, wounded and missing: c.7900

    Wounded evacuated: 1182

    Captured repatriated: 3900 known, plus maximum 1000 others

    Captured and fate unknown: at least 4100

    plus 62 aircrew killed, missing or died in captivity

    Estimated Vietminh casualties were between 25,000 and 30,000

Communist Chinese aid) evolve into an effective conventional army. Despite the shock, the United States (encouraged by its recent experience in Korea) attributed Giap's success largely to French weakness, dismissing it simply as a French defeat rather than analyzing its real nature as a Vietnamese victory. Since the USA would take over France's role in the region almost immediately, as protector of the new Republic of (South) Vietnam, this error returned to haunt American strategists in the 1960s. In his own way, however, General Giap also perhaps misinterpreted the lessons of his success.

Giap was not a talented conventional general – his battle tactics at Dien Bien Phu recalled the unimaginative sacrificial slaughters of 1914–18. His true success lay in motivating, deploying and sustaining many tens of thousands of Vietnamese fighters through long years of grinding effort and many bloody defeats, and in this he showed his superior understanding of his own people. Their tactical exploitation of the physical conditions was skilful, but counter-tactics can always be learned. What made the Vietminh (and their successors, the Vietcong, in the 1960s) unique was a deep-seated determination, acquired over centuries, to free their country of all and any foreign occupiers, whatever the cost. This time, Communism offered them the method, the instructor and the armourer that they needed; but even without it the Vietnamese would eventually have found a way to expel the foreigners – after all, in 1979 they would even join battle against their Chinese fellow-Communists.

KHE SANH – THE SIEGE THAT NEVER WAS

For 77 days, during a period that coincided with the Vietcong's Tet offensive against South Vietnamese cities, the 6800-strong garrison of the US Marine Combat Base at Khe Sanh was the focus of major North Vietnamese Army operations. At a time when the little-understood Tet fighting was dominating the US media, commentators seized on some superficial resemblances between Khe Sanh and Dien Bien Phu to make the public's flesh creep in the expectation of imminent disaster. Politicians were equally traumatized at the thought of US forces meeting the same fate as the hapless French; during the siege of Khe Sanh, President Lyndon B. Johnson angrily upbraided his military advisers: '*There isn't going to be any goddamn Din Bin Phu [sic] on my watch*'.

True, battles took place for outlying hills, where NVA artillery was emplaced to shell the airfield; road access was cut off, and the garrison relied upon air resupply, under constant bombardment. However, the differences between this so-called 'siege' and Dien Bien Phu were far more significant than their similarities. There is no doubt that General Giap sought to replicate his success of 1954, but he failed utterly; perhaps he simply did not grasp the significance of the hugely greater capability of the US air forces.

The Khe Sanh garrison was smaller and had slightly fewer howitzers, but was within range of powerful US external artillery. It had a much smaller and more compact perimeter to defend, and although two outlying positions were lost, these did not threaten its integrity. The Marines dominated the key surrounding hills for more than 4 miles (6.4 km) out, keeping NVA artillery (with far fewer guns than at Dien Bien Phu) between 5½ and 8 miles (9–13 km) away – twice or three times the distance in 1954.

The single greatest difference was in the scale of US air power, both fixed-wing and helicopter; this was tens of times greater than that supporting Dien Bien Phu, a whole generation more modern and capable, and flying from closer bases. The airfield was closed to most C-130 transports from 10 February, and to all of them from 20 February; but smaller fixed-wing transports continued to use it, and the 9000-plus helicopter sorties were unaffected. Altogether the US air forces delivered more than 19,000 tons of stores during the siege – 2½ times the total dropped at Dien Bien Phu, though the Khe Sanh garrison was only half the size of GONO. The French were lucky if they could amass three days' ammunition at a time, but at Khe Sanh the norm was 30 days' supply. At Khe Sanh casualty evacuation flights were never halted, lifting out at least 2250 of the roughly 2500 wounded, compared with only 324 successful French evacuations early in the siege of Dien Bien Phu.

Neither was there any comparison between the combat air support available in the two battles. On most days at Dien Bien Phu the French could not put up more than a couple of dozen sorties by fighter-bombers with two 500-lb bombs, and even fewer by medium bombers carrying about 4 tons; moreover, their ground/air control system was lamentable, so much of this effort was wasted. The US jet fighter-bombers and B-52 strategic bombers, with the latest targeting radar, dropped nearly 115,000 tons around Khe Sanh (for comparison, more than 1½ times the total tonnage of German bombs and V-weapons to strike Britain during the whole of the Second World War).

Exact figures for men killed at Khe Sanh are unknown due to confused criteria used in compiling them, but they seem to have amounted to some 730 US and 230 ARVN (South Vietnamese army) for the whole period from 1 November 1967 to 15 April 1968, which included some two months of combat before the siege itself. North Vietnamese casualty figures were never released, but were certainly several times greater and may even have reached 10,000.

GLOSSARY

abatis A barrier of felled trees, with branches facing outwards to impede attackers.

arquebus An early hand-carried *matchlock* firearm.

ashlar A block of dressed stone.

bailey An open, walled space in a castle, also known as a 'ward'.

ballista A Roman stone-throwing catapult.

bastion A protruding part of a defensive wall, usually at a corner.

battery A protected position for an artillery piece (or group thereof).

battlement The top of a defensive wall.

bombard A heavy siege gun of the 14th–15th centuries.

cannon A longer-barrelled artillery piece for shooting solid *roundshot* on a flat trajectory.

catapulta Roman arrow-shooting catapult.

cheval-de-frise (pl. chevaux-de-frise) An improvised defensive feature, made from a beam or plank closely set with sharp blades or spikes to impale attackers.

circumvallation A wall built by a besieger right around the besieged place to cut its defenders off from help or escape.

crenellations The notched top of a wall, with alternating shooting *embrasures* and protective slabs.

curtain wall The outer wall of a defended place.

embrasure A gap in a wall or *battlement* for defensive purposes.

enfilade fire Fire from a *bastion* sideways along the face of a wall, to hit attackers in the flank.

fascine A tied bundle of brushwood, used for building defences or filling in ditches.

firepot An early form of incendiary grenade, usually ceramic.

firing-step A ledge for defenders along the inside top of a wall.

flanking fire Weapons fire from one or both sides rather than from straight ahead.

flintlock An ignition system for firearms of the 17th–19th centuries, utilizing a spring-loaded flint wedge to strike sparks on a steel surface above a pan of gunpowder.

gabion A basket filled with earth, used for building defences or filling in ditches.

glacis A cleared slope outside a defensive ditch, designed to expose attackers to fire.

grapeshot Many small projectiles fired simultaneously from a *cannon* in a single discharge. Chiefly deployed as an anti-personnel weapon.

Greek fire An ancient flame-projector weapon, developed by the Byzantine Greeks.

grenadoe An early term for an explosive shell.

halberd A pole weapon combining a spike and an axe-blade.

howitzer A shorter-barrelled artillery piece, for firing explosive shells on a dipping trajectory.

Janissary Member of an élite corps of the Ottoman Turkish army, raised mainly from captive Christian boys.

keep The central tower or final redoubt of a castle, also known as a 'donjon'.

loophole A hole or slit through a wall, allowing defensive fire with small-arms

lunette A defensive position set outside the main walls of a defended place. Originally crescent-shaped (hence its French name, literally 'little moon'), lunettes later became pointed in shape

machicolation A slot in the floor of a *battlement* allowing projectiles to be dropped vertically onto attackers below

mangonel A man-powered beam-sling device for hurling stones, its arm swinging in a vertical plane.

mantlet A moveable shield or long shed-like structure for protecting advancing attackers.

matchlock An ignition system for firearms of the 14th–17th centuries, utilizing a smouldering cord thrust into a pan of gunpowder.

mortar A very short, large-calibre, smoothbore artillery piece for firing explosive or incendiary projectiles over obstacles at a high angle of elevation.

onager A late Roman stone-throwing torsion-powered catapult, its arm swinging in a vertical plane. The weapon's name means 'mule,' alluding to its recoil kick when fired.

outwork Any defensive position built outside the main perimeter of a defended place.

palisade A fence of timbers set vertically side by side.

parallels Systems of siege trenches built from side to side across the frontage of a defended place.

pike A long thrusting-spear.

postern A small gate, usually only wide enough for a single person, allowing exit and entry to a defended place while avoiding the danger of opening the main defensive gate.

rampart A defensive bank, originally made of earth.

ravelin A pointed *outwork*, usually built outside the *curtain wall*.

redoubt A defended position.

roundshot A solid cannonball, originally made of stone, later of cast iron.

salient An area of defences thrusting outwards or inwards, exposed to attack from its flanks.

sap A siege trench dug forwards towards a defensive place, usually in a series of zig-zag runs.

sepoy Indian infantryman of the British East India Company's army, later of the Indian army of the British crown.

sortie A raid outwards by defenders of a besieged place.

talus The solid, outward-sloping base of a defensive wall.

trebuchet A stone-throwing catapult powered by a counterweight at the forward end of an arm swinging in a vertical plane.

Vauban fort A generic term for a form of anti-artillery fortification perfected by Sebastien de Vauban, military engineer to the French king Louis XIV, in *c.*1667–1704. Vauban forts characteristically featured concentric systems of low, mutually supporting *bastions* defended by ditches.

INDEX

PICTURE CREDITS

akg-images
48 akg-images; 57 akg-images; 66 akg-images.

Bridgeman Art Library
6 © Guildhall Art Library, London.

Corbis
21 © Historical Picture Archive/Corbis;
39 © Julia Waterlow/Eye Ubiquitous/Corbis.

Photos.com
2–3; 105.

TopFoto.co.uk
4-5 ©2001 Topham Picturepoint/TopFoto;
12 © TopFoto; 30 © The British Library/HIP/
TopFoto; 76 ©2004 Topham Picturepoint/TopFoto;
86 ©2002 Topham Picturepoint/TopFoto;
96 ©2001 Topham Picturepoint/TopFoto;
114 © Print Collector/HIP/TopFoto;
124 © Ann Ronan Picture Library/HIP/TopFoto;
134 ©2004 Topham Picturepoint/TopFoto;
144 © Print Collector/HIP/TopFoto;
154 © The Image Works/TopFoto; 162 © World
History Archive/TopFoto; 172 © ullsteinbild/
TopFoto; 182 © RIA Novosti/TopFoto;
193 ©2004 Topham Picturepoint/TopFoto.

*Quercus Publishing has made every effort to trace copyright
holders of the pictures used in this book. Anyone having
claims to ownership not identified above is invited to contact
Quercus Publishing.*

Quercus Publishing Plc
21 Bloomsbury Square
London
WC1A 2NS

First published in 2009

A CIP catalogue record for this book is available from the British Library

Cloth case edition: ISBN–978–1–84724–831–2
Printed case edition: ISBN–978–1–84724–274–7

Printed and bound in China

10 9 8 7 6 5 4 3 2 1

Designed and edited by BCS Publishing Limited, Oxford.